The
Retail Jeweller's Guide

The
Retail Jeweller's Guide

c. 1

KENNETH BLAKEMORE

Editor of *Watchmaker, Jeweller and Silversmith*

Technical Adviser: G. F. Andrews
Formerly Secretary of the National Association of Goldsmiths
of Great Britain and Ireland,
and Secretary of the Gemmological Association
of Great Britain

NEWNES–BUTTERWORTHS
LONDON   BOSTON
Sydney   Wellington   Durban   Toronto

THE BUTTERWORTH GROUP

UNITED KINGDOM	Butterworth & Co (Publishers) Ltd London: 88 Kingsway, WC2B 6AB
AUSTRALIA	Butterworths Pty Ltd Sydney: 586 Pacific Highway, Chatswood, NSW 2067 Also at Melbourne, Brisbane, Adelaide and Perth
CANADA	Butterworth & Co (Canada) Ltd Toronto: 2265 Midland Avenue, Scarborough, Ontario, M1P 4S1
NEW ZEALAND	Butterworths of New Zealand Ltd Wellington: 26–28 Waring Taylor Street, 1
SOUTH AFRICA	Butterworth & Co (South Africa) (Pty) Ltd Durban: 152–154 Gale Street
USA	Butterworth (Publishers) Inc Boston: 19 Cummings Park, Woburn, Mass. 01801

First published in 1969 by Iliffe Books Ltd,
  for *Watchmaker, Jeweller and Silversmith*
Second edition 1973
Third edition published by Newnes–Butterworths, 1976

© K. Blakemore, 1976

ISBN 0 408 00266 2

Printed in England by Butler & Tanner Ltd, Frome and London

Preface

Since this book was last revised in 1973 many changes have taken place in the trade, necessitating the publication of this new and enlarged edition. Also my own association with the trade over a period of almost thirty years has made me aware of certain shortcomings in previous editions, which I have taken the opportunity to remedy.

The two major developments in recent years have been the new hallmarking legislation introduced in 1975 and the rapid developments in electronic watches and clocks.

The Hallmarking Act of 1973 has necessitated considerable revision of the information on hallmarking; those employed in the jewellery trade have to be familiar not only with the new legislation but also (because they are likely to have to buy and sell wares made before January 1975) the legislation in force before that date.

The rapid development in electronic watches and clocks, and the growth of a new industry in the United States, have made it necessary to include a separate chapter dealing with the types of clocks and watches the trade is likely to find itself selling in increasing numbers in the years ahead. It has become very clear that we are on the threshold of a timekeeping revolution.

There have been great changes also in the gem trade, brought about in part by fashion and in part by economics. Fine facetable gem material is nowadays in short supply, while there are more and more buyers bidding for what is available. As a result jewellery manufacturers have, in an endeavour to meet the demand for inexpensive jewellery, turned to a wide range of gem materials. These gem materials forced upon the trade by economic necessity have rapidly become fashionable. The result of this is that today those who work in the jeweller's shop have to familiarise themselves with many of the once less familiar gem minerals. At the same time new synthetic stones and new techniques for altering gemstones have brought new problems for the jeweller, of which he needs to be made aware. In the light of all these changes it was necessary not only to enlarge considerably the chapter on gems but also to rearrange it for the greater convenience of the reader.

Recent public interest in the jewellery of the past, resulting from such exhibitions as that of Tutenkhamun treasures and the treasures of Romania, makes it desirable for the jeweller and his staff to be at least aware of types of jewellery made in earlier times, while the growing public interest in jewellery design has made it necessary to bring the chapter on the history of jewellery up to date. That chapter has therefore been expanded to almost twice its original length.

One omission from previous editions, which now seems a glaring one, was a chapter on the boxes produced in the eighteenth and nineteenth centuries. Any jeweller with an antique department is likely to stock such boxes, while a jeweller doing valuation work would be expected to be familiar with them.

It is hoped that the expansion and updating of this book will make it more valuable both as a handbook of product knowledge, written primarily to provide new entrants into the retail jewellery trade with the necessary knowledge about the goods that they are likely to have to handle during their careers, and as a reference book for those who have been longer in the trade and who may wish to check up on some particular point.

There are a number of reasons why product knowledge is important to the jeweller's salesman. Customers expect the salesman to be an expert. Having themselves, for the most part, little or no knowledge of jewellery, watches, clocks and silverwares, they look to the jeweller and his staff for advice. A good salesman can give this, because he knows what he is talking about. By so doing he helps to increase the goodwill of the business in which he works.

Besides selling, one of the important jobs in a retail jeweller's shop is accepting goods for repair. Unless a salesman has a good product knowledge he cannot describe accurately the goods entrusted to him, or understand what may be involved in repairing them. Mistakes through lack of knowledge at this stage can lead to undesirable arguments, or even to legal proceedings, when the goods are collected. The Trade Descriptions Act also makes ignorance dangerous. If goods are improperly described on tickets or even in a sales dialogue prosecution could result. The various Acts relevant to the running of a retail jewellery business are given in the companion volume *Management for the Retail Jeweller*.

Almost every salesman hopes one day to be a manager, or a proprietor, when his job will entail buying as well as selling. If he buys well he will be serving his customers well and he will be playing an important part in making the business he works in successful. But he can only be a good buyer if he really knows his jewellery, his silver, his watches and his clocks.

This book inevitably has a great many facts in it, and I am indebted to the experts who have been kind enough to read the various sections and to suggest improvements. I am also indebted to a great many people, too numerous to' mention, who over the 30 years during which I have been editing the *Watchmaker, Jeweller and Silversmith*, have given of their time to show me how things are made, and to explain why they were made in a particular way.

K.B.

Contents

CHAPTER 1

The Metals

GOLD

Craftsmen have been making jewellery from gold for more than 6000 years, and it is not difficult to understand why the craftsmen of so many different civilisations have worked in this metal. Gold has a beautiful yellow colour, and it is a wonderful metal in which to work, being the most malleable of all metals; a troy ounce of it can be beaten out into a sheet 100 ft square. This sheet will be 1/280,000 in. thick, so thin as to be transparent. Gold is also very ductile; that same troy ounce could have been rolled down between grooved rollers and then drawn, and drawn again, through ever finer dies, to make 50 miles of gold wire.

When the craftsman produces a piece of jewellery from this sympathetic metal, the jewellery has a satisfying weight about it. Gold is a very heavy metal, considerably heavier than lead. Lead has a specific gravity of only 11·4 compared with gold's 19·3. But gold has much more to offer than beauty and weight. The physical characteristic which has probably had most to do with its importance in the history of mankind is its great nobility. It is almost certainly because gold does not tarnish like copper, or rust away like iron, that great men down the ages have used it to display their wealth to the world, loading their tables with gold plates and gold vessels, and decorating their women with gold ornaments, the beauty of which they knew would never diminish.

It was also, in part, the relative indestructibility of gold that persuaded so many nations in the past to mint their most valuable coins from it. Hoards of gold coins, unearthed after centuries in the ground, have come to light looking as bright as newly-minted pennies. People could have had confidence in such coins, the glory of which they knew time would not decay, and confidence has always been of prime importance where the coinage is concerned.

In the language of the chemist gold is a 'relatively inert substance';

it does not combine with the oxygen in the air. That is why oxide does not form on it, as iron oxide collects on the surface of iron to form what is known as rust. Even strong acids do not attack gold, with the exception of that potent mixture of hydrochloric and nitric acids that has been given the name *aqua regia*—royal water—because it can dissolve the noblest of metals, gold.

Although a rare substance, gold is to be found, in small quantities at least, in most countries. It is carried along in minute quantities, in the currents of many rivers, including the Rhine and the Danube, but these specks are not worth trying to trap.

Gold is to be found even in Britain. There is a gold mine on a hillside between Barmouth and Dolgelly in North Wales, which was originally worked by local village people as a co-operative. Later the royal family came to have first call on the gold found there, and every royal bride in this century has been married with rings made from gold from this Welsh mine. Mining there has always been sporadic and in recent years work has ceased altogether for there is not enough gold present to make it commercially worth while. Nowadays, anyone can apply for a permit, and on payment of a small fee pan the gravel there to his heart's content. This Welsh gold is in the form of grains and nuggets; the largest nugget to be found in this mine weighed about four ounces. Incidentally, Welsh gold has a characteristic colour, a reddish-yellow with a green tinge.

Gold has been mined in many countries at one time or another. Today, the main sources are South Africa, with a production of some 20 million ounces a year, the U.S.S.R., Canada, the U.S.A., and Australia.

ALLUVIAL GOLD

There was a time, in some parts of the world, when gold could be had merely for the effort of picking it up. If a man happened to be in the right place at the right time, he had merely to pan the sands and pebbles of a river bed or, at worst, sink a shallow shaft into the ground, to find a fortune in gold.

The gold found in this way was alluvial gold, sometimes called 'placer' gold. This alluvial gold had originally been what we call 'native' gold. That is, it existed in crystalline form in a matrix, usually of quartz. The gold and its attendant matrix came into existence as a result of changes in the earth's crust. It was formed by chemical reaction when hot magma from deep within the earth was forced up to the surface through fissures in the earth's crust many millions of years ago. Over the years the quartz reefs that contained the crystalline gold were weathered away, by rain and frost, and the debris from this weathering, which contained the gold, had been gradually washed down the hillsides, away from what prospectors call the mother lode.

Alluvial gold is sometimes found as 'dust', sometimes in the form of nuggets. A nugget is a lump of a quarter of an ounce or more, resulting from tiny grains of gold and sand being compounded together. Some really big nuggets have been discovered, perhaps the most famous being the Welcome Stranger, found in a cart rut in New South Wales, in the middle of the nineteenth century. The Welcome Stranger was two feet long.

GOLD RUSHES

It was the finding of placer gold that started the famous gold rushes of the last century, the first being the California rush of 1849. This was started as a result of a landowner in the Sacramento Valley sending out a party of men to harness a stream on the lower slopes of the Sierra Nevada to drive a sawmill. James Marshall, the foreman entrusted with the job, found yellow specks in the muddy bed of the mill-race that he was building. Word soon spread abroad. The first effect of Marshall's find was that the price of shovels rose from $1 to $10. Then 50,000 men set out to cross the United States on foot in search of a fortune. Another 50,000 booked passages on ships. These men, the 'forty-niners' came pouring into the Sacramento Valley like a swarm of locusts, destroying as they came. Ironically they ruined the man responsible for it all—the Swiss ex-army officer John Augustus Sutter. The colony he had founded in the fertile valley was laid waste and he died in poverty.

Most of those who came to California for the gold were content to pan the river gravels, watching the gold, which is much heavier than the gravel containing it, sink to the bottom of their pans. But there were some who realised that there was an even greater prize for the man who could find the mother lode from which all this alluvial gold had originally come.

In 1859 two Irishmen, Peter O'Riley and Pat McLaughlin found the mother lode, from which the gold in the Sacramento Valley had been eroded, on the slopes of the Sierras. The gold could be seen in an outcrop of quartz, the outward and visible sign of the richest reef that had ever been found. The reef was only a small one, and in ten years the Big Bonanza mine sunk there was worked out. But in that time it had produced £130 million worth of gold and the silver found in association with this gold was worth another £170 million.

The most famous and the most romantic of the gold rushes was that to the Yukon which began in 1896. It all started as a result of a salmon fishing expedition. A certain George Washington Cormack, a sailor who had deserted from an American ship, married a Siwash Indian girl and settled down to live with her family. He was fishing one day with his brothers-in-law in a creek of the Yukon river and while he was helping to set up the nets he noticed a glinting in the sand at the water's edge. Siwash George, as he was called, had found the first gold in the Yukon.

Word of Siwash George's find soon spread, and prospectors with their packs and pans began to arrive at Rabbit Creek on the Klondyke, where gold was there for all to see. The people from the little settlement of Forty Mile poured out of the town to pan the sand along the creeks. Rumours of the Yukon strike filtered through to the outside world. Then, in June 1896, two ships, the *Excelsior* and the *Portland*, arrived in Seattle harbour carrying the first of the gold from the Yukon. There was a ton of gold on board the *Portland* alone. The rush was on.

Men, many with no knowledge of gold or how to live in the wilderness, poured into the north-west corner of Canada, heading for the Klondyke river. A town began to spring up on the banks of the Klondyke—the famous Dawson City. In 1896 its population was 500. A further 1000 people arrived in 1897, and by 1898 there were over 30,000 inhabitants. In that year £3½ million worth of gold was taken out of the creeks, and for another 20 years men continued to find gold in the sandy banks of the Klondyke and its tributaries.

Australia, too, had her gold rushes in the nineteenth century. Gold was first found there in 1839, and as the century progressed nuggets were picked up here and there on that continent, but the great discoveries came after Edward Hammond Hargreaves, an unsuccessful prospector, returned from California to his native country in 1850, determined to discover gold there.

The following year he struck lucky at Ophir in New South Wales. Soon people were flocking to Australia from all over the world to dig for gold. Obscure places, such as Ballarat and Bendigo Creek, acquired a world-wide fame overnight and the population of Australia increased from 400,000 to 1,260,000 in the next decade.

BIRTH OF THE RAND

The great find of the century was, however, made neither in Australia nor in North America, but in the Transvaal. There are a number of versions describing how the great gold-rich quartz reef at Witwatersrand came to be found in 1886, but it is now generally accepted that it was discovered by a prospector called George Harrison, who had the bad luck to be killed by a lion before he could benefit from his good fortune. It is doubtful whether Harrison had even an inkling of the vast potential of the reef. What he found was a small outcrop. The reef stretched for nearly 300 miles from the Far Eastern Transvaal into the Orange Free State. In places this reef went 10,000 feet below the surface. It was by far the biggest gold-bearing reef that had ever been found, and not only is it still yielding gold in prodigious quantities, but even today new mines are being sunk into still untapped areas of it.

The Witwatersrand reef was unlike other gold-bearing reefs. The thinly sprinkled gold, which was alluvial and not native, was held in a conglomerate, the crystalline quartz of the original reef having been crushed and then reconstituted under enormous pressure. Such a reef could not be worked by individual prospectors. It called for mining and crushing operations that required both capital and industrial organisation. Men who had made fortunes in the diamond fields of South Africa, Cecil Rhodes and Barney Barnato among them, became interested in gold. The mines were dug, the machinery brought in, and a well-organised tent-town grew up to house the miners, a tent-town that was to develop into the great city of Johannesburg—the Rand gold-mining industry was born. Concentration became inevitable if the area was to be efficiently exploited. Once there were hundreds of mines in the Rand; today there are only 46 mines owned by seven large companies, but those 46 mines supply the world with most of its gold.

By the end of the nineteenth century alluvial gold was growing scarce. It was becoming increasingly unlikely that a man with nothing but a pan, a shovel, a grubstake and a good constitution would pick up a fortune in the wilderness somewhere. Gold mining had become an industry where rich men grew richer and poor men had little chance at all.

DOWN THE MINE

Some 300,000 coloured workers and about a tenth of that number of whites are employed at the mines of the Rand. Most of the coloured workers work below ground, going down in the cages suspended from the pithead gear, perhaps a mile or so to the tunnels, known as drives, that lead to the slopes where mining actually takes place. Here they drill holes in the rock face, and

Fig. 1.1. Western Deep Levels mine on the Witwatersrand Reef (by courtesy of De Beers)

in the holes place cartridges of explosive. In a year some 27,000 tons of explosive are detonated in the Rand, to loosen 50 million tons of gold-bearing rock.

Every ton of rock mined yields, on average, only about half an ounce of gold. The specks of gold in the quartz conglomerate are usually too small to be seen with the naked eye, and the extraction is a complicated business. First the rock goes to the stamping mills, where it is crushed in a series of great mechanical pestles and mortars. The crushed rock then goes to the tube mills, or the ball mills, where it is tumbled with large pieces of rock, or steel balls the size of cannon balls, to reduce it to a sludge. From this sludge the gold is then chemically extracted.

The capital required to put a gold mine into production today is enormous, but the rewards of course are considerable. The Western Deep Levels in the Transvaal (Fig. 1.1), which came into full production in 1970, had by 1960 already cost the Anglo-American Corporation £15 million. But this mine is expected to go on producing for at least 60 years, and to yield gold worth £800 million.

EXTRACTION

The concentration of the mines of the Witwatersrand reef was not solely the result of a need for more capital than the average prospector could provide. A contributory cause was a sudden and dramatic drop in yield in the year 1889, when many miners thought that the reef was worked out and sold their claims for what they could get. But the fault lay not in the reef, which was as rich in gold as ever, but in the amalgamation process for extracting the gold from the sludge. This consisted in putting the sludge containing the gold into barrels with mercury, which has a strange affinity for gold. Gold adhered to it, and the combined mercury and gold was then transferred to a retort and heated. The mercury, having a much lower vaporisation point than gold, was driven off as a gas leaving the gold behind. This method worked adequately for the gold-bearing ore from near the surface, but below 500 ft the character of the ore changed and the miners found less and less gold in their retorts.

In 1890, three Scotsmen came to the rescue of the miners of the Rand, but many of the small men had already given up gold mining and gone to search for diamonds round Kimberley, or had returned to their farms. The three Scotsmen were two brothers called Forrest and a man named MacArthur, who, with others, had been working for some time in Glasgow on an alternative method of gold recovery. In 1890, they arrived in Johannesburg to demonstrate the cyanide process that they had evolved. In this process the sludge containing the gold is put into tanks with cyanide of potassium which dissolves the gold. The liquid containing the dissolved gold is next filtered off and clarified. Zinc dust is then added to precipitate the gold, which is washed in sulphuric acid to get rid of excess zinc and then placed in an electric oven and roasted, or calcined. The calcine produced is only about 60 per cent pure at this stage, and is now mixed with a flux of sand, borax and manganese, and smelted in an electric furnace. During the smelting the impurities combine with the flux to form a slag, and the gold, being much the heavier, sinks to the bottom of the furnace. After the slag has been removed, the gold is poured into iron moulds to produce ingots each weighing about 1,000 ounces.

The mercury amalgamation process is still retained at some mines, as a first process, for it is a relatively cheap way of recovering about 40–50 per cent of the gold in a rich ore. But at most mines, the processed ore goes straight to the huge cyanide tanks, which dominate a modern gold mine.

REFINERS

The gold poured from the smelting furnace after the recovery process is still far from the 99·98 to 99·99 per cent purity needed for making carat golds for the jewellery trade. So it must be further refined. This fineness is necessary, not merely because pure gold makes it easier to arrive at the exact proportions of gold and base metals in carat gold, but also because the wrong impurities can affect the colour, or the working qualities, of a carat gold.

When the gold reaches the refinery it will contain some silver, some base metal including copper, and platinum and osmiridium perhaps. In the refinery, the gold is first subjected to the chlorination process, which exploits the relative inertia of gold. The gold is heated in a furnace to a molten state. Chlorine gas is passed down a tube into the furnace; it does not affect the gold, but it turns the silver and the base metals present into chlorides, which float to the top of the furnace where they can be ladled off. The gold left is 99·6 to 99·7 per cent pure; but still not pure enough, and it has therefore to go through yet one more process.

To get it into the right state for this process, the molten gold is poured from the furnace into a circular pit filled with water on the floor of the refinery. The rapid cooling solidifies the gold into granules which are placed in a large stoneware pan containing *aqua regia*. The gold and the combined acids are boiled together and the gold dissolves in the *aqua regia*. This gold-rich solution is allowed to cool for 6–8 hours, during which time any silver chloride left in the gold will, because silver chloride is an insoluble salt, have sunk to the bottom of the pan. The liquid containing the gold is now siphoned off leaving the silver chloride. To this liquid must be added an agent which will throw down the gold, but not the copper, platinum or any other metal dissolved with it in the *aqua regia*. Iron chloride is the agent mostly used to precipitate the gold. Following precipitation the liquid is siphoned off, and the gold, now in a sandy form, is washed with hydrochloric acid to get rid of any traces of iron chloride.

The platinum, the copper and the other metals left in the *aqua regia* are subsequently extracted, for the refiner obviously does not waste any of the valuable by-products acquired in the refining of gold.

CARAT GOLDS

The refiner now has almost pure gold ready for alloying. Gold has to be alloyed because, in its pure state, it is unsuitable for working, being not only heavier but also softer than lead.

The refiner has to achieve three things when he alloys his gold with other metals for use by the jewellery trade: working properties, the necessary degree of purity, and the right colour. He aims at providing the jeweller with a metal suitable for the job that it will be required to do. He must also provide gold which will pass the rigid tests at the assay office. He will further have to be prepared to offer his gold to the jewellery manufacturer in various colours, ranging from a natural yellow to purple.

Let us first deal with quality. In Britain there are four legal standards for gold: 22 carat, 18 carat, 14 carat and 9 carat. In some countries 8 carat gold is legal, in others 15 carat, while yet other countries employ metric standards that cannot be expressed by the carat system. The carat system is merely a method of expressing the proportion of gold to other metals in a particular alloy. Pure gold is reckoned as 24 carat, 22 carat gold contains 22 parts of gold to 2 parts of other metal, while 9 carat gold contains 9 parts of gold to 15 parts of other metal.

The law requires that 22 carat gold shall contain not less than 22 parts of gold, or 14 carat not less than 14 parts of gold, and so on. There is nothing to prevent a jeweller from selling a gold which assayed at 17 carats, but since the assay office would have marked such gold at 14 carat there would be no point.

Copper and silver are the principal metals used to alloy gold, though nickel, zinc, cadmium, iron and aluminium are also used. The refiner's problem is to reach a satisfactory compromise between working qualities and colour for each different carat quality. Copper produces a hard alloy, with good wearing qualities and a red colour; silver gives a more malleable gold of a yellow colour.

Fig. 1.2. Precious metal, sheet, wire, tube and findings supplied to the manufacturing jewellery trade by the refiners

So the refiner has to balance one consideration against the other. If hard gold is needed for pins and snaps, he will include as much copper as possible, using only enough silver to give him the colour required. If malleability is called for, such as for deep drawing in a press, then he will use more silver than copper.

The taste of various markets, and the fashion of different periods, influence the demand for the various colours of gold which the refiner can produce. On the Continent, for instance, people have tended in the past to like their gold redder than have people in Britain. Recently there has been a swing towards white gold, both in Britain and abroad, and every now and again there is a fashion for multi-coloured gold jewellery.

Red and yellow gold, as has been shown, are the result of varying the proportions of copper and silver in the alloy. A low-carat white gold can be produced by alloying with a high proportion of silver, but for the higher carat white golds nickel or palladium must be introduced. A blue gold is produced by adding 6 parts of iron to 18 parts of gold. Purple gold is the result of adding 6 parts of aluminium to 18 parts of gold, while an alloy of three-quarters gold and one-quarter zinc produces a lilac colour. Silver and cadmium are used to produce green gold.

When the gold has been alloyed to produce the various carats, colours and grades—special grades for deep spinning and deep stamping, for casting, for enamelling and for making chain—the refiners then process these golds to produce the materials needed by the jewellery trade. They turn the golds into sheet of various gauges, into plain and fancy wires, into tube and into solders, for even the solders used by the jewellery trade must pass the assay (Fig. 1.2). They make findings, too, such as snaps and catches and settings, ear-ring wires and bolt-rings and even eternity rings all ready to take the stones.

GOLD COINS

Many countries have at some time had a gold coinage, and gold coins were in daily use in Britain over many centuries. Henry VII gave us our sovereign at the end of the fifteenth century; it was the equivalent of the 20 silver shillings, which had been the basis of our monetary system. The guinea came later, so named because it was made from gold from the Guinea coast of West Africa. At first the guinea, too, was the equivalent of 20s., but at the end of the seventeenth century, after the Restoration, silver was in such short supply that silversmiths began clipping the silver coinage to obtain enough raw material to fulfil the flood of commissions from the new court.

Eventually, things deteriorated so that no one would exchange a good golden guinea for 20 of these decimated pieces of silver. People began to demand an extra shilling to make up for the bits that had been clipped off, and in 1717 the guinea was officially proclaimed to be worth 21s. And so it remained for the next 100 years, after which it ceased to be minted.

By the early nineteenth century it was becoming widely recog-nised that a 21s. coin was unwieldy—an unsuitable unit for the complicated calculations of an aspiring commercial nation. In 1817, therefore, the old sovereign, worth 20s., was brought back again. The new sovereign was made of 22 carat gold and weighed 123·27447 grains. Sovereigns were last used as currency in 1917.

The law relating to the melting down, retention and use of coins as jewellery will be found in the companion book, *Management for the Retail Jeweller*, in the chapter 'Law and Insurance'.

GOLD AND ECONOMICS

The gold used for jewellery represents only a small fraction of the world output. A considerable part of the gold mined every year is put to economic uses. This means that it goes back into the ground again, into great vaults such as those at Fort Knox in the U.S.A. Gold remains the currency of international trade, and lying in a country's vaults it serves to prop up the economy of that country.

Britain was 'on the Gold Standard' until 1931. This meant, in simple terms, that our national as well as our international trading was based on gold. Our currency was closely linked to gold, which was maintained at an official standard price of 84s. an ounce from 1717 to 1931, except for the ten years between 1915 and 1925. While we were on the Gold Standard, anyone owning a piece of gold could, in theory at least, take it along to the Mint and exchange it for sovereigns at the standard rate. Also, it was laid down by the Bank Charter Act of 1844, that for every pound note issued, the equivalent in gold must exist in the vaults of the Bank.

World War I upset this established order. Between 1915 and 1920 the price of gold fluctuated wildly, soaring to 120s. an ounce. Authority had lost control, and the law of supply and demand had taken over.

In 1925, authority reasserted control, and Britain returned to the Gold Standard, but only until the slump in 1931. In that year our paper currency and gold finally parted company. Since then gold has had no fixed price; like that of any other commodity its price has fluctuated according to supply and demand.

THE PRICE OF GOLD

The price of gold rose less during six centuries than it has risen during the past 30 years. In 1344, gold was worth 22s. 9½d. an ounce. By the sixteenth century the price had risen to 45s. an ounce. During the seventeenth century it rose as high as 86s. an ounce, and then came the long period when the price remained stable at 84s. The quoted price of gold is normally for fine gold, which is of a minimum fineness of 996 parts in 1000.

When Britain left the Gold Standard the price of gold rose rapidly to 130s. in 1932, and 140s. by 1935—the period known to retail jewellers in those days as 'the gold rush'. The then Chancellor of the Exchequer appealed to the patriotism of the people to sell their sovereigns to the banks for the face value of 20s. Avarice prevailed over patriotism and hoards of sovereigns were unearthed and brought into jewellers' shops to sell for from 25s. to 27s. 6d. each. And it was not only their sovereigns that people brought to the jeweller—they brought their old watches, their Victorian jewellery, their old spectacle frames, and disused dentures. Many jewellers in those days were too busy buying to have time to sell.

The price of gold has continued to rise. By 1945 it was 172s., by 1949 it had risen to 248s., and in December 1975 was £69 per ounce.

INDUSTRIAL USES

In addition to its use by the jewellery trade, and its economic role, gold has many industrial applications today—for electrical contacts, for radio valves, for instrument springs—while its resistance to corrosion makes it especially desirable in the chemical engineering and the textile industries, and for space satellites.

SUBSTITUTES FOR GOLD

Ever since rich men began to use gold to boast their wealth to the world, there must have been a market for jewellery and holloware that had the appearance of being made of gold but were within the means of the majority. The bronze jewellery of early civilisations was the costume jewellery of the day. Joan Evans, in her *History of Jewellery*, when writing of the post-Roman period differentiates between the sophisticated jewellery of the mediterranean culture using 'materials that were inherently precious', reserved for the governing classes, and the 'barbarian technique of gilt bronze of the governed'.

PINCHBECK

By the eighteenth century the use of copper and zinc alloys to imitate gold was an established practice, and the most famous of these alloys was pinchbeck. Its inventor was a watchmaker who had a workshop in London's Fleet Street. Christopher Pinchbeck

(1670–1732) evolved his alloy of 83 parts copper to 17 parts zinc, with the idea of marketing an expensive-looking watch case at an attractive price. In the years that followed, however, many jewellers worked in pinchbeck, and made more use of it than did the watch trade. In the early eighteenth century there was a considerable vogue for pinchbeck chatelaines, for instance, and these were manufactured in their thousands.

GILDING-METAL

Pinchbeck was what today would be called gilding-metal. The jeweller now has a range of copper and zinc alloys available to him: 90 copper to 10 zinc gilding-metal, 85–15, and 80–20. All these are strong, corrosion-resistant alloys of good colour, with slightly different working characteristics, those with more zinc being the more malleable. A softer grade still is used for wire, normally a 75–25 alloy, while for casting, which since the development of centrifugal casting has replaced stamping as the principal fabrication technique of the costume jewellery industry, lead and tin replace some of the zinc, to provide better flow.

Though gilding-metal has a golden colour it is seldom used nowadays in its naked state. The customer of today expects imitations of gold to look as golden as the real thing, and so the manufacturer puts a veneer of gold on his gilding-metal.

ROLLED GOLD

Until the recent development of the hard gold plating technique, the most satisfactory method of putting a veneer of gold on to gilding-metal was to make rolled gold. Rolled gold was a British invention, dating from 1817. It is made in the same way as Old Sheffield Plate, and was a logical development of this process which Thomas Bolsover invented in 1743. Under great heat and pressure a block of gold is fused on to a larger block of base metal to make an open sandwich, which is then rolled out repeatedly between highly polished rollers, the sandwich becoming ever thinner and thinner, until sheet of the required gauge is achieved. It was this rolling process which gave rolled gold its name.

In Pforzheim, which has throughout this century been the rolled gold city of Europe, rolled gold having gold on one side only is called 'doublé'. Rolled gold with gold on both sides is known as 'treblé'. The situation is confused, however, by the fact that 'doublé' is also used as a description of quality (see page 16).

Rolled gold wire is made by producing a gold seamless tube. This is done by first deep-drawing sheet gold to form a cup. The end of this cup is sawn off to produce a short fat tube. This then has a base metal core inserted in it. After this it is drawn down in the same way as gold wire.

Great care has to be taken in the production of rolled gold sheet, tube and wire, because only a limited amount of polishing can be done on this material, otherwise the gold veneer will be penetrated and the metal beneath brought to light. So dust is just as much the enemy of the producer or rolled gold manufacturer as it is of the watchmaker.

Silver is sometimes used in place of gilding-metal as the basis for rolled gold, and so are bronze (an alloy of copper and tin) and nickel silver (an alloy of copper nickel and zinc). When silver is used a two-colour decorative effect is sometimes achieved by cutting through the gold to show the silver beneath. Modern textured finishes, achieved by diamond milling, also result in the gold surface being penetrated. Articles decorated in this way are subsequently plated, and are sometimes marked 'R.G.Pl.'. But rolled gold is not really a suitable raw material from which to make this type of jewellery. It is preferable to make it in a base metal and then gold plate it with a deposit comparable to the gold layer on rolled gold.

Various qualities of gold are used for rolled gold. A British Standard, published in 1960, advocated a minimum standard of 9 carat, and Johnson Matthey describe 9, 10, 12 and 14 carat rolled gold as 'the more usual qualities'. All these qualities are supplied in a choice of three colours: red, yellow or white.

The thickness of the gold veneer is usually measured in microns (a thousandth part of a millimetre). The established standard for a good quality rolled gold watch case is 20–30 microns. This should mean that no part of the case is covered with less than a thickness of 0·02 millimetre of gold. To test these cases, samples are taken from every batch and the base metal backing dissolved away with acid, leaving a case-shaped skin of gold which is measured all over with a micrometer. It is generally reckoned that a 20 micron case will give 20 years of wear—a year for every micron.

Standards based on the micron were, in the past, generally reserved for articles such as cigarette cases and cuff links as well as watch cases, where it is essential for the gold to be evenly distributed, because the edges are subjected to considerable wear. When this even spread of gold was less important, the gold content was often expressed in milliemes. This merely indicated the proportion of gold to base metal, and nothing about its distribution over the surface of the article. Jewellery, which is described as of 10 millieme quality, will have 10 grams of fine gold to every kilogram. The well-known doublé, advertised by the Pforzheim manufacturers, was a 10–12 millieme rolled gold. Charnier had 25 grams to the kilo, and Union 50 grams to the kilo. Today the micron unit of measurement is being increasingly used for jewellery, whether produced from rolled gold or by gold plating.

GILDING

The idea of covering base metal with a skin of gold goes back centuries before Bolsover's time. No one knows who invented gilt, or when, but it is known that from very early in history craftsmen were applying gold to the surface of other metals using a bonding agent similar to niello. Later, mercurial gilding was invented. We have seen this process operating in reverse when discussing gold recovery from the Witwatersrand reef. In the recovery process gold is amalgamated with mercury to separate the gold from the rock. In mercurial gilding the amalgamation was done with the idea of attaching the gold to another material. The combined gold and mercury were applied to, say, a base metal chalice, and then the mercury, which has a low vaporisation point, was driven off by heating, leaving the gold fused to the chalice. This process, which is still used occasionally, is very effective. Pieces of silver exist, made 400 or more years ago, that still have the original gilt clinging to them.

ELECTRO-GILDING

Following the taking out of a patent in 1840 by G. R. Elkington, the electro-deposition of metals began on a commercial scale, and before many years had passed the plating bath had become a familiar piece of equipment in the jeweller's workshop.

The plating bath is filled with a solution containing gold potassium cyanide. The plater hangs the jewellery to be plated in the bath, so that this jewellery becomes the cathode. If the bath is thought of as a battery, the jewellery is doing service as the negative pole. The plater switches on the current, and the gold atoms in the solution all move along and attach themselves to the cathode. The solution would, of course, eventually become exhausted of its gold; sometimes this is overcome by making the positive pole of the bath, the anode, from a sheet of gold. When the current is switched on, gold atoms are detached from the anode, go into the solution, travel across the bath and attach themselves to the cathode, and it becomes a continuous process until the anode is stripped of its gold. Nowadays, however, it is usual to use platinum, or platinum-plated anodes, that are permanent, and either to replace the solution when the gold content drops below a certain level or to top it up with a replenisher. This method allows much closer control of the plating solutions.

In the past electro-gilt has had some disadvantages when compared with rolled gold. As 24 carat gold was normally deposited in the plating bath, the gilt was very soft. Also gilding mostly gave only the yellow colour associated with pure gold. With rolled gold, it was easy to produce any of the colours in which carat golds are available. Further, the technique of electro-gilding allowed the deposition of infinitely thin coatings of gold, and offered a temptation that was not always resisted. There is at least some basis of fact to the stories circulating in the trade about parsimonious electroplaters. A great deal of gilt jewellery has come on to the market having had only a very thin plating of soft gold which would not stand up to much wear. Moreover, plating was sometimes done in primitive conditions, often in a bucket in a back room. Standards of cleanliness were not high, and unless all the grease is removed from a piece of jewellery before plating, the gilding will simply peel off.

As a result of recent developments, some of the drawbacks to electro-gilding have disappeared. Today, new processes allow carat golds of various shades to be deposited by the addition of copper, silver, and other metallic salts to the bath and by varying the current density, while it is now possible to deposit gold which is a great deal harder than the electro-gilt of the past.

HARD GOLD PLATING

The relatively new technique of depositing a plating of hard gold is now widely used both in the watch case industry and the jewellery industry.

The details given by Johnson Matthey in their electroplating data will suffice to explain what the process achieves. The salts and anodes that they supply give a deposit of 98 per cent gold and 2 per cent silver, with a Vickers hardness of between 115 and 120 as compared with a hardness of between 65 and 70 for normal electro-gilt. The plating 'can be produced to any normal thickness required'. In other words, by using this technique a coating of a known micron thickness can be applied that will have better wearing qualities not only than gilt, but better even than rolled gold. It has been said that a 20 micron hard gold plated case will wear as well as a 30 micron rolled gold case.

Hard gold plating is carried out in laboratory conditions (Fig. 1.3). Success depends on very careful control of pre-cleaning and of the contents of the plating bath. Care has also to be taken to control

Fig. 1.3 A computer-controlled plating bath. The timing of the various stages of the process is programmed; all the operator needs to do is load the jigs.

temperature current density and the rate of agitation of the pieces being plated. Plating with a gold alloy is more exacting than plating with pure gold. After plating there are more cleaning operations, and then the thicker platings are heat-treated.

This process, like any other, can of course be debased. The production of cheap hard gold plated jewellery, just flashed with gold and produced without the necessary strict control, could make the public as suspicious of this as they are of gilt and rolled gold. Efforts are being made within the trade to establish minimum standards for hard gold plate to prevent this loss of reputation, but at the time of writing there are no legally imposed standards.

Since the Trade Descriptions Act was passed jewellers have become increasingly aware of the necessity for differentiating between a rolled gold article and one which has been gold plated. While five major Pforzheim producers now market their plated lines as Guaranteed Gold Plated, some smaller German firms continue to market plated wares as 'rolled gold' or 'doublé'.

GOLD CORE AND GOLD SHELL

In the past a number of descriptive names were given by the trade to gold-covered articles, which are now not permitted by the assay offices. One of these was gold core. This was a 9 carat rolled gold, a fifth of which was gold when it was despatched from the refiners. Some of the gold was, of course, bound to be polished away in the process of turning the sheet metal into jewellery.

Gold shell was a name sometimes given to an electroplated article having gold of sufficient substance deposited on it to stand up by itself, if the base metal were etched away.

GOLD BACK AND FRONT

This is best explained by describing a gold back and front heart-shaped locket. This consisted of a hollow heart-shaped frame of gilding-metal to which two heart-shaped pieces stamped out of gold, usually 9 carat, had been attached. When the locket was closed, all that could be seen was made of gold. The manufacturer was thus able to offer what appeared to be a gold locket at a considerably lower price than would have been possible had the whole been made of gold. Gold back and front articles are now also declared illegal by the assay offices.

LACQUER

Lacquer is a synthetic resin suspended in a volatile solvent which evaporates, leaving the resin behind as a film over an article. Lacquer can be either clear or coloured. Gold-coloured lacquer is used to simulate gold on very cheap jewellery. Coloured lacquers are used to simulate enamel. Colourless lacquer is used to protect other finishes. It is not unusual for gilt jewellery and compacts to be given a coating of colourless lacquer. Provided that it is not subjected to too much wear, lacquer can last for quite a long time.

SILVER

It is not known when men first started to turn silver into ornaments and vessels, but it was used by the ancient Egyptians and the Sumerians. Athens was founded on silver, just as in the nineteenth century Johannesburg was founded on gold. When the mines that had made the Athenians rich were eventually worked out, the silversmiths of the classical period, including the Romans who were great lovers of silver, got their raw material from the mines of Thrace and of Spain.

The European silversmiths of the Middle Ages got their silver, from which they wrought plate for the great new Gothic cathedrals, from Germany and from Bohemia. In the sixteenth century the Spanish conquerors of Mexico discovered there the seemingly inexhaustible lodes, and started to send back to Spain galleons laden with bullion. They enriched not only their mother country, but England as well. English privateers flourished for over a century on the Spanish Main, bringing into Plymouth Sound many a bright cargo belonging to the King of Spain.

Silver from Mexico, and from South and Central America, satisfied the needs of silversmiths and coiners of Europe until the nineteenth century, when the great finds and silver rushes in the U.S.A. began. Harry Comstock's famous lode was discovered in 1859, and the first shaft of the great Anaconda mine was sunk in 1894. And there were many more smaller finds. In Australia, too, there were silver rushes as well as gold rushes. The most famous find there was Broken Hill, which the miners gradually reduced to rubble, so that today there is no sign of a hill.

RECOVERY TODAY

The leading silver-producing nation is still Mexico. She produces 35 per cent of all silver mined this side of the Iron Curtain. The U.S.A. comes next, contributing 25 per cent, followed by South and Central America, where 20 per cent of the total is mined. Canada contributes 10 per cent and Australia 5 per cent. The total world production, excluding that mined in Russia, in China and the other Communist countries, which the U.S. Bureau of Mines estimate to be about 10 million ounces a year, was over 220 million ounces in 1966. Silver is the commonest, and therefore the cheapest, of the precious metals.

SILVER FROM LEAD

Apart from its widespread occurrence, there is another reason why silver is relatively cheap. Most of what is recovered is a by-product of the mining for other metals. Between 80 and 85 per cent of all the silver recovered today is found in lead, zinc, copper, nickel, tin or gold ores. The most important of these sources is lead ore. Where lead is found, so almost invariably is silver. About 45 per cent of all silver comes from lead mines.

SILVER IN BRITAIN

At one time or another silver has been mined in most countries of the world. In Britain silver has been recovered, in small quantities, over a long period. In olden days, it was a by-product of the Cornish tin and lead mines. More recently the lead mine at Mill-close in Derbyshire has produced a few thousand ounces a year, but this closed down in 1961, and recent statistics do not include Britain as a source of silver. But the British Isles may soon be included again, for a lead mine has been opened up at Tynagh in Eire, which is yielding a concentrate containing 40 per cent lead, and is expected to yield 4 ounces of silver for every ton. There is also some talk of re-opening an old lead mine in Scotland which contains silver.

THE PROPERTIES OF SILVER

The craftsman finds silver a particularly sympathetic metal in which to work. It has many properties in common with gold, and for some purposes the smith even finds it preferable.

Like gold, silver is a malleable and ductile metal. It cannot be beaten out quite as thin, or drawn quite as fine, as gold but it has excellent working qualities none the less. It can be rolled down to make sheet 0·0005 in. thick, or a troy ounce can be turned into a mile of wire. It bends easily without a tendency to crack, so that it is a good metal from which to make boxes. It can be tempered to make blades for fruit and butter knives, while its malleability means that it can be raised under the hammer or deep drawn in the press to make hollowares.

Silver is a noble metal, second only to gold in nobility. It does not combine readily with the oxygen in the atmosphere, and is resistant to the attack of many corrosive substances. It is unaffected by the acetic acid in fruit juices, or by hydrochloric or weak nitric acid. But it is attacked by strong nitric acid and by sulphuric acid, neither of which attacks gold.

Advantages of silver over gold are its greater tensile strength, its relative lightness and its greater reflecting power. Its strength, and the fact that fine silver has a specific gravity of only 10·5 compared with 19·32 for fine gold, means that it is a better metal than gold for making into domestic hollowares. A pint tankard made of gold would be quite unwieldy and less strong than one made of silver.

We tend to think of silver as having a soft white beauty, but in fact silver is the brightest of all the metals when newly polished. It reflects 95 per cent of the incident light that falls on it, compared with 92 per cent for gold, 82 per cent for copper, only 66 per cent for chromium (a good sales point this) and 62 per cent for rhodium.

Silver, unlike chromium and steel, is not unattractive when scratched. Because it is a soft metal the scratches that it acquires do not have such sharp edges as the scratches taken by harder metals. Also the scratches on silver become blurred with wear and with polishing, and it is this process of scratching and blurring which, over the years, imparts to silver that unique patina which collectors set such store by.

A disadvantage of silver is its affinity for sulphur. Silver eggspoons are particularly vulnerable. The sulphur in eggs attacks silver, turning the surface a nasty black-brown colour. This tarnish was not easy to remove with the cleaning methods of the past.

Unhappily, not only eggs but the air around us is full of sulphur, in the form of sulphur dioxide, a gas which pours out of domestic and industrial chimneys. This is the main cause of tarnish on silver, and was a contributory factor in the decline in silver sales in the years after the last war. Fortunately, the chemist has done much to solve the tarnish problem and to make silver acceptable in a servantless age, by inventing various forms of tarnish protection, a subject which will be considered again later in this chapter.

A further drawback of silver for the craftsman is its susceptibility, in the alloyed form in which it is used in the trade, to firestain. Here again, however, the scientist has helped, and the problem has been minimised.

The silver used by the trade is alloyed with copper, and during annealing and soldering, when the alloy is heated, the copper oxidises and a black stain appears on the surface of the metal. As operation succeeds operation the stain tends to penetrate the metal, and if this happens the firestain can be extremely difficult to remove. Surface stains can be removed by rubbing with a stone or by pickling in acid, but if the stain is deep-seated the silver has to be electroplated to hide it. Today, however, the refiners anneal their sheet and tube in an oxygen-free atmosphere, so that the material at least reaches the manufacturer unimpaired by firestain. Such stain as the silver now acquires in the workshop is usually easily removed, and the old practice of plating to hide firestain is today used far less widely. Plating, incidentally, imparts slightly greater tarnish resistance to an article, because pure silver resists tarnish a little better than sterling silver.

REFINING

Although most of our silver today is a by-product (a small percentage of the metal is present in ores rich in other metals) there are lodes, particularly in Mexico, rich enough to be mined for their silver alone.

To recover the silver from these silver ores, they are crushed, and the silver recovered by the cyanide process. The crushed silver ore is dissolved in a cyanide solution, usually a calcium cyanide solution, and the silver precipitated by the addition of zinc. The resulting precipitate is between 75 and 90 per cent pure. After being washed with acid to remove surplus zinc, this impure silver is melted in a stream of air, which results in the oxidising of any base metal present. The oxides are then skimmed off the surface of the silver which will now be about 98 per cent pure, and ready for despatch to the refinery.

When the silver is a by-product, other methods of recovery are used. As stated earlier, the most important source of silver is lead ore, and two processes are used to separate the silver from the lead. These are known as the Parkes process and the Betts process.

The Parkes process uses the fact that zinc has a greater affinity for silver than lead, and so any copper, tin and other impurities are first separated out, then the lead containing the silver is melted, and zinc added. The zinc combines with the silver and is removed from it by distillation.

The Betts process is electrolytic. The lead containing the silver is cast into sheets which serve as anodes in a bath containing lead fluosilicate. The passage of an electric current through the bath etches away the lead from the anode leaving a silver slime which can be scraped off and refined. This and the Parkes process both give a silver about 90 per cent pure.

The 90 per cent pure silver has to be further purified at the refinery before the various grades of alloyed silver, with the required working properties, can be produced. This purification can be achieved by further cupulation, that is, by oxidation of the base metals present by heating the silver in a stream of air. Nowadays, though, most of the refining of silver is done electrolytically. The silver is cast into anodes, and these are placed in refining cells. The passage of an electric current through these cells results in crystalline silver of a purity of between 99·95 and 99·99 per cent being deposited on the cathodes.

The refiners produce silver of three qualities. They produce sterling silver, consisting of 92·5 per cent silver and 7·5 per cent base metal, mostly copper. Small quantities of Britannia standard silver, which contains 958·4 parts in 1000 silver, and which was introduced in the seventeenth century to discourage the clipping of the coinage by the silversmiths, is still used for the occasional piece today. Then there is 800 silver, which, as will be gathered from its name, is only 800 parts in 1000 silver, or 80 per cent pure. This standard is still widely used on the Continent, but it is not permitted to offer wares of this standard for sale in Britain unless one is careful not to describe them as silver.

In addition to these different qualities the refiners supply the manufacturing silversmith with different types of silver for different jobs. Cadmium is often added to silver when sheet suitable for spinning is to be produced. Then high melting point alloys, free of zinc and cadmium, are made up for enamelling.

Nowadays the manufacturer can buy a vast range of materials from the refiners. There is the sheet silver of various gauges which he can turn into coffee pots, cruets, napkin rings, sports trophies and spoons. Sheet silver gauges are expressed in B.M.G. (Birmingham metal gauge). This is an irregular scale of measurement. The difference between 40 B.M.G. at the top of the scale and 39 B.M.G. is a hundredth of an inch. The difference between 1 B.M.G. and 2 B.M.G. is only a thousandth of an inch. Besides sheet, the refiners supply the trade with tube of various cross-sections, with plain wires and with fancy wires produced by stamping or rolling. They supply rod, too, and the flakes, grain or shot used for casting. They supply finding as well, and the various solders with different melting points. Just how these materials are turned into hollowares, flatwares and smallwares will be described in a later chapter.

SILVER COINS

Silver had great importance in the past as a coin metal. Most countries had a silver coinage. In Britain this dates back hundreds of years. The term 'sterling' is said by some to have derived from the name 'starling', or 'sterling', given to the silver pennies used in this country 700 years ago. They are said to have got the name because they were made by Easterlings, coiners from Hansa in North Germany. Other derivations suggested for the term are that it was the name of a twelfth century silver coin bearing a star, or that it came from the starlings on the coat of arms of Edward the Confessor, that appeared on coins minted in his reign. It is not known which, if any, of these legends is true.

We, in Britain, lost our silver coinage in 1947, though deterioration had started 25 years earlier. Until 1922, British silver coins had been made of 925 silver, the same standard as the legal standard for wrought plate. In 1922, coins which were only 50 per cent silver began to be minted. During the next quarter of a century various alloys containing 50 per cent silver were used at the mint, and then finally in 1947 silver disappeared altogether as a result of the coinage act of that year. Since then our 'silver' coins have been made of an alloy called cupro-nickel, which consists of 75 per cent copper and 25 per cent nickel.

If, however, there is no longer a demand for silver from the mint, this has been more than compensated for by the growing demand from industry. The great popularity of photography nowadays results in an enormous demand for silver nitrate, the light-sensitive chemical used in the preparation of photographic emulsions. Silver is also important to the electrical and electronics industries, because besides being the best conductor of heat of any metal, it is also the best conductor of electricity. Its nobility recommends it to the food and pharmaceutical industries.

PROTECTION AGAINST TARNISH

From time to time experiments have been carried out in an effort to produce a silver alloy that would not tarnish, but so far without success. If tarnish is to be avoided, therefore, silverwares must be protected in some way from the sulphur dioxide in the atmosphere. Until recently this could only be done by plating the silver with a metal that did not tarnish, or by coating the silver with lacquer.

Silverwares have been plated with gold down the centuries, but presumably in the early days when the atmosphere was less polluted with sulphur dioxide, the object of this was to enrich rather than protect the silver. Anyway, as any museum curator will confirm, mercurial gilt is not particularly tarnish resistant. Electro-gilding offered better protection, but it had two drawbacks. It was very soft, and therefore did not stand up to wear very well. Also, of course, it changed the silver's appearance, and not everyone liked their silver to look golden. Hard gold plating overcomes the first of these objections but does not overcome the second.

Lacquer is a much cheaper way of protecting silver without greatly altering its appearance. Modern transparent lacquers are a quite satisfactory way of protecting decorative silverwares for a number of years. Lacquer, of course, cannot be used for any article likely to be subjected to hard wear like flatware, or for anything that will be subjected to heat, such as an entrée dish or an ash tray. Even the lacquer on decorative silver will eventually wear off, and if silver treated with lacquer is accidentally cleaned with an abrasive, this will scratch the lacquer and cause peeling, and the unprotected areas of the silver will then tarnish.

Recently, the scientists have evolved new and better ways of protecting silver. One technique is to plate the silver with a rhodium-based alloy. Rhodium, one of the platinum group of metals, provides very good protection; it is both a hard and a noble metal, and, when alloyed, its colour if not acceptable to antique collectors is not sufficiently unlike silver to dissuade less exacting owners from ridding themselves of the burden of regular cleaning. It is not a cheap way of protecting silver, or rather the initial cost is fairly high, but if properly applied a plating of rhodium alloy should give years of protection even to pieces having to stand up to a good deal of rough usage.

Another of the new methods of protection is to give the silver a coating of silicones. This is cheaper than rhodium plating, but the protection does not last nearly so long. On the other hand the silicone coating alters the appearance of the silver only very slightly. Treated pieces tend to yellow with age, however, and the length of time which silicone protection lasts depends upon the amount of wear on the silver. It could be months, it could be a year or more.

Besides the silicone treatment, which is carried out in a workshop, there are domestic cleaners on the market that leave a silicone coating behind, which prevents tarnish for perhaps one or two months, depending again on the amount of wear and also on the amount of sulphur dioxide in the atmosphere.

A third modern answer to tarnish is a chemical containing sulphur in a form that does not cause tarnishing. It is applied to the silver and, as it were, satisfies the silver's appetite for sulphur so that it does not combine with the sulphur dioxide in the air.

Silver not in daily use can be protected simply by storing it in the special papers or bags available. These all work in much the same way. The paper, or the fabric, from which the bags are made is impregnated with a substance (colloidal silver is sometimes used) which combines readily with sulphur dioxide. The paper or bag acts as a filter extracting the sulphur dioxide from the air before it reaches the silver.

CLEANERS AND POLISHES

There is some confusion, understandable as there are so many products on the market today, between the silver cleaners and the silver polishes. The early cleaners worked on the principle of scouring the tarnish off the silver. They were abrasives hard enough to remove the tarnish but not to cut the silver. The rubbing involved also polished the silver; they were combined cleaners and polishes. Since the war a number of 'dips' have appeared on the market. These liquids, in which the silver was placed, dissolved the tarnish away and took the labour out of cleaning, making it possible to live with decorative silver in a servantless age. But for silver to look really nice it still had to be polished, though this involved no more trouble than polishing any other household possession. More recently, foam polishes, similar to those used for cars, have made their appearance, and these clean and polish at the same time. The domestic tarnish-preventative liquids on the market also clean and polish the silver in one operation.

SUBSTITUTES FOR SILVER

PLATED WARES

The most convincing imitations of silverwares are base metal articles plated in some way with a coating of silver. An early technique for doing this was called 'close plating'. The article to be plated was first dipped in molten tin, and pieces of silver foil were applied and fixed in position by burnishing or hammering. A bond between the foil and the tin was effected by passing a soldering iron over the surface which melted the low melting point tin. A variation on this technique was known as 'French plating'. In this process the tin was omitted and the silver foil heated to a high temperature and burnished directly on to the base metal article.

OLD SHEFFIELD PLATE

Sheffield plate, invented by Thomas Bolsover in 1743, was a far more satisfactory technique than either of these earlier ones.

Bolsover's invention came at a propitious time. In the early years of the eighteenth century the middle classes were assuming an importance they had never had before. The merchants were growing rich, some of them very rich indeed, and they were beginning to ape their betters, the aristocracy, by setting fine tables laden with plate. They bought candlesticks and epergnes, tea-pots and coffee-pots, salts and dredgers from the great Huguenot silversmiths and from the native English smiths. Bolsover's invention made it possible for the slightly less successful members of the middle class to put on a show. Old Sheffield plate, as we call it, looked like silver and cost a great deal less, and was soon in great demand. In the years following 1765, that is from the time when the invention began to be fully exploited, Sheffield became a boom town.

Old Sheffield plate was made, like rolled gold, by fusing a block of noble metal, in this case silver, on to a block of base metal, usually copper, and then rolling out the block to form sheet of various gauges.

Much of the Sheffield plate was made in the neo-classical style, usually known as the Adam style, and new techniques had to be developed to impart to it the necessary decoration. The traditional techniques of chasing and engraving could not be used, because they would have cut into the silver surface and brought to light the copper underneath, so the decoration had to be stamped or rolled on to the metal. If engraving was called for, shields of silver were soldered into the pieces.

Old Sheffield plate is attracting collectors in growing numbers. Unfortunately many of the old pieces became worn in use and were restored by electroplating when the copper began to show. This, of course, reduces the value of the piece from the collector's point of view.

ELECTROPLATING

Old Sheffield plate was eventually superseded by George Elkington's exploitation of electroplating in the 1830s and 40s. In this process the silver is deposited either on brass or nickel silver. Nickel silver made its appearance in Europe in the 1820s, but it was not new. The Chinese had been using a similar alloy for centuries. The nickel–copper alloy which they used was known to European travellers to the Orient as white bronze.

In the early years of the nineteenth century experiments to discover a satisfactory alloy were carried out in Germany, which is why nickel silver is sometimes called German silver. The Germans evolved an alloy consisting of nickel, copper and zinc, the nickel providing hardness and tarnish resistance, the zinc giving a low melting point and improving the ductility. This alloy was originally used unplated as a silver substitute, and is still used in this way to produce very cheap flatware.

A similar metal was evolved in Sheffield in the eighteenth century. This metal which consisted mostly of tin, with some antimony and copper, was called white metal or Vickers metal after James Vickers who first used it to make holloware and flatware in the 1780s. It was later called Britannia metal.

Nickel silver* began to be important when Elkington started to use it as the base metal foundation of e.p.n.s., electroplated nickel silver. The principles of electroplating have already been described in connection with gold plating. The only difference is that, for silver plating, silver salts are used in the bath and a silver anode to replenish the solution.

PLATING STANDARDS

There are unfortunately no legal standards for silver plating. The term A.1 is used by most firms for their top quality, but as a *Which?* report published a few years ago revealed, A.1 means very different things to different firms. A good A.1 quality would have a plating 0·001 in. thick, about the thickness of tissue paper. Some firms express this as so many pennyweights per dozen tablespoons, or so many pennyweights per square foot. A plating of 16 pennyweights per square foot will give a lifetime's wear. [The pennyweight was abolished on 1st February, 1969 under the Weights and Measures Act, 1963—but old usages die hard.]

Recently, hard silver plating has been introduced, and this promises even better wearing properties than normal silver plating, but at the present time only one company, a German one, offers hard silver plated cutlery and flatware.

PLATINUM METALS

In 1731, a Spaniard, Don Antonio de Ulloa, wrote *A Narrative of a Journey to South America,* which contains a reference to 'platina', the diminutive of the Spanish word for silver. This 'little silver' was sometimes used by the Indians to make beads, but for the most part the Indians considered platinum to be a nuisance. Its high

*This description may well prove to be unacceptable under the Trade Descriptions Act 1968.

melting point meant that the native craftsmen found it unworkable, and the platinum that was found in the gold and silver mines in the Choco district of Colombia was dumped with other refuse in the Bogota river to await the miners of the nineteenth century.

The first platinum known to have reached England was sent here by a Jamaican assayer, Charles Wood, in 1741, and scientific work on the metal was first carried out by William Watson, who described its interesting properties in the Philosophical Transactions of the Royal Society in 1750. Then, in 1789, came the first recorded use of platinum for a ceremonial vessel. In that year Charles III presented Pope Pius VI with a platinum chalice.

The problem of working platinum continued to limit its use until the invention of the oxy-hydrogen blowpipe by the American scientist, Robert Hare, in 1847. Meanwhile, it had been discovered that platinum was not a single metal, but a family of six metals. In 1800, William Woolaston and Smithson Tennant had established a partnership to try to produce a malleable platinum for commercial use. This partnership was to prove fruitful in a way neither man could have anticipated. In 1802, as a result of his study of platinum, Woolaston isolated palladium, naming it after the planet Pallas, which had also just been discovered. Next, he isolated another of the platinum metals, rhodium. Its name derives from the Greek word for rose, because its salts are rose coloured.

Smithson Tennant's contribution was his discovery of osmium and iridium. Then a Russian scientist named Claus discovered ruthenium, Ruthina being the Latin name for Russia. The platinum family was now complete.

Until 1916 the biggest source of our supply of platinum metals, which are almost always found together, were the alluvial mines of South America, including the tailings of old gold and silver mines and the bed of the Bogota river. Another source was the Ural mountains in Russia, where platinum had been discovered in 1823. Today, most of our platinum metals come from Canada, as a by-product of the nickel and copper mines in Ontario province, and from Rustenburg in South Africa. The refiners refuse to give output figures, for reasons best known to themselves, but the world output of platinum must be in excess of 500,000 ounces.

The recovery and refining of platinum differ only in detail from the recovery and refining of gold already described, an important factor in determining refining techniques being that platinum like gold can be dissolved in *aqua regia*.

Platinum recommends itself to the manufacturing jeweller for a number of reasons. Once the problem of melting it had been overcome it proved to have good working properties, being almost as malleable and ductile as gold. It does not oxidise during working. Its strength and colour make it ideal for mounts for diamond jewellery. Further recommendations are its nobility (it resists the attack of almost everything except *aqua regia*) and its reflective power which, though not as good as that of silver and gold, is acceptable.

Platinum has one disadvantage as a metal for making jewellery. It is very heavy indeed. It has a specific gravity of 21·43, and a large platinum brooch will weigh down a light fabric, while to wear sizeable platinum earrings is a real labour of love.

The lower specific gravity of palladium, only 12·16, was one of the arguments urged for its adoption by the jewellery trade. Another argument was its relative cheapness. It offers many of the same physical properties and much the same appearance at about a third of the price of platinum. For some reason, however, palladium has never become popular except for settings for diamond rings.

The only other platinum metal of much importance in the jewellery trade is rhodium, which is harder and whiter than platinum, and the most reflective of all the platinum metals. It is widely used for plating. Silver jewellery is often rhodium plated, and it is a common trade practice to plate platinum and white gold jewellery with rhodium.

Like gold and silver, platinum has to be mixed with other metals to improve its working qualities. Palladium, iridium and copper are the metals most commonly used for this purpose. Platinum has been assayed and hallmarked in Britain since January 1975, following the Hallmarking Act of 1973. The standard for platinum is 950 parts in 1000 pure. Tests carried out by one of the refiners in the 1950s revealed that some manufacturers were at that time using platinum considerably below the accepted standard.

There has been a considerable increase of interest in platinum among jewellery manufacturers recently. The rise in the price of gold has meant that nowadays platinum is very little dearer than 18 carat white gold. Also the mining interests have set up a publicity body, the Platinum Guild, to stimulate public interest in the metal. Supplies, too, are nowadays more readily available than they have been in recent years, mainly from the mines at Rustenburg in South Africa.

Like the other noble metals, the platinum metals have many industrial uses today. To cite just a few, it is used for vessels for the chemical industry, for electrodes, and for the decoration of china and book covers.

BASE METALS AND THE JEWELLER

Apart from the noble metals and their imitators, the metal most likely to be found in a jeweller's shop, nowadays, is stainless steel. It is less than 60 years ago that this was discovered by a Sheffield man, Harry Brearley, almost by accident, while he was experimenting to find a non-rusting steel that could be used for rifle components. That was in 1913.

At first, no one was much impressed by Brearley's discovery that an alloy containing 13 per cent chromium, 3 per cent carbon, and 84 per cent iron did not rust. One reason for this cool reception was that the new steel proved difficult to work. Also, the experimental knife blades made from it were insufficiently hardened and proved to be poor tools. These early stainless steel knives, made before the working of this metal was fully understood, gave rise to the myth that stainless steel blades do not take as good an edge as the old carbon steel blades. In fact, recent tests carried out in butchers' shops have shown that not only are stainless steel blades sharper but they also keep their edge four times as long as carbon steel blades.

Until the 1950s the most important use of stainless steel connected with the jewellery trade was for the making of knife blades. Even before the war, however, a handful of firms had been far-sighted enough to realise that this new metal had a great future. They began to produce stainless steel hollowares and flatwares, but sales in those days were small. Only in the past 20 years has this metal really come into its own, challenging silver-plated wares for pride of place on the average British table.

We tend to talk about stainless steel as though it were one alloy only, but in fact there are a number of stainless steels. They all contain a proportion of chromium, for it is the presence of this metal that gives stainless steel its resistance to rust, but the proportions of the constituent metals are varied to provide the different working qualities demanded by various industries. The stainless steel most commonly used for flatwares and hollowares is what is called 18/8. This contains 18 parts of chromium and 8 parts of nickel. This alloy has good working properties and a high resistance to rust.

The terms 'austenitic' and 'martensitic' are sometimes seen in descriptions of stainless steel. Austenitic steel, named after the Assayer to the Mint, Sir W. Roberts Austen, is the 18/8 carbon-free stainless steel already described. Martensitic steel is stainless steel with a small carbon content, about a half per cent, used for making knife blades.

The term stainless steel is not really accurate. Rustproof would really be a better name for it. Certain foodstuffs, salt and vinegar for instance, do stain stainless steel but most stains can be easily removed, simply by washing in soapy water. Solid detergents if they are not completely dissolved can, however, cause pitting. More permanent stains also sometimes appear on knife blades.

One of the drawbacks to stainless steel as a metal for making domestic hollowares and flatwares is that it scratches, and because the metal is hard these scratches are unsightly and permanent. They do not polish out like the scratches on silver. So highly polished stainless steel does, after a time, look the worse for wear, and this has led to a great increase in the popularity of the satin-finished stainless steel to which there was some initial resistance. Scratches do not mar its appearance to anything like the same extent as they do the bright-finished wares.

PEWTER

Pewter is a mixture of tin and lead, nowadays mostly of tin, often as much as 95 per cent, and very little lead. Indeed the Board of Trade restrict the lead content in pewter measures and tankards to not more than 10 per cent, in the interests of public health.

Our ancestors were not so mollycoddled. The tankards they used often contained as much as 30 per cent lead; indeed they were sometimes made of that villainous looking 'black metal', that was 50 per cent lead and 50 per cent tin. And there is really no evidence to show that anyone's health suffered from drinking out of these leaden vessels.

Not only lead was used in the old days to alloy tin to make pewter. 'Common pewter' consisted of 83 per cent tin and 17 per cent antimony, while 'fine pewter' was an alloy of 81 per cent tin, and 19 per cent copper.

Until the eighteenth century, pewter was a very important metal; everybody ate off it and drank from it. Then the increased production of china, and the invention of Sheffield plate, resulted in a decline in the craft of the pewterer, and by the middle of the nineteenth century it had almost died out altogether.

The marks to be found on pewter vessels are as interesting in their own way as those on silver. In 1503 it became obligatory for every master pewterer to stamp his wares with his touch mark, and this marking continued to be obligatory until 1824. The early marks consisted of heraldic devices embodying the maker's initials. The touch marks were all stamped on a plate kept by the

Pewterers Guild. Unfortunately, the first plate was destroyed in 1666, during the Great Fire of London. Later plates, however, have been preserved.

After 1690, the master pewterers were allowed a little more latitude in the form that their touch mark could take, and some decided that it would be better advertising to use their whole name instead of just their initials, while some also added the word 'London' to give their wares a metropolitan cachet. Others went too far. They began to use marks that bore too close a resemblance to the hallmarks stamped on silver at Goldsmiths Hall, and the Goldsmiths Company had to take out an injunction restraining the pewterers from attempting to deceive the public in this way.

Countless pewter vessels and pewter plates must have been made in the old days, when every household had its garnish of pewter, but surprisingly little remains for the collectors of today. When pewter lost its popularity in the eighteenth and nineteenth centuries, thousands of unfashionable plates and tankards and jugs must simply have been melted down for scrap, for the owners could hardly have been expected to foresee that there would be a pewter revival in the second half of the twentieth century.

BRONZE

Bronze, the oldest alloy known to man, has been highly regarded at many periods in history. It had many uses—for spears and armour, hammers and cannon. The craftsmen of ancient China cast great bronze incense burners and bells; the sculptors of ancient Greece cast their graceful statues in this brown metal, a mixture of copper and tin, with usually some zinc. The Phoenician traders of the Bronze Age came all the way to Cornwall to obtain the tin which their craftsmen at home, in what is now Syria, needed to make the bronze for fashioning into jewellery and weapons. The manufacturers of the nineteenth century also regarded bronze highly, making clocks and mantelpiece statuary for Victorian drawing rooms from it. Nowadays, however, bronze is a neglected metal, used only occasionally for the sculpture created to adorn some new office building. One day, however, bronze may stage a comeback; once again there may be bronze jewellery, bronze figurines and bronze vases.

CHROMIUM

Chromium is normally met only in the form of chromium plate, which, like so many other things, has a bad name simply from being badly used. Many have suffered from the shoddy chromium plating only too often supplied by motor car manufacturers, and as a result 'chrome' is regarded with suspicion and is expected to pit and peel and rust. Properly applied, chromium plate can provide a hard, tarnish resistant, bright finish that will stand a great deal of wear. It has, however, a rather bluish look compared with silver, and many people, perhaps because of its associations, think of it as cheap looking. Chromium plate is met with in the jewellery trade nowadays only on cheap watch cases, cheap powder compacts, spoons and on very cheap costume jewellery. Experiments some years ago resulted in the production of coloured chromium plate, but this has proved to have little commercial importance.

CHAPTER 2

The Gems

Fashion and economic considerations have over recent years brought great changes to the world of gemstones. There is a great demand these days for real jewellery in the medium price range, and to meet this demand the jewellery manufacturers have had to employ a wide range of relatively inexpensive gem material in place of the faceted stones, which have become increasingly expensive. The reason for this rise in the price of fine facetable gem material is that such material is becoming scarcer at a time when world demand is increasing. More and more people throughout the world are now buying jewellery. The Japanese, for example, who only a few years ago showed little interest in gems, are now buying them in great numbers. The rise in prices due to increasing demand and diminishing supply applies not only to fine emeralds, rubies and sapphires, but to all fine facetable material. Between 1970 and 1975, for instance, the price of good-quality aquamarine rose from £60 per carat to £140 per carat. The results of escalating prices are that nowadays gemstones are being scattered more thinly over more metal, and many more types of gemstones are being used in jewellery than at any time since the Victorian period.

There is every likelihood that the trend will continue. Julius Petsch in Idar Oberstein told a party of British jewellers, when he talked to them in 1974, that facetable stones were going to become scarcer, and that they would in the future often have to persuade their customers to accept jewellery set with cabochons. Though the jewellers in question expressed doubts that their customers would in fact find cabochons acceptable, it must be remembered that only a century ago the cabochon enjoyed a great vogue and some of the most attractive Victorian jewellery featured cabochon garnets and amethysts. Since Julius Petsch made his prediction many more cabochons are seen on the continent, and more recently in this country there has been an increasing use of cabochons. During this period, too, beads and polished slices of a variety of gem materials have been used to enrich jewellery, notably jade, coral, dyed agate, rhodonite and rhodochrosite.

So whereas the average jeweller a quarter of a century ago dealt with little else in the course of trade except the 'big four' (diamond, emerald, ruby and sapphire), in future he is likely to find himself dealing with a host of gems. He will have to be more open-minded about what constitutes a gem, more receptive to the new and unfamiliar and, of course, more knowledgeable about gem minerals generally. And not only will he be dealing with gemstones set in jewellery, he will probably also be selling more gem minerals in the form of *objets d'art* and shelf specimens. Every year more and more people are becoming interested in mineral specimens, and more and more people are using specimens and *objets d'art* as decorations in their homes.

With the scarcity of major stones of fine quality, it obviously behoves the jeweller to educate his customers to accept alternatives. Two new and very attractive alternative stones have made their appearance in recent years. These are the mauve form of zoisite, found in Tanzania and known as tanzanite, and the gem-quality grossular garnet of a fine emerald colour called tsavorite, found in both Tanzania and Kenya. One hopes that supplies of both these stones will be increasingly available in the future and that they will become increasingly acceptable to the public as they become more familiar. There is, however, some doubt about the supply of these and indeed many other stones found in the developing countries. The governments of these countries are inclined, understandably perhaps, to nationalise their natural resources. Having done so, however, often they fail to exploit these resources and (as in the case of tanzanite) the supply tends to dry up or to become sporadic and unpredictable.

Besides needing to be familiar with the whole range of gem minerals, the jeweller in the future will also have to be very much on his guard where gems are concerned. New ways of altering gem minerals and new and ever more plausible reconstituted and synthetic gems are an ever-present problem. Altered stones or synthetics can result in the jeweller losing his money or jeopardising his reputation, or both. Even plastic simulants of such gem materials as amber can deceive the unwary.

Altered gem minerals are nothing new. The vast majority of aquamarines have for years been heat-treated to turn them from the more commonly found green colour to the more desirable water blue. Commercial citrine and cairngorm have been produced for a long time by heat-treating inferior amethyst, while the heat-treating of zircons (turning them from brown to colourless crystals) goes back centuries. Agate has also been dyed in Idar Oberstein for a century or more, while such materials as jade, lapis-lazuli and turquoise are often stained. These alterations are more or less permanent, and jewellers (if they have been aware of it) have come to accept the practice of heat treatment as a necessary and useful way of improving on nature. In the past few years, however, there has been a good deal of experimentation, and some commercial colour alteration by means of X-rays, neutron bombardment and so on. While it is generally felt that such methods of improving stones would be just as acceptable as heat-treatment if the results were permanent, in practice it seems that this is not always the case. In 1974 a number of very experienced Idar Oberstein dealers paid high prices for some parcels of topaz that exhibited a beautiful deep aquamarine blue coloration. Unfortunately after a matter of days the colour faded away altogether. The best known example of the use of these new techniques is the coloration of diamonds. Diamonds bombarded in cyclotrons and atomic piles have been coloured green, blue, brown and yellow. X-ray bombardment has been used to turn kunzite green, and to deepen the yellow of yellow sapphires, albeit only temporarily.

The new and more sophisticated synthetic gemstones are a problem to the jeweller, because he could be deceived by them. It must be borne in mind, however, that those who produce them do not do so with intent to deceive the jewellery-buying public. These synthetics are seen by their producers as a less expensive substitute for natural stones, which are rare and expensive. One suspects though, that the desire of men like Pierre Gilson and Carroll Chatham, who have been the most successful workers in this field, to reproduce natural minerals as accurately as possible is also motivated by the scientific challenge this presents.

A question posed by the existence of synthetic gems almost indistinguishable from real ones is whether the jewellery trade should accept such stones as part of its stock-in-trade. The reactions of individual jewellers to this question vary considerably. Many would prefer to continue to sell only natural gems, others are less certain of their position. The fact is that synthetic gems are already being used fairly extensively in jewellery in the United States, and to a lesser extent in Britain. It must also be borne in mind that the cultured pearl, over which there was once a similar controversy, has now gained universal acceptance, and natural pearls have almost ceased to exist as a commercial proposition. Today one sees cultured pearls used side-by-side with diamonds, and few people see anything wrong with this. One could argue of course that cultured pearls, unlike gems produced in a laboratory, are at least partly natural.

Another interesting question for the jeweller is what his attitude is going to be towards the reconstituted coral, lapis-lazuli and turquoise that has come on the market. This material has been produced because the demand for coral, lapis and turquoise (stones that are being increasingly used in jewellery) exceeds the supply. Small and unusable material is reduced to powder and then pressed into disc-shaped blocks. From this reconstituted material stones and beads are cut that are very plausible imitations of natural ones. The makers of the compressed lapis have even gone to the trouble to include the specks of iron pyrite one would expect to find in natural lapis, and some of the turquoise is veined to simulate matrixed material.

In discussing the various stones that are most likely to come the jeweller's way in his day-to-day business it is convenient to consider them under four headings. First the 'big four' are described, then the rest of the gemstones and decorative minerals. The third section is given over to a description of those gems and decorative materials that derive from living substances, the so-called 'organic gems' such as pearl, jet and amber. Lastly the various synthetic stones are reviewed. The list of gemstones and organic substances included in this book is not exhaustive. At one time or another all kinds of minerals and natural substances have been mounted in jewellery or used to decorate *objets d'art*, but many of these are met with very infrequently. For those who wish to widen their knowledge of gemstones to take account of all the various substances, a number of specialist books exist, notably Robert Webster's *Gems*.

DIAMOND

Diamond is crystallised carbon, and chemically speaking is the simplest of all the gem minerals. It is not particularly rare. Since the discovery of the diamond pipes in South Africa in the last century, diamonds have been recovered in much greater numbers than have emeralds, rubies and sapphires. But if the diamond is neither a rare nor complicated mineral, it is nevertheless a unique and a wonderful one. It is not the result of some caprice of fate that diamond has assumed its paramount position among gemstones—its position is a tribute to its qualities.

HARDNESS

The best known of these qualities is hardness. Diamond is the hardest of all natural substances. To say that it is immeasurably hard is not just to use a figure of speech. It is impossible to measure the hardness of a substance that is harder than anything else. A Vickers hardness of between 10,000 and 50,000 has been suggested as a possible figure for diamond, and just how hård this is can be appreciated when it is realised that the Vickers hardness of steel is around 500. It is this characteristic, the great hardness of diamond, which makes it so valuable to industry today. For every carat of diamond sold to the jewellery trade, four carats are sold to industry for use as a cutting and grinding medium—in almost all forms of high-precision engineering.

The hardness of diamond is the result of its closely packed atomic structure; the atoms are so tightly packed that it is virtually impossible to pack them any tighter. It is interesting here to compare diamond with that other well-known form of crystalline carbon, graphite, used in the manufacture of pencil leads. It is as soft as diamond is hard, and this is because the atomic structure of graphite is very loose.

The name diamond derives from the Latin *adamantem*, and the Greek *adamantos*, both meaning unconquerable; but diamond is far from unconquerable. It can be conquered by flame (in air at about 800°C), and whereas it was once thought that diamond would resist any blow, this belief has proved to be false. A diamond can be shattered into pieces by a blow, and it can be cleaved, that is, split with a steel blade along one of the cleavage planes. These cleavage planes run parallel to the four faces of the octahedron, the classic, though not the only, form in which diamond crystals are found.

That diamond can be cleaved in this way is most useful to the diamond cutter, for by cleaving he can do with one blow what it might take days to do with a saw. But the diamond cutter has to remember that a blow delivered in the wrong place can break a diamond into pieces. The story of the cleaving of the 3106 carat Cullinan is one of the legends of the trade. The cleaving of this stone was carried out in 1908. The task was entrusted to Joseph Asscher of the famous house of Asscher, who studied the stone for months, fully aware that the slightest error could reduce this great stone to a heap of fragments. The day came, and he stood over the stone and struck the cleaving blade. The blade broke. He tried again. This time he was successful. From the cleaved pieces a number of fine stones were cut including the 530 carat Cullinan Great Star of Africa, now in the Royal Sceptre, and the Cullinan II of 317 carats, now in the Imperial State Crown.

OPTICAL PROPERTIES

Diamond has unusual optical properties, which are responsible for its adamantine lustre and its celebrated fire. Because diamond is so hard it takes a very high polish. As a result of this the table facets of a cut stone reflect 18 per cent of the light falling on them perpendicularly, compared with the 4 per cent reflected by the table facets of a glass imitation.

Diamond is also highly refractive. Refraction is what happens when light passes from one substance to another. If a stick is partly immersed in a pool of clear water, the stick will appear to be bent. This is because the light rays travelling to the eye from that part of the stick which is below water level are bent in passing from the water to the air above it. The angle of bend which a substance imparts may be expressed by a figure called an index of refraction. The refractive index of diamond is 2·419. That of quartz is only between 1·53 and 1·54, while that of the corundum gems, ruby and sapphire, is between 1·765 and 1·773.

Both the high reflectivity and the high refractivity of diamond are exploited by the brilliant-cut with its 33 facets above the girdle and 25 below. These facets are so angled that the light entering the top of the stone is refracted on to the pavilion facets at such an angle that these facets will reflect a high proportion of this light back through the table. On leaving the stone the white light is also broken up into its constituent colours to give the 'fire', a characteristic for which diamond is famous.

Diamond is singly refractive. Some minerals are doubly refractive, that is they not only refract a light ray entering them but also split it in two. The mineral which demonstrates double refraction most clearly is Iceland spar (calcite). Another mineral which is doubly refractive is zircon, which sometimes poses as diamond.

FIRE

Minerals refract different coloured light at different degrees, so that the various colours that make up white light, red, orange, yellow, green, blue, indigo and violet, are separated one from another. This colour dispersion is especially high in diamond. That is why this usually more-or-less colourless stone appears scattered with bright colours. This flashing of colours is known as the 'fire' of a diamond.

Though one tends to think of diamonds as colourless gemstones, most are in fact at least faintly coloured. Many of those sold to industry are of an unattractive brown, green and grey, though a tinge of yellow or green is far from uncommon in gem diamonds. The blue–white diamond is a stone much talked about but seldom seen.

Diamonds of many colours have been found, and those which

have a distinct and pleasing coloration are often valuable, more valuable sometimes than colourless stones of the same size. Most common among the coloured diamonds are the lightly tinted stones, the canary yellows, the pinks, the pale greens and the topaz browns. Rarer are the strongly coloured stones, the deep green of the Dresden Green, the blue of the Hope and rich reds, as strong as, but more brilliant than, the red of a fine ruby.

VALUATION

The value of a diamond depends on four factors, what De Beers call the four Cs—carat weight, colour, clarity and cut. The assessment of these qualities is not easy, however. As Norman Harper, the well-known authority, wrote in an article, 'Putting a price on diamonds' (*Watchmaker, Jeweller and Silversmith*, April 1966): 'Many jewellers with years of experience behind them are extremely cautious of such matters, others with more nerve and less enlightenment throw caution to the winds and sometimes bring discredit to their trade.'

It might seem, for instance, to be a simple matter to arrive at the carat weight of a stone, and so it is if the stone is unmounted, for it is only necessary to weigh it to the second decimal place, on an accurate balance. But, as Norman Harper points out: 'Diamonds usually have to be valued when they are mounted, so that an assessment of the weight has to be made and these assessments are frequently wildly inaccurate. In many cases as much as 25 per cent out. If one considers a stone said to weigh 2 carats, which is in reality 1·50 carats, and assumes the value to be £350 per carat, the error is in the order of £175. "It spreads 2 carats" is a phrase often heard, and one must know that a stone spreading 2 carats with a diameter of 7·4 millimetres and a depth of 5·4 millimetres can weigh 2 carats, but another with the same diameter and a depth of 3·4 millimetres will probably only weigh 1·25 carats. This would increase the error mentioned above to £262.'

Errors of judgement about the cut, or the 'make' as it is called, can lead to equally devastatingly wrong assessments. There are many common faults of make, such as a stone with a too thick or thin table, or a pavilion that is too deep or too shallow, a too large culet, incorrect height of the crown and so on, and such faults can affect the price of a diamond by as much as 50 per cent.

Clarity, or quality, again has a big influence on value, and is not an easy thing to assess. Most diamonds have inclusions or flaws, which need an expert to evaluate them. A diamond is generally accepted as flawless if it shows no imperfections when examined under a glass which magnifies 10 times, but the job of deciding whether a stone showing flaws is more, or less, valuable than another, calls for considerable experience. Scales of clarity do exist, and they are a help, but they are no substitute for experience.

Olivine and garnet are two of the important inclusions in diamond. Others are ilmentite, bronzite, chrome-diopside, chrome-enstatite, diopside and graphite. Some cavities in diamond are coated with graphite and occasionally an octahedron of diamond is seen within a diamond. The term 'carbon spots' is too loosely used in the trade to describe what may be other included materials.

Some dealers use the terms 'very slightly imperfect' (v.s.i.) or 'slightly imperfect' (s.i.). The word 'imperfect' is a derogatory term and the use of 'very slight inclusions' (v.s.i.) or 'slight inclusions' (s.i.) is more sensible when the presence of inclusions is being referred to.

Colour is the most fugitive of the four Cs; it is a relative thing, and is affected by the light in which a stone is examined, by the setting in which the stone is mounted and by any other stones surrounding it. A diamond surrounded by sapphires will be flattered by the blue light reflected by them. A diamond in a gold setting may well look more yellow than it really is.

To quote Norman Harper again: 'When considering colour it has to be appreciated that colour is not a thing in itself; it is a sensation conveyed by the eye to the brain by vibrations of varying wavelengths and velocities. Eyes vary and so do brains, and just as some people have a well-educated sense of tonal differences so some others have a highly developed sense of colour. No matter how developed a sense may be it can always be improved with practice.'

A widely used classification of diamonds by colour is: river, top wesselton, wesselton commercial white, fine or top silver cape, silver cape, light cape, cape, dark cape, fine light brown, light brown, brown and dark brown. The use of the term 'cape' implies a yellow tinge. To relate the colour of particular stones to such a scale requires, besides skill and aptitude, a known source of light and a set of standard stones to use for comparison.

By some dealers 'commercial white' is regarded as meaningless. In the U.S.A. the Gemological Institute of America in the past used a grading system based upon the alphabet, D being the top grade and R the lowest. The American Gem Society uses a numerical form of grading, from 0 to 10. Both systems are open to objection because they tend to downgrade desirable stones in the eyes of the customers—grade 2, or grade B, sounds much worse than it is. The Scandinavian countries use the terms river, top wesselton, wesselton, top crystal, crystal, top cape, cape, light yellow, and yellow or the colour grades which correspond to the American numerals and letters for stones of half a carat and above. For diamonds under this weight the terms rarest white, white, tinted white, yellowish, and yellow are used. Some argue that these latter terms are to be preferred. In the U.K. there is no uniformity of practice.

The Diamond Committee of the European Organisation CIBJO (Comité International des Bijoutiers, Joailliers et Orfèvres) has been working for the recognition of standard categories for diamonds, and so far (1975) has obtained an interim agreement among ten European countries on standardised categories for colour and clarity. The accepted categories for colour are:

> Exceptional white
> Rare white
> White
> Slightly tinted white
> Tinted white
> Yellowish

The categories for clarity are:

> Internally flawless
> V.V.S. (very very small inclusions)
> V.S. (very small inclusions)
> S.I. (small inclusions)
> Piqué I
> Piqué II
> Piqué III

The clarity standards are dependent on 'the examination by an experienced professional under ten-power magnification in normal light by means of an achromatic aplanar lens'.

Acceptance of the CIBJO standards is recommended by the trade organisations for use in the U.K., and obviously many advantages would accrue to the universal adoption of such categories, but it must be borne in mind that experienced professionals can differ with one another, particularly over borderline stones. A totally objective judgement of subtle variations in colour and clarity is just not possible.

SOURCE

The first diamonds were, as far as we know, found in Southern India, probably among the sand and pebbles on the banks of the Kistna river, and it was from India that many of the great historic stones, such as the Koh-i-noor, the Orlov, the Sancy and the Hope, came.

By the early seventeenth century, when the French jeweller

Tavernier visited India on his travels on behalf of Louis XIV, the mining of alluvial diamond on the banks of the rivers of Southern India was on a formidable scale. 'The first time I was at the mine,' he wrote, 'there were about 60,000 persons at work, men, women and children, the men being employed to dig, the women and children to carry the earth.' At Golconda he found a market established where the diamonds changed hands, most of them being bought by the emissaries of Indian Princes to decorate their masters' thrones and their masters' persons.

In the eighteenth century diamonds were discovered in the gold mines of Brazil, and subsequently were found in the alluvial gravels along the rivers of that country, and Brazil gradually replaced India as the principal source of diamonds.

The most important chapter in the history of the diamond was, however, written in the last century in South Africa. The first diamond was found there in 1866, by the son of a Boer farmer. The boy was playing on the banks of the Orange River when an unusual pebble attracted his attention. He picked it up and kept it. This bright pebble of 21¼ carats, later to be known as the Eureka, was obviously something unusual, and was passed from hand to hand. But no one set much store by it until Dr Guybon Atherstone, an amateur gemmologist, identified it as a diamond. It was then sold to Sir Phillip Wodehouse, the Governor of the Cape, for £500, and subsequently put on show at the Paris exhibition.

No one seemed at first to appreciate the importance of the discovery of the Eureka, but another and bigger diamond was found elsewhere on the Orange River three years later, this time by a shepherd boy on the Zendfontein farm. The boy was given five hundred sheep, ten oxen and a horse for his stone. A few days later that same stone, the Star of South Africa, was sold for £10,000. This discovery triggered off the great South African diamond rush.

The prospectors who flocked there found very little to begin with; but in 1870, at the Jagersfontein farm in Orange River Colony, the overseer found a diamond in the dried-up bed of a stream. Then there was a find on the Dutoitspan farm, another on the Bulfontein farm, and another on the De Beers farm. These farms, which families of Boer immigrants had won from the wilderness, were soon to be world famous as the names of great diamond mines.

On these farms, large areas of yellow ground were discovered which proved to be rich in diamonds. Miners poured into the country, and the bonanza was on. Then suddenly, about 50 ft below the surface, the yellow ground ran out. Disappointed, many miners sold their claims for what they could get for them and moved away. But some people stayed and bought, and among these were a musical hall entertainer, Barney Barnato, and an Oxford graduate, Cecil Rhodes.

One day someone discovered that the ground below the yellow ground was richer in diamonds than that which the miners had dug on top. It was realised that the yellow ground had been the cap of an enormous volcanic pipe, going down into the depths of the earth, and packed with a grey-blue volcanic rock which was to become famous as the 'blue ground'. The pioneers had laboriously uncovered the Aladdin's caves of South Africa.

Barnato and Rhodes took stock of their investment, and they were not over-happy about what they saw happening in the mines. There were still too many miners, and too many claims. The tops of the pipes were shrouded in a spider's web of cables, carrying each man's little daily collection of blue ground to the surface. To men like Rhodes and Barnato such inefficiency must have been painful. But that was not the worst of it. Men undermined their neighbours' claims. There were falls and men died. The pipes began to flood, and work had to stop until the water could be got rid of. Rhodes and Barnato decided that the time had come for all the little claims to be consolidated, and they began to buy them up. But soon it became apparent that the Kimberley diamond fields were not big enough to hold two men with a thirst for power. The battle was bitter but brief, and in the end it was Cecil Rhodes who won.

Cecil Rhodes was the chairman of a company called De Beers, and in 1888 purchased for £5,338,650 control of the great Kimberley mine. 'We had to choose between the ruin of the diamond industry and control of the Kimberley mine', Rhodes said after the battle had been won and he had emerged as the virtual dictator of diamond mining in South Africa. An outcome of the consolidation of the South African mining interests was the establishment in 1890 of the Diamond Syndicate, whereby the entire diamond production was sold on a percentage basis to certain buyers. From these basic origins Sir Ernest Oppenheimer, who had become chairman of De Beers, formed the Diamond Corporation Ltd in 1930, when the great depression had forced the closing of virtually all the diamond mines. The idea behind the forming of this body was the realisation that some at least of the diamond's attraction lay in its being not just a thing of beauty, but a saleable asset. It became obvious, therefore, that it was desirable to see the value of diamonds controlled. So the company was formed to control the price at which diamonds were sold. Contract buying was also started, and the miners had the guarantee that their diamonds would be bought at a fixed price even when there was a slump. This policy of price control through centralised selling is still pursued, and today not only South African diamonds, but those found in other parts of Africa, come to De Beers in London to be sorted and sold at the 'sights'. These sights, which are held four times a year, are attended by leading dealers from all over the world, who take the parcels of rough that they have bought, back to their respective countries to be cut.

Today, African diamonds are recovered from the blue ground in Tanzania as well as South Africa by mining, from alluvial deposits in South West Africa, the Congo, Angola, and Sierra Leone, by dredging the sea-bed at the mouth of the Orange River for diamonds that have been carried there by the current (Fig. 2.1), and by sifting the marine terraces where beach mining techniques are used. Some idea of the cost of this last form of recovery can be judged from the fact that, on average, 25 tons of sand and gravel have to be moved and processed for every carat of rough recovered.

Besides Africa, Brazil remains an important source of diamonds. An increasing number of diamonds are nowadays coming out of Russia, but figures of Russian production are not available.

DIAMOND SIMULANTS

The physical characteristics of diamond are so distinctive that it might be thought unlikely that anyone could succeed in passing off any other colourless and transparent stone as a diamond. Certainly anyone who has handled a lot of diamonds would be unlikely to be deceived by any simulant, but members of the trade with less experience can be taken in.

The natural stone that has been most often passed off as diamond is zircon; the colourless zircon produced by the heat-treating of brown zircon can, unless one is on one's guard, easily be mistaken in poor light for diamond. Zircon certainly looks more like diamond than any other natural stone, though compared with a good diamond a zircon really appears rather lifeless. There is a simple test that the jeweller can apply if he has any reason to suppose that a stone might be a zircon. All he has to do is to look down through the table of the suspected stone using a magnifying glass. Because zircon is doubly refractive the edges of the facets at the base of the stone will usually appear to be doubled. The edges of the back facets of a diamond, because it is singly refractive, will appear as single lines. The jeweller must, however, be careful when carrying out this test to rotate the suspected stone, because if a zircon is viewed in one particular direction this doubling of the facet edges is not seen.

Two other colourless stones which could conceivably be mistaken

48

Fig. 2.1. Stripping the overburden from the marine terraces at the mouth of the Orange River to recover alluvial diamonds eroded from the blue-ground and carried down the river (by courtesy of De Beers)

for diamond, though there is really little excuse for doing so, are rock crystal, the colourless form of quartz, and colourless topaz. Rock crystal has comparatively little fire, while topaz, which has more fire, has a characteristic slippery feel to it. Both these stones are also much softer than diamond.

In addition to natural stones a number of man-made stones have been passed off as diamonds. These synthetics are described in the third section of this chapter. However, among these man-made simulants is paste. Paste stones are made from a very soft lead glass, and while admittedly they often have considerable fire when new, their softness and the presence occasionally of distinctive bubbles make it difficult to understand how anyone in the trade could mistake paste for diamond.

DIAMOND CUTTING

The aim of the diamond cutter is to make the most of the diamond's high reflectivity and refractivity. The cutter too has often to make the most of an imperfect rough stone given to him for faceting. In his *The Art of the Diamond Cutter*, A. Monnickendam wrote: 'The master cutter is constantly on the alert for ways of eliminating marks and imperfections of all kinds, and at the same time aims at the best possible weight consistent with correct proportions.'

It will be appreciated from this that the diamond cutter has first of all to study his stone. This is usually the job of the designer, who is often the head of the firm. After he has studied the stone, he will mark it with Indian ink as a guide to the men who will do the actual work on it.

Suppose that the rough diamond to be cut is an octahedral crystal, the classic shape, and not one of the irregularly shaped stones that make up a considerable proportion of all the diamonds recovered. An octahedron is like two pyramids joined at their bases, and to obtain the profile of a brilliant-cut stone the top of one of the pyramids must be removed (see Fig. 2.2). The technique of shaping a rough diamond is by splitting it along one of the cleavage planes with a steel blade, but the removal of the point of an octahedral crystal is more usually done by sawing than by cleaving (Figs 2.3 and 2.4). In a diamond-cutting factory there are batteries of saws, and the operative in charge of these mounts the rough stone in cement and fits it between two holders. The stone is then held, by the pressure of a counterweight, against the edge of the saw. The saw, consisting of a paper-thin disc of bronze

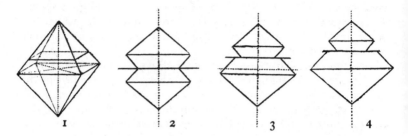

Fig. 2.2. When cutting an octahedral the designer will be influenced by any faults or inclusions in the stone when he decides whether to get one big stone and a small one out of the rough, or two smaller stones. If he decides to get two equal stones out of the octahedron (2) he will lose 60 per cent of the rough. If he cuts to obtain the two cut stones outlined in (4) he will lose only 51 per cent of the valuable material

Fig. 2.3. A cutter dividing a diamond by cleaving

impregnated with a paste made from powdered diamond, rotates at 6000 revolutions a minute. Surely, but very slowly, diamond cuts diamond. It takes five eight-hour days to saw through a ten-carat stone.

Fig. 2.4. A diamond being divided by sawing

The next operation is to round off the stone to create the girdle dividing the top, or the table as it is called, from the base, or pavilion. This rounding operation is known as 'bruting', and is done by rubbing one diamond against another. One stone is held in a lathe and the other is cemented into a handle so it can be held against the stone in the lathe with the necessary force.

Once the stone has been rounded the faceting begins. This is done on a turntable called a 'lap', which is impregnated with a mixture of diamond dust and olive oil. The diamond is held in a 'dop', a small metal cup with adjustable claws. People who visit diamond factories are often disappointed by the faceting department; the rows of laps look just like rows of gramophones playing silent music.

In the first faceting operations, which are carried out by the 'cross-worker', the flat table is polished on the top of the stone, and four facets are polished above, and four below, the girdle. The angles of these, and indeed those of all the facets, are critical.

Fig. 2.5. The process of polishing a diamond on a 'lap'

Unless they are correct they will not fully reflect the light falling on them through the table, and the stone will lack brilliance.

Next, the stone passes to the brillianteer (or brilliandeer, or finisher). He puts on the other 48 facets to make up the total of 57. When the brillianteer has finished, the sides of the stone will be broken up into a pattern of stars and kites.

Apart from the round brilliant-cut, there are oval brilliant-cut stones, pear-shaped brilliant-cut stones, sometimes called drops or pendaloques, and there are the nowadays very fashionable boat-shaped or marquise-shaped brilliant-cut stones (Fig. 2.6). The cutting of these fancy shapes calls for more skill and knowledge than the cutting of round brilliant-cuts, and this is reflected in the

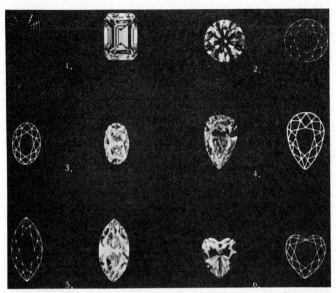

Fig. 2.6. Some cuts commonly used for diamonds: 1—step-cut, or emerald-cut; 2—brilliant-cut; 3–6—variations on the brilliant-cut; (5—the fashionable marquise)

relatively high price asked for them. The cutting of emerald-cuts, sometimes called square-cuts or trap-cuts, is also very exacting. An emerald-cut stone has 16 traps above and 24 below the girdle. A diamond much used in modern jewellery is the long rectangular baguette. This is a simplified step-cut.

From time to time the jeweller will also come across diamonds in other styles. In older pieces he will find many rose-cut stones, having flat bases, and a pointed top on which 24 triangular facets have been cut. This is an old Indian style of cutting which was introduced into Europe during the seventeenth century, being very popular until it was superseded by the modern brilliant-cut (Fig. 2.7).

Then, too, there are simplified versions of the brilliant-cut which are used for small stones. Among these is the eight-cut which, as its name suggests, has eight facets on the table and a further eight on the pavilion.

Diamonds have been cut in many other and sometimes very

54

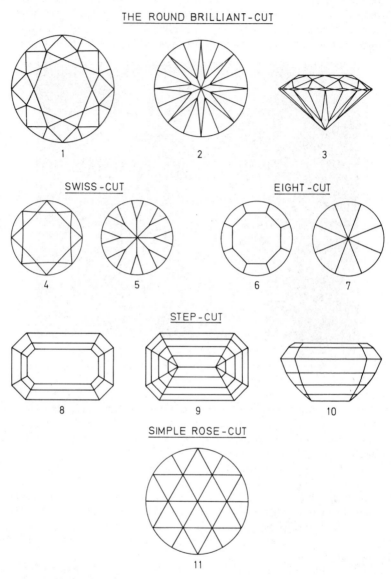

Fig. 2.7. *Diagrams of cuts used for diamonds: 1, 4, 6, 8, 11—crown; 2, 5, 7, 9—base; 3, 10—side. The rose-cut was very popular in the eighteenth and nineteenth centuries*

complicated ways, such as the Jubilee-cut in celebration of Queen Victoria's Jubilee; this has a pointed top like a rose-cut diamond, but is also faceted below the girdle. Then there is the so called Royal-cut, which has no fewer than 144 facets. But stones cut in this way are seldom met with. Perhaps, however, a recent experiment in diamond cutting should be mentioned. In 1961, A. Nagy introduced the profile-cut. Nagy had taken thin slices of diamond, and had cut ridges on them at right-angles to one another so that the stones looked rather like miniature reflectors, similar to those used on bicycles. After some initial interest in this cut, which was very economical of material, the trade has shown little enthusiasm for it. More recently a new cut has been developed for the flat triangular crystals, known as macles, that imparts considerable brilliance to them.

RUBY AND SAPPHIRE

Ruby and sapphire are both corundum gemstones. They both consist of crystalline aluminium oxide, the only difference between them being their coloration, which is caused by trace elements of alien metallic oxides. Ruby is the red variety of corundum. All the other different coloured corundums, the green, brown, orange, yellow, pink, violet and purple, as well as the blue corundum, are known as sapphire.

The red of ruby is caused by the presence of chromic oxide, and the amount of this in a crystal decides whether it is pale red in colour, or the much more desirable rich crimson. The blue of blue sapphire comes from titanium and iron oxide in the stone, and again the colour varies according to how much of these oxides are present. Blue sapphires are found having no more than a pale watery tinge of blue in them. Others, like many of the sapphires found in Australia, are almost black. Some people think that the deeper the colour the more valuable the blue sapphire, whereas it is in fact the middle blues, the cornflower blue and the French blue stones, that fetch the highest prices.

The traditional source of the best rubies is the district around Mogok in Upper Burma. Stone-age tools have been found there, testifying that rubies have been mined in the alluvial gravels of the Mogok region for thousands of years. Dr Edward Gübelin, the eminent Swiss gemmologist, made a film there a few years ago, which revealed that the mining methods used are still extremely primitive. The women, dressed in their colourful national costume, still pan the streams with flat wicker baskets, while the men dig pits, called twinlons, 20–40 ft into the gravel. They work away in these confined twinlons digging out the gravel and sending it up to the surface, in baskets suspended from primitive bamboo cranes, to be sorted.

The rubies found in Thailand, near Cambodia, the next most important source, are usually a rather brownish-red in colour, or sometimes violet-red. Rubies are also found in Sri Lanka, and more recently there have been worthwhile finds in Tanzania. An important ruby find has also been made recently in Kenya, by a geologist looking for chrome garnets. Rubies of facetable quality from this source have been said to compare in colour with those from Burma, although the majority of the stones recovered would seem to be suitable only for cabochons. Cabochons from this area exhibited at the Basle Fair in 1975 tended to be of a sugar-pink colour and to have many inclusions, but there is a strong possibility that the best material is not being released on the market and that this find is indeed an important one. The find is interesting because it illustrates the fact that major finds of gemstones are still likely to be made even today. The mining of coloured stones is still very much in the hands of freelance prospectors who work in remote areas with primitive equipment, and systematic geological surveys are the exception rather than the rule in gem prospecting.

Ruby is found in very few places because chromic oxide is a comparatively rare substance, and, because the ruby-bearing areas of Burma, Thailand and Sri Lanka have been systematically mined for longer than anyone can remember, good rubies are becoming very scarce. It is hardly surprising, therefore, that a fine ruby today is extremely expensive.

Sapphires are much more widely distributed over the earth's crust than are rubies. They are found in Burma, in Thailand and in Sri Lanka, and sapphires of a fine cornflower blue colour have been found in Kashmir, in a small valley in the Himalayas. Sapphires of many colours are found in Australia, which has recently become an important source of the blue sapphire so popular today as an engagement ring stone, though much of the material found there is very dark. Australia also produces some very attractive pastel-coloured sapphires. These are by no means the only sources of sapphires. They are also to be found in the U.S.A., in Africa and in the U.S.S.R.

RUBY AND SAPPHIRE SIMULANTS

Besides synthetic rubies and sapphires, which are dealt with in the section on synthetics, the jeweller has to watch for other natural stones posing as real rubies and sapphires. Red spinel could be mistaken for ruby by the unwary. This used to be called 'balas ruby', the most famous being the so-called Black Prince's ruby in the Royal Regalia. A good red spinel is, incidentally, a rare and valuable stone in its own right. A much less valuable stone sometimes mistaken for ruby is the almandine garnet. Natural and synthetic blue spinels, blue tourmalines, deep blue aquamarines, the rare deep blue benitoite, and even blue paste stones, could all possibly be mistaken for blue sapphire.

Besides these natural stones the jeweller should also keep a lookout for doublets. A careful study of a suspected stone with a lens will reveal the joint between the natural crown, often garnet, and the fake pavilion. Doublets are obviously more difficult to detect if they are set in rub-over settings.

CUTS, CABOCHONS AND STARS

The mixed-cut is used for rubies and sapphires, and indeed for most transparent coloured stones. It is a mixture between the brilliant-cut and the emerald-cut, being usually brilliant-cut on the table and emerald-cut on the pavilion. Many rubies and sapphires are cut cabochon, because a large proportion of the stones recovered are not of facetable quality. Cabochon cutting consists of polishing the crystal to produce a smooth dome with a flat base. Such cutting is always used for stones showing the optical effect known as asterism. The asteria, or star, seen in these stones is caused by bunches of needle-like crystals, which lie at 120 degrees to one another, catching the light.

Star-stones are very highly prized in the U.S.A., where they are produced synthetically in considerable numbers. The value of a natural star-stone depends on the colour, on how clearly defined the star is and how central it is in the polished gem.

EMERALD AND OTHER BERYLS

Many people think that a fine emerald, which is a rich velvety green in colour, is the most beautiful of all the coloured stones. Today, fine emeralds are extremely rare and expensive.

Emerald is a beryl, a silicate of aluminium and beryllium, the latter being a metal which has many specialised industrial uses. Emerald owes its colour to traces of chromic oxide, the rare substance that is also responsible for the red of ruby and the green of demantoid garnet.

The colour of emerald varies from a deep green to a pale and watery green, and has a big effect on its price. So has the clarity of the stone. Emeralds are very often flawed and usually contain many inclusions. A really clean stone is a rarity. Because most emerald crystals are more or less flawed, it is usual practice to protect them during cutting by soaking them in oil, which fills up any fissures and acts as a bonding agent. The oily smell of a sack of emerald crystals is quite distinctive. The danger, of course, is that if all this oil is removed, by ultrasonic cleaning for example, the stones may become extremely fragile.

Emeralds were mined in Egypt, in the Cleopatra emerald mines near the Red Sea, as early as 2000 B.C. These mines have long been worked out, and the main sources of fine emeralds today are mines in Brazil and in the Andes, in Colombia. The Andean mines were worked by the Incas, and by their Spanish conquerers after them. Although emeralds are still being recovered in fair quantities, it can be appreciated that after so many years of working there is not much good-quality emerald left.

Russia has some emerald mines in the Urals. The stone was first discovered there in 1830, when a peasant noticed a green stone among the roots of a tree that had been toppled by lightning. Emeralds have also been found in Australia, Africa, Pakistan and India, and there have been small finds in both Norway and Austria.

OTHER BERYLS

Emerald is not the only beryl that has been cut as a gemstone. Almost as famous is aquamarine, a sea-blue or sea-green beryl. Unlike emerald, aquamarine often has a remarkable freedom from inclusions, and clear and clean crystals of very considerable size have been found. Aquamarine has been found in Brazil, in Russia, in Malagasy, in the U.S.A., in Burma, in India and in a number of other places, and enormous crystals have been found recently in Mozambique. Most aquamarine is green rather than blue when found, and is subsequently changed to the favoured blue by heat-treatment.

Another famous beryl is the pink morganite, named after the American financier, J. P. Morgan, who collected pink beryls. Some of Morgan's stones came from the U.S.A., others from Brazil and Malagasy.

Yellow beryls and brown beryls exist as do green beryls which the gemmologists distinguish from emerald because their coloration is not due to the presence of chromic oxide.

The emerald-cut, known sometimes as the trap-cut or the square-cut, got its name because it is the most common cut and that

which most flatters beryl gemstones. To produce it 16 rectangular
cuts are placed round the table, and another 32 on the pavilion.

BERYL SIMULANTS

Soudé simulants were made in the past by cementing a piece of green
gelatine, or a sintered copper compound, between a table and a pavilion of rock crystal or two pieces of colourless synthetic spinel. A new
soudé simulant has now appeared in which a layer of an unrevealed
green substance is placed between a crown and a pavilion of colourless
beryl. Doublets have been made from a top of almandine garnet and
a pavilion of green glass. Also, rock crystal has been stained green
to imitate emerald, and natural emeralds are sometimes stained to
improve their colour.

Glass imitations have been passed off as aquamarines and so have
pale-blue synthetic spinels.

Synthetic emeralds are discussed in the section on synthetic gemstones.

OTHER COLOURED STONES

While ruby, sapphire and emerald are by far the most important
coloured stones, an increasing interest shown in other coloured stones
makes it imperative for the jeweller to know about what are often
misnamed semi-precious stones. This is an unfortunate description,
for to call a ruby precious and, say, a topaz semi-precious can confuse
the public about relative values. With gemstone, quality can be more
important than a name. A fine topaz could have 10 or even 20 times
the value of a poor ruby.

What a great many people, even in the jewellery trade, do not fully
appreciate is that fine coloured stones have always been exceptional.
When a prospector discovers that ruby or sapphire, say, is present
in a particular area, he still does not know whether it will be worth
investing in their recovery. The gems may be of poor clarity, translucent or heavily included, and so unsuitable for use in jewellery at
all and not worth the cost of extracting them. Only a small proportion
of finds prove to be economically viable to mine.

BLUE JOHN

Blue john would be scarcely worth mentioning were it not our most
famous native gem material. Blue john is the massive form of

fluorspar. It is an attractive stone, usually having a transparent, or translucent, colourless ground through which striations meander, usually blue in colour. A green massive fluorspar is also sometimes found.

There is also a cubic crystalline form of fluorspar found in England (and elsewhere in Europe), but the bold pastel-shaded crystals of this mineral, though very attractive, are seldom cut as gemstones because they are too soft to withstand wear. Blue john, on the other hand, has been used for jewellery since the Roman occupation. For many years this jewellery has been sold to tourists visiting the little town of Castleton, in Derbyshire, outside which, on one of the tors, the Blue John Mine is situated. The mine is almost worked out now, but in the past some very large pieces of blue john have been recovered from it.

CHRYSOBERYL

Like beryl, chrysoberyl is a beryllium gemstone, an oxide of beryllium and aluminium. It is usually a rather yellowish-green in colour. There are two types of chrysoberyl that show curious optical effects. They are the beautiful chrysoberyl cat's-eye, containing needle-like inclusions that produce the characteristic chatoyant streak, and the very rare alexandrite, that looks green in daylight and red in artificial light. The split personality of the alexandrite is due to the fact that the stone absorbs both red and green light with equal facility, therefore the colour which the stone shows depends on the colour of the light in which it is seen. Unfortunately, one very seldom sees a natural alexandrite; most passing under this name are merely synthetic corundum simulants. Apparently, even in Russia, one of the main sources of the stone, these synthetic imitations are sometimes sold as alexandrites.

DIOPTASE

The copper silicate dioptase has been used in jewellery in recent years, mainly in the form of uncut crystals. It is occasionally faceted or cabochoned, though with a hardness of only 5 on Mohs's scale it is not really hard enough to use as a jewellery stone. The attraction of this mineral for jewellery designers is the beautiful emerald-green colour of the trigonal crystals, often contrasted with the white of the translucent massive rock-crystal matrix with which it is frequently associated. Dioptase is found in many mineral-rich areas, including Russia, the Congo, Chile and the U.S.A.

FELDSPAR

Feldspars are a complicated and a geologically interesting group of minerals, but only a few members of the family are of interest to the jeweller. These are the mysterious moonstone, sunstone, amazonstone and labradorite.

The most important of these, moonstone, is an orthoclase feldspar, a potassium aluminium silicate. The pure form of orthoclase is adularia named after the Adular mountains in Switzerland where clear crystals are to be found. Moonstone, which is invariably cut cabochon to bring out its beauty, has a blue shiller in it. This is caused by reflection of light from layers of albite, another feldspar, contained in the orthoclase. The most important source of moonstone is Sri Lanka.

Sunstone, which as its name suggests has a yellow glow in it, is an orthoclase containing the iron mineral hematite. Amazonstone is a green microcline feldspar, another potassium aluminium silicate, but slightly harder than orthoclase. It is named after the Amazon, but although it is found in Brazil it has never been found anywhere near the Amazon itself. Its main source is India.

Labradorite is a plagioclase feldspar, a soda-lime mineral. It is noted for the iridescent play of colour shown when looked at from the right angle; a play of colour not much different from that displayed by gem opal. Labradorite is basically a rather drab grey stone, and the blue and copper colour it shows is due to interference effects caused by its laminated structure, when light falls on the stone. Labrador is the main source of the mineral, but it is also found in Finland, the Finnish material being called spectrolite.

GARNET

To try to sum up the garnet family in a few paragraphs is very difficult, simply because it has so many members. Of the six distinct types of garnet five are polished and used in jewellery.

The garnets most often seen by the jewellers are the deep-red almandine and the blood-red pyrope. At one time the source of most of the pyropes was the area once known as Bohemia. Archaeological finds suggest that a jewellery industry existed in this part of Europe as early as the fifth century A.D. which set the local garnets in gold. The garnets were polished as shaped slabs and set *cloisonné* to produce a stained-glass-window effect. In the nineteenth century, when garnets were immensely popular, a thriving industry grew up in Bohemia, and today government-owned factories in Czechoslovakia turn out quantities of garnet jewellery, mostly in the nineteenth century style, set with a profusion of rose-cut stones.

Pyrope garnet is a magnesium aluminium silicate. Almandine garnet, which has been found in Australia, India and Sri Lanka, is an iron aluminium silicate. When there is a lot of iron present in almandine garnet it tends to be brown rather than red in colour.

The rarest and the most beautiful of all the garnets is the green demantoid, a species of the andradite garnet. This is a calcium iron silicate, and the grass-green colour is due to the presence of chromium. The best demantoid garnets come from Russia but few are found there nowadays. Some have also been found in Italy, Switzerland and the Congo. There are also yellow and black andradite garnets, the latter having occasionally been used for mourning jewellery.

The grossular garnet, which is calcium aluminium silicate, derives its name from the botanical name for gooseberry—*grossularia*. This is rather confusing as most of the grossular garnets seen by the jeweller are orange or yellow in colour, the green grossular garnets not usually being sufficiently transparent to be cut as gemstones. (There are also red grossular garnets, but they are seldom of gem quality.)

Some transparent green grossular has been found in Pakistan, and there has been a very important find recently of facetable green grossular garnets coloured by chromium in both Kenya and Tanzania. These stones have been christened tsavorites by Henry Platt of Tiffany's, who also christened tanzanite when this came on the market. Platt first saw the tsavorites in the tanzanite mines in Tanzania, but was unable to buy them there. He became convinced, however, that the vein containing these beautiful emerald-green stones crossed the Kenyan border. Eventually he was proved to be right, for they were found in considerable quantities in the area of the Tsavor National Park, hence their name. Supplies of these stones are now coming out of both Kenya and Tanzania, and they make very attractive and relatively inexpensive centre stones for cluster rings.

Another garnet only occasionally used for jewellery is a manganese aluminium silicate. This is the spessartite garnet, the name deriving from Spessart, the district in Bavaria where this stone is found. The few spessartite garnets of gem quality are usually orange-red in colour.

NATURAL GLASS

The natural glasses are not of great importance to the jeweller as they are only rarely cut as gemstones, but the exhibition of the work of the famous Swiss designer Gilbert Albert, in London in 1966, drew public attention to them, because Gilbert Albert used natural glasses as the central stones in some of his most lavish pieces.

There are two distinct types of natural glass: those which, like obsidian, are the result of the fusion of silica during the cooling of volcanic lava or of other earthly upheavals, and those which came to us from space.

Obsidian is usually black or grey. Like flint and jade it was important to early civilisations as a raw material for tools and weapons. The Aztecs and the American Indians sank deep shafts to recover obsidian. As well as using it for weapons and tools, the Aztecs also used obsidian for ornaments, and occasionally down through the ages it has been cut and used for jewellery.

The extra-terrestrial glasses arrived on earth, it is believed, as a result of the disintegration of stars. The most famous of these glasses is moldavite, named after the Moldau river in Bohemia, where this mysterious glass was first found at the end of the eighteenth century. Similar glass has been found in many other places. It is often a rather interesting green colour, sometimes brown, sometimes black.

JADE

There are two quite different jades: nephrite which was at one time used for tools and weapons, and the more colourful jadeite.

Nephrite was used for tools and weapons because, like flint, when fractured a sharp edge is created. The Maoris of New Zealand used it, as did the stone-age people who inhabited the lake villages of Switzerland; so, too, did the ancient peoples of Mexico, who also carved representations of their gods in this tough, fibrous material. The Chinese used nephrite to make tools and weapons, and when metal superseded nephrite as a raw material for knives and axe-heads, they perpetuated their past by producing ritual weapons, and a whole range of amulets, from jade. In the early days, the Chinese carvers are believed to have cut their jade with bamboo drills and silica sand. Later, metal drills were used with powdered corundum, and later still carborundum was used as a cutting agent. At some time during the eighteenth century the Chinese carvers started to use jadeite instead of nephrite. They obtained jadeite from the rivers of Turkestan.

Nephrite is a silicate of magnesium and calcium, and is found in a limited range of colours. It is usually either dark green, a mutton-fat white, a greenish-grey, or brown. Jadeite, a sodium aluminium silicate, is found in a much greater variety of colours, green, black, orange, mauve, yellow, blue, pink, tomato-red even, brown and white.

Today there is on sale a lot of bowenite serpentine—a soapy green stone. It is usually quite wrongly described as 'new jade', a name given to it by the Chinese themselves, who now produce rather mannered and lifeless carving from it. Another common jade simulant is the massive green grossular garnet. This is sometimes wrongly described as Transvaal jade. One also sometimes comes across jade doublets and triplets, employing a thin slice of natural jade bonded to a less precious material.

LAPIS-LAZULI

One of the earliest gemstones to be used in jewellery was lapis-lazuli. The ancient Egyptians used it in conjunction with turquoise and cornelian *cloisonné*-set in their symbolic jewels at least as early as 3000 B.C. Today lapis is more frequently used as a decorative mineral for boxwares and dishes. Lapis owes its beautiful blue colour to the presence of haüynite; also usually present in this complex mineral are sodalite, noselite and lazulite. Often lapis exhibits tiny gold-coloured specks, which are in fact tiny crystals of iron pyrite. Sources include Afghanistan, where the deposits have been worked on and off ever since the ancient Egyptians obtained their supplies from this area. It is also found in Chile, Burma, Pakistan, the U.S.A. and Canada. Reconstituted lapis that includes specks of iron pyrite has recently made its appearance on the market.

MALACHITE

There has been a vogue in recent years for setting polished slabs of this beautiful green striated material in jewellery, though in the past its role has been rather as a mineral from which *objets d'art* were carved than as a jewellery stone. Malachite is a hydrated copper carbonate, and it has considerable commercial importance as a copper ore. It is found in veins, in botryoidal masses and in the form of stalactites, and usually displays a series of concentric striations of various shades of green. Malachite is not infrequently found in conjunction with a blue mineral of similar habit, another copper carbonate, azurite. When the combined minerals are polished together the material is known as azurmalachite and is most attractive.

The main source of malachite in the past was the copper mines in the Urals in Russia. It has also been recovered from copper mines in Australia, Africa and North and South America.

MARCASITE

What is known in the jewellery trade as marcasite is really pyrite. Both marcasite and pyrite are sulphides of iron, but they have different crystal structures. In the eighteenth century, when marcasite first enjoyed a wide popularity, the difference between these two minerals was not recognised. So the small-faceted pyrite which the eighteenth century jewellers set in gold, silver and pinchbeck, was given the name marcasite.

Pyrite is to be found in Britain, but most of that used by the trade comes from the Jura mountains. There it is found in the form of cubic crystals, the cubes interpenetrating one another at all angles. Often these crystals are of a golden colour, and sometimes actually contain traces of gold. It is pyrite which is known as 'fools' gold'—glinting among the pebbles in a pan it must momentarily have raised the hopes of many a prospector.

Pyrite is also found in massive form, and nodules of this massive pyrite are sometimes picked up in the South of England. Pyrite has been imitated both by cut steel and by faceted glass, and it was, in fact, the cheap imitations of marcasite jewellery which finally brought an end to the great post-war marcasite boom.

OPAL

Opal, besides existing in its own right, is also the bonding material that cements together the microscopically fine quartz crystals of which chalcedony is composed. It is a hardened gel, consisting of microscopic silica spheres mingled with infinitely tiny droplets of water, and so is known as a hydrous compound.

Most of the opal found is of non-gem quality, a rather dull stone. The opal scattered with brilliant colour is much rarer, very rare indeed today. Australia has produced most of the gem opal in recent years, but many of the opal diggings in the Australian outback are worked out. From these diggings came the fine black opals, looking like the wings of tropical butterflies, as well as less spectacular but not less beautiful milky-white opals.

The iridescent colours in precious opal, which are like the colours seen in oily water, are considered to be due to interference effects, caused by reflection of light from the minute spheres of amorphous silica of which opal is composed.

Besides the iridescent opal there is a beautiful translucent orange-coloured opal found in Mexico and other places, and known as fire opal. An apple-green translucent opal is also found in South America.

Most of the opal that is exported from Australia these days consists of opal doublets and opal triplets. The doublets are made by cementing a slice of opal to a base of common opal. The triplets also have a slice of rock crystal cemented over the top of the thin precious opal layer. The doublets when mounted can be difficult to detect, but the triplets have a characteristic glassy appearance that once seen is easily recognised again.

The French chemist and industrialist Pierre Gilson has also produced synthetic opal which could often easily be mistaken for genuine opal (see the section on synthetic gemstones).

PERIDOT

Peridot is a magnesium sulphate, a green stone, the colour of which Oscar Wilde described as 'pistaccio green'. The island of Zeberget in the Red Sea, the traditional source of this stone, was once known as Topazios, which resulted in peridot being called topaz in the early days.

Peridot, which is also found in Burma and the U.S.A., is another of those stones which is getting rarer. This may to some extent be because the expeditions to the island of Zeberget, which used to bring back this mineral, are nowadays more and more infrequent.

THE QUARTZ GEMSTONES

The most common of this vast family of gemstones is the colourless variety of quartz, known as rock crystal. Like all the other members of the family, rock crystal consists of crystalline silicon dioxide. The Greeks called rock crystal *krustallos,* meaning ice, and the stone certainly has an ice-like quality.

Crystals of colourless quartz are found that stand as high as four feet or more, while others are so small that they look like a sprinkling of frost on the mother rock. These crystals are found all over the world, including Britain. They are not very often cut as gemstones, but attractive beads are made from them, and the Chinese have a long tradition of rock crystal carving. They make snuff bottles and small dishes from this stone, and they have always had a particular affection for the variety known as Venus hair stone, which contains long needle-like rutile crystals. They also carve colourless quartz containing slender black tourmaline crystals, and that containing green actinolite needles.

To the jeweller, the most important variety of quartz is the yellow quartz known as citrine. This is the stone which is still sometimes wrongly described as quartz-topaz, or even just topaz, though the two gems belong to quite distinct species.

Citrine is a not unattractive yellow stone, varying in colour from a light golden-yellow to a red–yellow, the colour being determined by the amount of iron present. Natural citrine is not so common as its availability might suggest. Most of the so-called citrine in the trade is in fact amethyst, the purple variety of quartz, that has been heat-treated.

Amethyst suffered for a long time from the taint of Victorian popularity, but it is a very beautiful stone at its best, rich and royally purple, and it is now firmly back in favour. It is a stone which has had many legends woven round it, and has been used by more than one civilisation as a symbol of dignity. Amethyst wine cups, or cups with amethyst placed in the bottom, were supposed by the ancient Greeks to protect from drunkenness those who drank from them. The name of this stone is, in fact, derived from a Greek word that means 'not drunken'. The Germans at one time used amethyst as a symbol of power, while the Roman Catholics and the Buddhists of Tibet have both used it as a symbol of sanctity.

Scottish regalia is often set with another form of quartz, the smoky-grey–brown quartz known as cairngorm. Another beautiful quartz is the cloudy-pink rose-quartz, used both for beads and carving. This is usually found in massive form, but occasionally crystalline rose-quartz is recovered.

Some quartz has a multitude of fine yellow or blue asbestos fibres in it, which create a cat's-eye effect. This quartz cat's-eye is not to be confused with the more beautiful chrysoberyl cat's-eye. Tiger's-eye or crocidolite is a massive quartz that also contains asbestos.

Recently, quartz has assumed a new role. It is used to control very accurate timepieces. One of its properties is that if an electric current is passed through a thin slab of it, this will pulsate at a regular rate. A physicist, G. A. Marrison, took advantage of this fact when he designed the first quartz-crystal clock in 1929, the clock which revolutionised our ideas of accurate timekeeping.

Besides the quartzes already mentioned are a whole group of microcrystalline, or cryptocrystalline, quartzes. These consist of microscopically fine quartz crystals bonded together by opal, which is incidentally another silica gemstone. These microcrystalline quartzes are usually known as chalcedonies, among which are the apple-green chrysoprase, the flesh-red cornelian, the black or black-

and-white banded onyx (nowadays usually simulated by staining agate), and the dark green plasma, which when speckled with red flecks of jasper is called bloodstone. The most famous of the chalcedonies is, however, agate, used by the jewellery trade both in its

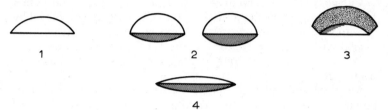

1   2   3

4

Fig. 2.8. Different profiles of coloured stones cut cabochon: 1—simple; 2—double; 3—hollow (section); 4—tallow top

banded and its dendritic form. The latter is the so-called moss agate, the inclusions in which look like fronds and leaves. Agates are usually cut cabochon or as flat slabs (Fig. 2.8). Staining is often employed to improve banded agates, and most of the agate used by the jewellery trade today is stained.

RHODONITE AND RHODOCHROSITE

These are the two most popular opaque red stones to be used for *objets d'art*, and more recently for jewellery as well. A number of designs nowadays feature beads or slabs or even cabochons of one or other of these two most attractive minerals.

Rhodonite is a silicate of manganese, at its best exhibiting a deep rose-red coloration. The red areas are usually divided by areas of black, which consist of oxidised manganese. The stone is moderately hard, about 6 on Mohs's scale, and is perhaps seen to best advantage when carved to form bowls. It is found in many areas in the U.S.A., and in Russia, Mexico, Australia and Africa.

Rhodochrosite has a flesh-pink colour quite distinct from the colour of rhodonite, though it also owes its colour to manganese, being a manganese carbonate. Rhodochrosite is striated like agate or malachite, the striations resulting from its stalagmitic formation. Rhodochrosite is appreciably softer than rhodonite, only 4 on Mohs's scale. Main sources are Eastern Europe, India and the U.S.A., but there was also an important find in Argentine in the 1930s.

Both rhodonite and rhodochrosite are very occasionally found in crystalline form, the beautiful translucent pink cubic crystals of rhodochrosite being particularly attractive. These crystals, although of no importance as gem material, are very desirable acquisitions by those who collect mineral specimens.

SODALITE

This attractive blue decorative stone is today widely used for *objets d'art* and occasionally in jewellery. Sodalite has been called 'poor man's lapis', and is in fact one of the constituent minerals of lapis-lazuli. It never attains, however, the rich dark blue characteristic of good-quality lapis.

Sodalite is a sodium aluminium silicate containing sodium chlorite and is moderately hard, $5\frac{1}{2}$ to 6 on Mohs's scale. It is widely distributed, being found in North and South America, India and Africa. Like other mainly massive minerals sodalite is found in crystalline form, the crystals being cubic and exhibiting a range of colours including green and red as well as blue.

SPHENE

Sphene, a silicate of titanium and calcium, is cut to produce green, yellow and brown gems. They are not very hard, only $5\frac{1}{2}$ on Mohs's scale, but they show considerable fire when faceted. Sphene is found in Austria, Canada, Malagasy, the U.S.A. and Brazil, and is one of the very limited number of gem minerals found in the Swiss Alps.

SPINEL

Spinel is a gem which occurs in several colours, the most usual being red, pink, orange-yellow, green and blue. It is a gem which crystallises in the cubic system. It is fairly hard, being 8 on the Mohs's scale, and therefore well suited for use in jewellery. It is found mainly in Ceylon, Burma, Thailand and the U.S.A. The white or colourless spinels encountered in jewellery are almost invariably synthetic and they should not be described other than as 'synthetic spinels'. The term 'white spinel' sometimes seen in jewellers' shops is inadequate if the stones are, in fact, synthetic. The jeweller also has to be on the lookout for spinel doublets, including doublets with a natural spinel top in a variety of colours, sometimes bonded to a synthetic spinel base.

TOPAZ

It may at this stage seem unnecessary to stress the importance of making it clear to the public that topaz is not citrine, and that citrine is not topaz. One does, however, sometimes come across that confusing description 'quartz-topaz', applied to citrine, and some irresponsible jewellers flagrantly display citrine labelled 'topaz', or 'real topaz'. The only gem that can properly be called topaz is topaz.

Citrine is nothing more nor less than the yellow variety of quartz. It is crystalline silicon dioxide. Topaz is a fluosilicate of aluminium. It is much harder than quartz, much more brilliant and a much rarer stone.

Topaz, like most gemstones, is found in a variety of colours. The best known, the one that is confused with citrine, is the beautiful sherry-coloured topaz, most of which comes from Brazil.

There are also very attractive blue, green, yellow and pink topazes, and there is colourless topaz. Natural pink topaz is very rare, and most of the pink topaz that has been found has acquired its colour as a result of heat-treatment of the brown stones.

Besides being simulated by citrine, topaz is also simulated by synthetic corundum, by tourmaline and by aquamarine, and by synthetic spinel doublets.

TOURMALINE

The beautiful long crystals of tourmaline are found in many colours: blue, red, pink, green, yellow and brown. There is even an opaque black tourmaline. Some crystals of tourmaline are parti-coloured and are cut as parti-coloured stones. Some crystals also show, when sectioned, different coloured centres like a piece of seaside rock. In fact, no other gem species is found in such a variety of colours as tourmaline.

The chemical composition of this stone is so complex that many gemmological textbooks do not even give a formula for it. It is basically another aluminium gemstone, a borosilicate of aluminium, but many other ingredients are present, and it is the presence and the proportions of these which determine the colour.

Tourmaline is moderately hard ($7-7\frac{1}{2}$ on the Mohs's scale), and the stone may be transparent or translucent or even opaque. Like aquamarine the colour is often improved by heat-treatment.

Russia, Brazil, Africa, Malagasy, Pakistan and the U.S.A. are all sources of tourmaline.

Transparent tourmalines are usually mixed-cut, and they can make very attractive gemstones, particularly the pink and the acid-green tourmaline. Those tourmalines showing a cat's-eye effect are, of course, cut cabochon, and inferior tourmaline crystals are sometimes turned into beads.

TURQUOISE

There have been very few periods when this opaque blue stone has been out of favour. Often the demand has exceeded the supply, and to fill the gap simulated turquoise has been made down the ages, going back to the days of ancient Egypt. It is thought, in fact, that turquoise was the first gemstone to be simulated. The jeweller has therefore to be on his guard against imitation turquoise made from glass, from plastics and from clay, and against natural stones with their colour improved by staining or oiling.

The name turquoise means Turkey stone, though most of this gemstone has always come not from Turkey but from one quite small mountain area in Persia. This sky-blue stone has a complicated chemical composition. It is, like opal, a hydrous compound, i.e. a hydrous copper aluminium phosphate containing iron. The colour, which has considerable bearing on the price of this stone, is due to the copper and the iron. Turquoise is usually cut cabochon and takes a good polish.

ZIRCON

Zircon has already been mentioned as the most convincing natural simulant of diamond. It is a silicate of zirconium found in a variety of colours, the most common natural colours being brown and green. It is the brown stones that the Sinhalese heat in crude native furnaces to produce the colourless and blue zircons used by the trade.

ZOISITE AND TANZANITE

The crystalline form of zoisite was not in the past of great interest to anyone except mineralogists. The usually (though not invariably) colourless orthorhombic crystals, though attractive in form, were seldom cut as gems. In 1967, however, a new find of zoisite crystals in a range of colours was made in the Meralani Hills in Tanzania. Some of the crystals were blue, and it was found that the others, the green, yellow and brown crystals, could be turned blue by heat-treatment. These stones, christened tanzanites by Henry Platt of Tiffany's, are of a most attractive mauve colour. They have become much in demand as ring stones despite the fact that they are not particularly hard (6 on Mohs's scale), inclined to be easily fractured, and particularly averse to ultrasonic cleaning. Since their first discovery the tanzanite mines have been nationalised, and supplies of good-quality stones have tended to be sporadic.

Two other forms of zoisite are of importance, the massive green and pink varieties. The massive green zoisite, which often contains hexagonal ruby crystals, also comes mainly from Tanzania, and is used mostly for bowls or as polished slabs intended as shelf specimens or table mats. The pink variety is called thulite, after Thule, the ancient name of Norway, from where it is obtained. It tends to be found most often as variegated stone with the pink contrasted with white areas.

THE ORGANIC GEMS

The so-called organic gems owe their existence to living organisms: pearls to oysters, mussels and so on, jet to primeval trees, and amber to prehistoric pines. By far the most important of the organic gems is, of course, the pearl.

NATURAL PEARLS

Natural pearls are those which grow in oysters, and other molluscs, without assistance from man. Oysters are the best known source of pearls, which are, however, also found in mussels and in other shellfish such as the giant clam.

There are a number of different species of oyster. Oriental pearls, famous for their pink-white colour, their regular shape and fine lustre, are found in the *pinctada vulgaris*, a small oyster which lives in the Persian Gulf and in the Gulf of Manaar. These oysters usually measure not more than $2\frac{1}{2}$–3 in. across, and seldom produce pearls of more than 12 grains in weight. The grain used as a measure for pearls is 0·05 gram ($\frac{1}{4}$ metric carat). Bigger pearls are found in the *pinctada margaritifera* which live in the waters off the northern coast of Australia, and some as big as 40–60 grains in the *pinctada maxima*, also found in Australian waters and off the coast of Malaysia.

Freshwater pearls, from unio mussels found in our rivers, were treasured by Roman invaders of Britain, and have had many admirers during the centuries since the Romans left our shores. Chief among these were the Scots who used, and indeed still use, them in their jewels and their regalia. For although these freshwater pearls do not have the majesty or the lustre of the pearls found in oysters, they do have a charm of their own. They are sometimes very colourful, being found in a variety of pastel shades, the grey and pink pearls being the prettiest of them.

The pearls found in oysters may also display subtle tinges of colour. Some have a pink, some a blue and some a green tinge. The *pinctada martensi*, found round the shores of Japan and widely used for cultured pearl production, tends to produce a greenish pearl. The early cultured pearls had a distinct green tinge like that associated with the natural Japanese pearls. Later, however, cultured pearls of a better colour began to come out of Japan, once the Japanese farmers had evolved a technique for improving their pearls by dyeing and bleaching. Oysters also produce beautiful, natural black pearls, though 'black' does not adequately describe these, as they are as full of subtle colouring as the so-called black opal. Black pearls, which fetch high prices, should be viewed with care, for some on the market were not black when they came out of the oyster; their colour will have been due to artificial treatment, possibly with silver bromide, the light-sensitive chemical used in the coating of photographic films.

Some pearl fishing in the Persian Gulf and off Sri Lanka is still carried on sporadically in the traditional way, though there are virtually no full-time divers working the oyster beds nowadays. The divers used to go out to the oyster beds in boats, most of those who fished in the Persian Gulf sailing there in the stately but often decrepit dhows of Bahrain. Before the war, as many as 600 of these dhows tacked down from Bahrain to the reefs of the Gulf, some with perhaps 100 men on board. Today this fleet is decimated. The oil industry offers alternative employment and, understandably, there are few young men nowadays prepared to take up the arduous and dangerous work of pearl fishing.

Certainly, pearl fishing in the Indian Ocean was not an easy way to make a living. The divers sometimes went down to a depth of 90 ft, on the end of weighted ropes, to prise up the oysters from the rocks. An average of only one oyster in 40 contained a pearl. An experienced diver had some indication of the presence of pearls from the outward appearance of the oysters, those containing pearls tending to be mis-shapen, but this was not an infallible guide. Each diver had to bring up as many as 500 oysters a day, the result of perhaps 30 dives of 1–1½ minutes duration, if the trip was to be profitable.

Off Australia the divers now go down in diving suits, and the future of pearl fishing probably depends on these shambling men in their cumbersome suits and cyclopian helmets, rather than upon the romantic and naked diver whose only equipment is a knife and a string bag hung round his neck.

The oysters brought up from the beds in the Persian Gulf and in the Gulf of Manaar were left to rot on the decks of fishing boats, and the pearls were eventually extracted. Often only one pearl was found in an oyster; in fact, the best were found singly. Usually not more than three were found in the sun-rotted remains of one oyster, but as many as 87 tiny seed pearls have been found in a single oyster.

The price of a pearl is calculated from a base price, which is arrived at by inspecting the pearl and assessing its quality. Its colour, its shape and the presence or absence of flaws are taken into account. The standard base price is 5p. A good pearl might be assessed as having, say, a 50p base price, a particularly fine one a £1.50 base price. The weight of the pearl then enters into the calculations. This is squared to arrive at the actual price of the pearl. A 2-grain pearl with a 50p base price would be valued at £2 ($2 \times 2 = 4$, then $4 \times 50p = £2$). A 20-grain pearl of the same base price would be valued at £200 ($20 \times 20 = 400$, then $400 \times 50p = £200$).

The value of a pearl depends on its size and colour. It also depends upon its shape and its lustre. The more nearly spherical, the more valuable is the pearl, though drop-shaped pearls, particularly a perfectly matched pair suitable for making into a pair of earrings can be very valuable. Least valuable are the knobbly and misshapen baroque pearls, and the blister pearls that grow, like wens, attached to the inside of the shell. Lustre, sometimes called 'orient', is caused by the refraction of light by the edges of the overlapping plates of nacre of which the pearl is composed. A pearl having a good lustre is termed ripe, a lustreless pearl, unripe. It must also be borne in mind that pearls wear out and may decrease in value over the years.

Pearls are created by the secretory cells in the robe-like mantle enfolding the organism of the oyster. The primary function of these cells is to produce the two hinged shells in which the oyster lives. Some of these cells secrete a liquid which solidifies as a horny black or brown substance which becomes the outside of the shells. Other glands secrete calcium carbonate, which solidifies in a crystalline form, to build the iridescent layer, the smooth lining of the shell known to the layman as mother-of-pearl, and to the gemmologist as nacre. The small calcium carbonate crystals are embedded, or attached to each other by a substance known as conchiolin, similar to the material of which our fingernails are composed.

Mother-of-pearl and pearl are both composed of the same substance, crystalline calcium carbonate, secreted by the self-same cells. No one is quite sure what causes these cells to perform their secondary role, that of producing pearls. Some people believe it is the result of a tumour, others that it is caused by a tiny worm sucked into the oyster during the process of opening and closing the shell to draw in sea-water containing the plankton on which the oyster feeds. Many people believe it is the result of a disease. Whatever the cause, once a nucleus of nacre is formed in the mantle of the oyster it continues to coat this nucleus with nacre, perhaps because it acts as an irritant. As a result a pearl grows inside the oyster layer by layer. A pearl cut in half and looked at through a lens shows distinct layers of nacre, so that it appears rather like a sliced onion or a tree trunk that has been sawn through. A stronger lens reveals that the layers are made up of those plate-like formations of calcium carbonate looking like a terraced vineyard on a hillside, and it is these plate-like formations that refract the light and give the pearl its lustre.

CULTURED PEARLS

The ancient Chinese were the first people to discover that an oyster will coat with layers of nacre any object inserted into it. They are known to have placed tiny carvings of the Buddha into oysters to produce little mother-of-pearl ornaments. It was the Japanese, however, who first used this technique to produce a simulant for natural pearl. They placed a mother-of-pearl bead in a little sac

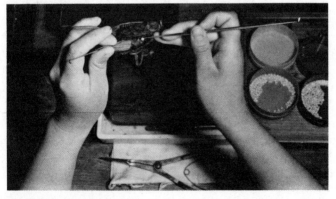

Fig. 2.9. Mother-of-pearl beads being inserted into the mantle of an oyster to produce cultured pearls. This is a very delicate operation

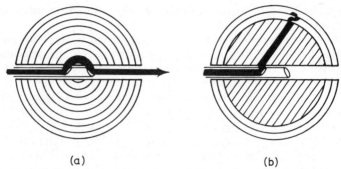

(a)   (b)

Fig. 2.10. Testing pearls with an endoscope. In the natural pearl (a) the light passes straight through the drilled hole, while in the cultured pearl (b) the light is not reflected back and is dispersed

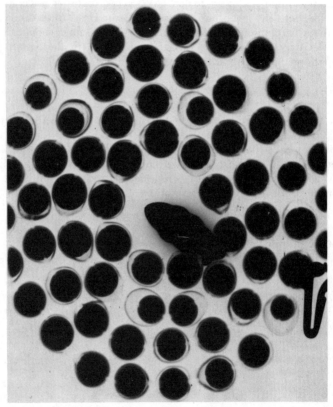

Fig. 2.11. An X-ray picture of a cultured pearl necklet, revealing the presence of the nuclei (by courtesy of Robert Webster, F.G.A.)

of mantle, and then placed this in the mantle of a live oyster (Fig. 2.9). The man who first made pearl farming a commercial proposition, though he was not the inventor of the technique as many people believe, was that strange and dedicated man Kokitchi Mikimoto. Many of Mikimoto's fellow countrymen laughed at him in the early days, but his beautiful diving girls and his cultured pearls were soon to become famous. His first cultured pearls were blisters, but before many years had passed he was producing spherical cultured pearls.

The first round cultured pearls were seen in Britain during the First World War, but it was not until the early 1920s that they began to arrive in any quantity, when they created a problem for the pearl trade. It was by no means easy in those days to distinguish between them and natural pearls, but soon gemmologists evolved techniques for identifying them. Drilled pearls intended for necklaces were tested with an endoscope, which made use of the fact that the spherical layers of nacre of which the natural pearl is composed reflect back light (Fig. 2.10). The parallel layers of a mother-of-pearl bead in the centre of a cultured pearl do not. Today pearls are tested by X-ray examination. This reveals the mother-of-pearl bead in the centre of a cultured pearl (Fig. 2.11).

The development of the cultured pearl industry, which at first seemed to be a threat to the jewellery industry, turned out to be a boon. It came at a time when natural pearls were becoming ever rarer and more expensive, and also when more and more people wanted to buy pearls. Japan needed foreign currency at this time to buy capital goods to carry out her programme of industrialisation, and she was prepared to export her cultured pearls at any price. Soon millions of women in the West were wearing necklaces made up from Japanese cultured pearls.

Another type of cultured pearl has appeared. This is the non-nucleated cultured pearl grown by the Japanese in a species of freshwater mussel living in Lake Biwa. They are supposed to use a tiny piece of mantle, which eventually disintegrates, as the nucleus. Non-nucleated pearls have been produced by Australia's rapidly developing cultured pearl industry, using the *pinctada maxima*. The first non-nucleated cultured pearls to arrive in this country were characteristically barrel-shaped, but subsequently some more spherical pearls have been encountered.

The Japanese pearl farmers used to destroy substandard or misshapen cultured pearls, but recently a number of jewellery designers have been incorporating baroque cultured pearls in their designs. The source of these baroque cultured pearls is Hawaii, where they are being produced by an expatriate Japanese. These often beautiful pearls are sometimes strongly-coloured, the peach-coloured and grey pearls being particularly attractive. The cause of this coloration is possibly trace elements of chemicals present in the waters around Hawaii.

ARTIFICIAL PEARLS

Before Japanese cultured pearls appeared on the market, people who could not afford natural pearls bought artificial pearls. These have been made for centuries. The Chinese produced artificial pearls at an early date, so did the French as early as the seventeenth century, while Roger Griffiths in *A Description of the River Thames,* published in the middle of the eighteenth century, tells us that the fishermen who got their living from the river: 'take the fish merely for their scales which they sell to make beads'. The scales of fish are still the usual basic raw material of the artificial pearl industry, which today produces untold millions of artificial pearls every year. Suspended in lacquer, the tiny crystals which are found attached to these fish scales are coated on to glass beads, by dipping, to give them an iridescent appearance very similar indeed to the appearance of natural pearls.

The identification of artificial pearls is not difficult. The simplest test is to run pearls, suspected of being artificial, across the teeth. If the pearls feel smooth they are artificial. If the teeth detect the gritty texture of the edges of the plates of nacre, then the pearls are either natural or cultured. Artificial pearls used for necklaces also often show a flaking of the.coating around the drill holes.

AMBER

Amber is not a gemstone but an organic gem. Like the other organic gems, pearl and jet and coral, it owes its origin to something that was once alive—to an organism. With amber, the organism was a species of pine which once covered much of northern Europe, but no longer exists today. Amber is the fossilised resin which was exuded by those pines.

It is an attractive substance in itself, and is sometimes still more attractive because of natural objects contained in it. When the resin ran down the trunks of those prehistoric pines it often entrapped insects, foliage, even small lizards, and these have been eternally preserved in a transparent golden tomb. At Kalingrad in Russia, where a great deal of amber has been found, is a museum housing a collection of 50,000 specimens of prehistoric flora and fauna preserved in the gem.

Amber used to be plentiful along the east coast of the British Isles, and in the Bronze Age was exported. It can still be found among the pebbles along this coastline, but today only a few fragmentary pieces are likely to reward a beachcomber.

It is light in weight, and if rubbed it acquires an electric charge, and will then attract bits of paper as a magnet attracts iron filings. Both these characteristics are useful in differentiating between natural amber and some of its many simulants. Plastic imitations are produced in great quantities, and sometimes the manufacturers even enclose natural flies in their spurious amber. If a fragment of one of these plastic imitations is whittled off with a knife and burnt, the smell given off will be the acrid smell of burning plastic and not the aromatic smell of burning amber.

Glass imitations are also common, but these are markedly heavier than natural amber, and do not develop an electrical charge. More difficult to identify, unless one is used to handling amber, is pressed amber, small fragments of natural amber often being compressed together to form a lump of useable size.

CORAL

Coral is a kind of tenement dwelling secreted by the coral polyps, for their own convenience. This communal dwelling place is made of calcium carbonate, and grows on the sea-bed like a forest of pink or white trees.

Coral has been dredged up from the bottom of the sea for centuries and was probably first used in jewellery in Hellenistic Greece. One of its main sources used to be the Mediterranean coast of Italy, and the craft of coral carving flourished in Naples. Coral carvers are to be found there to this day, but they now depend upon imports from Japan for most of their material which they turn into beads or carve into charms. A black variety of coral comes from Hawaii.

Pink coral, some of it improved by staining, is being increasingly used for jewellery in the form of slabs, often contrasted with agate dyed to simulate onyx. Reconstituted coral, made by powdering and subsequently pressing natural material, has made its appearance on the market.

JET

Jet, another organic gem, derives as does amber from trees. It is fossilised wood, a close relative of coal. Jet is a native British gem, and its source is the area round Whitby in Yorkshire. Millions of years ago, trees there became covered by the sea, as a result of some shift of the Yorkshire coastline. The trees were enfolded in the mud of the sea-bed and gradually, as the mud turned into rock, they became fossilised.

Jet has been used for jewellery at least since the Bronze Age; some has been found in graves dating from that period. The Victorians rediscovered jet, and it was the great demand during that period for it for mourning jewellery that caused the Whitby area to be finally denuded. In recent years only the odd fragment has turned up to reward the patient collector. Jet has also been found in France and Spain.

This sombre substance is either black or brown in colour, and though it is quite soft it takes a good polish. Like amber it acquires an electrical charge when rubbed, and it burns like coal. It has been imitated in glass and in plastic.

SYNTHETIC GEMSTONES

Whether one considers the existence of extremely plausible synthetic stones as a boon or a menace depends on one's point of view. Most retail jewellers understandably see synthetic gems other than in the form of watch jewels as a problem, and the more difficult they are to identify the greater problem they represent. But today a wide range of synthetic gems do exist, and the jeweller is left with no choice but to live with them, learn to cope with them and perhaps exploit them increasingly for his own profit.

VERNEUIL SYNTHETIC CORUNDUM

The commercial production of synthetic gemstones goes back to the end of the last century when, as the culmination of a number of small-scale and not particularly successful experiments, Auguste Verneuil, a French chemist, invented the flame fusion process. This synthesis was carried out in the famous 'furnace' that still bears Verneuil's name. The furnace consists in simple terms of a hopper in which the chemicals to be fused are placed, with a trip hammer above it that taps the chemicals into a tube, which is an oxy-hydrogen blowpipe. Below this pipe is a 'candle', which can be lowered as the cylindrical boule of fused chemical grows on top of it.

The furnace was first used to produce synthetic corundum, the powder placed in the hopper being aluminium oxide, with trace elements of other metallic oxides to produce differently coloured boules.

The most important, and indeed the first, synthetic stones to be produced commercially as a result of this process were synthetic red corundums containing chromic oxide, that is to say synthetic rubies. Subsequently blue corundum was produced by the addition of titanium and iron oxides. Later, synthetic corundum came to be produced in a great variety of colours: white corundum, which sometimes masquerades as diamond, purple corundum simulating amethyst, yellow corundum simulating topaz, and even synthetic corundum simulating alexandrite, which shows a colour change in different types of light.

It is necessary to draw a distinction between a synthetic and a simulant. Synthetic red corundum has the same chemical composition as natural ruby, and similar physical characteristics. It is therefore correctly described as *synthetic* ruby. Synthetic purple corundum does not have either the same composition or the same characteristics as amethyst. All that it has in common with amethyst is that it is the same colour. So purple corundum is a *simulant* of amethyst. The same is true of the synthetic purplish-green corundum that has been sold as alexandrite; natural alexandrite is not a corundum, but a chrysoberyl. (Incidentally, a synthesis of chrysoberyl has been achieved, and a synthetic alexandrite does exist, but it has never been produced on a commercial scale.)

Of all the synthetic corundums, far and away the most useful has been synthetic ruby, because of its role as a watch jewel. Untold millions of watch jewels had been produced in the Verneuil furnace before, in recent years, alternative techniques came to be adopted.

Verneuil synthetic ruby has also been widely used in jewellery during the course of the present century. Fortunately Verneuil synthetic rubies, because of their method of growth in the form of circular boules, have fairly easily recognisable characteristics under magnification, in the form of curved lines and distinctive clouds of gas bubbles. Synthetic star rubies and star sapphires are also produced by the Verneuil process.

SYNTHETIC SPINEL

One of Verneuil's students, L. Paris, was responsible for first producing synthetic spinel, but this material was not produced commercially until the 1930s. Synthetic spinel's role has been mainly as a simulant of other gemstones, as only red spinel has any importance as a gemstone.

Synthetic spinel is produced in boule form in the Verneuil furnace, and the colourless form of it has been the most widely used synthetic in the British market as a diamond simulant. One of the most popular uses of this synthetic has been for eternity rings. In France it has been extensively used for engagement rings.

Spinel is a magnesium aluminium oxide. Though it is relatively hard (8 on Mohs's scale) it is of course much less hard than diamond. Synthetic spinels rarely display the characteristic curved bands associated with the Verneuil boules, but the stone has none of the fire of diamond, though it has considerable lustre.

Blue, green, pink and red synthetic spinels have been produced simulating such stones as blue zircon, green tourmaline and peridot. The red version is of course a true synthetic of natural red spinel. In the 1950s a synthetic spinel simulating lapis-lazuli was produced in Germany, some of this material even incorporating the characteristic gold specks of iron pyrite. A synthetic spinel imitating moonstone has also been produced.

SYNTHETIC RUTILE

The last thirty years have seen rapid developments in the synthesis of gem minerals, and the production of synthetic simulants. One of the first of these to make its appearance was synthetic rutile. This material was again produced in a blowpipe by the flame-fusion process, from titanium dioxide, but the technique of production is more complicated than that needed for the production of synthetic corundum. The boules that were produced were black, like the crystals of natural rutile seen as inclusions in rock crystal. Subsequent heat-treatment was necessary to turn these black boules blue, green or yellow. The only synthetic rutile likely to come the jeweller's way, however, is a very pale blue stone simulating diamond, which was produced in the past but is not currently being made. These stones had six times the colour disperson of diamond and therefore had tremendous fire; they were in fact too good to be true. They were also comparatively soft, only 6 to $6\frac{1}{2}$ on Mohs's scale.

STRONTIUM TITANATE

A relatively new synthetic simulating diamond, first seen in 1955 and also produced by the flame-fusion process, is strontium titanate. This substance has no natural equivalent. Again, this stone is much too soft to be mistaken for diamond by anyone on their guard, being only 6 on Mohs's scale. It is, however, singly refractive like diamond, and has a great deal of fire, again far more than that exhibited by diamond.

The original boules produced in the blowpipe furnace are, like synthetic rutile boules, black in colour and have to be heat-treated to turn them colourless. The resulting material when faceted is rather brittle, and the cut stones tend to become flawed if subjected to ultrasonic cleaning. Strontium titanate is usually sold under the trade name 'Fabulite'.

YAG

Another simulant of diamond is YAG, standing for yttrium aluminium garnet. This is not in fact a synthetic garnet, but is so called because of its garnet-like structure. YAG is produced by what is called the 'pulling' technique, which consists of drawing a rotating seed crystal out of a melt of yttrium aluminium oxide.

These stones are nothing like so hard as diamond, only $8\frac{1}{2}$ on Mohs's scale, but optically they are closer in character to diamond than either synthetic rutile or strontium titanate. They are usually sold under a trade name, the best known of these in the U.K. being 'Diamonair'. Coloured versions of YAG have been produced, including a green version simulating the rare demantoid garnet.

THE HYDROTHERMAL SYNTHESIS OF QUARTZ

During the last war, because of the difficulty of obtaining adequate supplies of natural quartz from Brazil, the hydrothermal synthesis of quartz became an important commercial process in the U.K. The process involves the use of an autoclave, which has been described as 'a sophisticated pressure cooker'. The method dates back to experimental work carried out by G. Spezia in the first decade of this century. The technique consists of causing substances to crystallise out of mineral-rich solutions by superheating, which results from heating the liquid under pressure. Crushed quartz is placed in a chamber filled with water, and as a result of the superheating the water becomes mineral-rich. When the solution cools it becomes supersaturated and crystallises out round seed crystals placed in the solution. The conditions closely resemble those under which natural quartz crystallised out in rock fissures and in spherical chambers to produce geodes.

Synthetic quartz produced by this method is likely to become increasingly in demand if the quartz watch achieves the popularity predicted for it.

Hydrothermal synthesis has been used for the production of other synthetic stones, notably emerald, and more recently rubies in increasing numbers. Carroll Chatham has stated that his 'Chatham-created emeralds' are produced by this process. Doubts have been expressed about this, however, and it is now generally believed that the Chatham stones result from a different process known as melt-diffusion, that is from chemicals heated in a crucible.

Whatever the method he uses, there is no doubt that Chatham produces fairly large quantities of very plausible synthetic emeralds with physical characteristics very close to those of natural emeralds. They are by no means easy to identify, though identification is possible by laboratory testing. Though far from cheap, because good-quality natural emeralds are scarce Chatham's synthetics have been used extensively in jewellery in the U.S.A. As well as faceted stones, some jewellery designers have also used uncut Chatham synthetic crystals.

Chatham has produced other synthetic beryls, the blue aquamarine and the pink morganite, and also synthetic rubies by either the hydrothermal or more probably a melt-diffusion process. These present similar difficulties of identification.

Sophisticated synthetic emeralds have also been produced in Europe, by Pierre Gilson in France and various people in Germany. No detailed information about the method of production of these stones has been released, but it is believed that it is a flux-melt technique. An American firm, Linde, has also produced synthetic emeralds.

The chemists who have produced these plausible synthetic emeralds and rubies are continually experimenting with new synthetics, and there seems no reason to suppose that there is any limit to their ingenuity. Gilson has produced synthetic turquoise, and more recently synthetic opals that are remarkably like natural opals. So far the gemmologists, like those working in the Chamber of Commerce Pearl and Precious Stone Laboratory in London, have been able to find characteristics that enable them to distinguish from natural stones all the synthetics that have been produced. For the jeweller, however, without the know-how, the time or the equipment, the situation is very worrying, and likely to become more so in the future.

SYNTHETIC DIAMOND

Potentially the most important of all the synthesis methods is that of gem diamond, a synthesis probably first achieved in Russia in the late 1960s, and then in the Western world in 1970 by American G.E.C. Fortunately the trade seems unlikely to have come to terms with these stones in the near future. Though G.E.C. have produced stones of a carat and upwards in weight, they have stated that such diamonds were appreciably more expensive to make, by the use of very high pressure and temperature, than it costs to mine stones of similar size and quality. It seems unlikely that such diamonds of high clarity, which can be white or coloured as required, will be commercially synthesised in the near future. As the late Robert Webster rightly said, however: 'One cannot be complacent, for with the advances of science today there must surely come a time when synthetic diamond becomes a commercial reality.'

The fact that synthetic industrial diamonds are nowadays being produced in considerable quantities implies that there is a growing body of knowledge being accumulated about diamond synthetics. There seems every reason to suppose therefore that this will one day be applied to gem-diamond synthesis. For the present, however, the jeweller has only the simulants that may masquerade as diamond to worry about, and not synthetic diamond itself.

MODERN CUTTING METHODS

The faceting of coloured gemstones has been traditionally carried out by hand on a lap. The crystalline material to be cut is inspected to see which way to orient it in order to maximise the colour present, the colour in coloured stones tending to be unevenly dispersed. Then the material is fixed into a stick called a peg. The lap, having been charged with a diamond paste that acts as the abrasive, is turned by means of a handle. The peg with the stone fixed in the end of it is inserted in one of a series of holes in an upright stake called a jam-peg. Then working entirely by eye the cutter grinds on the facets and subsequently polishes them.

One factory in Idar Oberstein in Germany has recently mechanised this process, however, for cutting the less expensive stones such as amethyst. The stones are first oriented for colour, as in hand cutting, then attached to metal holders that fit into a continuous belt carrying the stones to an automatic grinding machine. This reduces all the material to a standard size. The standard-sized stones are then mounted on a holder, which looks like a comb. The combs are placed in specially designed machines that are programmed by computer to cut all the facets on the stones. They then pass through similar machines that polish the facets. Any shape of stone can be produced, but the process is obviously wasteful of material. For this reason it is not likely to be applied to stones of high value.

The same factory has also mechanised the polishing of agates, which is carried out against a revolving sandstone wheel by applying automatically fed stone-holders to the wheels. Previously this was also an operation carried out entirely by hand.

In a number of factories in Idar Oberstein nowadays one can see the automatic polishing of gemstone beads being carried on. The drilling of these beads is then carried out ultrasonically: hollow needles vibrate rather than cut their way through the gem material. Ultrasonics are also being employed to produce crests on seal-stones, once a job that could only be done laboriously and with infinite patience by a gem engraver using tiny dentist's drills.

CHAPTER 3

Antique Silverwares

The dating of a piece of silver by the hallmarks alone can be dangerous, for there are always fakes on the market. Pieces will be found with feet or lids that do not belong to them, and many pieces of early silver were 'improved' during the nineteenth century. Fortunately, few fakers have had much historical sense. The improvers who repoussé-chased plain Georgian cream jugs were more concerned to appeal to the tastes of their Victorian customers than to deceive anyone, so that this added decoration is nearly always out of period. Also, those who replaced missing lids or damaged feet often made errors of style. It is obvious, therefore, that anyone dealing with antique silver will find it invaluable to become familiar with period styles and not simply depend on the hallmark. Otherwise he is bound sooner or later to make mistakes.

There are many excellent books available on the subject which provide a good basic guide. There are fine collections in the principal museums which may be studied, the best probably being that in the Victoria and Albert Museum. Then there are illustrated catalogues put out by the top-ranking auctioneers to attract buyers to their sales. Much can be learned about both style and value by trying to date the illustrated pieces and checking the result against the text, and by trying to value the pieces in advance of a sale.

The silver of the past was not created in isolation; it was made to appeal to the taste of the period in which it was produced. Silversmiths were influenced by the manners and the new learning of their age, just as furniture makers and architects were influenced, and some understanding of the influences, and of the social habits, of the past is a great help in understanding antique silver.

Silver made before the reign of Elizabeth I is so rare that it can be ignored here, and a start made with the silver of the last years of the sixteenth, and the early years of the seventeenth, centuries. The silver of this period is Renaissance silver. The Renaissance, the rebirth of the classical traditions of Greece and Rome, had begun in Italy two centuries earlier and had travelled slowly northwards through Europe. By the time it reached England it had lost much of its early conviction. The Elizabethan craftsman paid lip-service to it. For him its imagery had become a collection of clichés. The classical columns had lost their perfect proportions, the representations of human figures had become stiff and stylised, and the fruit and flowers and leaves were no longer vigorous growths,

Fig. 3.1. Standing salt, made London 1583, typifying the debased baroque style of much of the silver of the period

but had become flabby and lifeless parodies of nature (Fig. 3.1). Not that the overwrought steeple cups and standing salts that have survived from this period are devoid of beauty or charm. Some of them are very attractive, but they are the late flowerings of a great tradition and the products of an ostentatious and often shallow age (Fig. 3.2).

Perhaps, however, we judge silver made during the reign of Elizabeth I and James I harshly, because we have so little by which to judge it. Much of it was sold and melted so that the noble families of England could buy powder and shot and men and horses to fight one another in the Civil War. Little of the sensible everyday silver with which earlier generations had decked their tables survived this holocaust. At the end of the Civil War there remained only the important pieces which their owners thought worth while hiding against better days, and a few pieces that survived by accident.

The Civil War destroyed not only the silver of the past, but also virtually destroyed the craft of silversmithing. Silversmiths depended on the patronage of the great and noble families. For eighteen years the owners of the great houses spent their money with the armourers and not with the silversmiths, and when the war ended the Lord

Fig. 3.2. Bell salt, made 1599, illustrates the charm of simplicity present in some of the silver of Elizabeth I (by courtesy of the Worshipful Company of Goldsmiths)

Fig. 3.3. A goblet of 1657 having the plainness usually associated with the Commonwealth period

Protector set his face against the ostentations of the past. Puritan England was a utilitarian age and as such did not prosper the silversmith (Fig. 3.3).

When Charles II came into his own in 1660, he and his court were eager to live again like gentlemen. After years of privation abroad, they were in haste to surround themselves once more with the symbols of gracious living, and soon the hammers were again

Fig. 3.5. A Charles II ginger jar (by courtesy of Sotheby & Co.)

heard in the workshops of those silversmiths who had survived. But there were too few silversmiths and too many orders, and much Caroline silver, as the silver of the Restoration period is called, shows signs of being made in a hurry for a not-too-exacting clientele. Some of it is frankly shoddy.

The restored court of Charles II had acquired foreign tastes during its sojourn abroad, and it attracted Continental craftsmen to London to cater for these tastes. Also at this time English merchants were trading farther from home, bringing back tea and coffee from the East, and importing china and other wares decorated with the alien imagery of China and Persia. Chinoiserie became fashionable, and the silversmiths engraved their wares with peacocks and strange little men in oriental costumes, and eastern-looking trees, all scribed with the rather uncertain strokes of the engraver and chaser on cups and bowls and dishes (Fig. 3.4). This Caroline decoration looked like a child's conception of a distant land, and the silversmith's designs were but pale copies of the lacquer decoration applied by Chinese craftsmen to the long-case clocks and cabinets of the period. Side by side with this chinoiserie, Dutch craftsmen and their English contemporaries were appealing to the acquired taste of the court by producing silver repoussé-chased all over with flowers and birds, and big ragged tulips so beloved by the Dutch often dominated the designs (Fig. 3.5).

In addition to producing new styles of decoration the silversmiths working in the second half of the seventeenth century produced new vessels for the new beverages. The first silver tea-pot appeared in the 1670s and the first coffee-pot in the 1680s. Porringers, too, were produced with handles in the form of female figures, often so stylised and so emaciated as to be scarcely recognisable for what they are. There was a great demand for tankards, and the Caroline tankard was often a huge vessel holding sometimes as much as two or three pints, fitted with a flat hinged lid, a bold scroll thumbpiece, an S-scroll handle and a big spreading foot.

The last years of the sixteenth century might be called the age of the gadroon and the flute. The gadroon was a lobed border, and this decoration was almost invariably applied to the silver made during the reign of William and Mary (Fig. 3.6). The form of much of the silver of this period was derived from the balusters, the moulded columns making up the balustrades so much in evidence in the new baroque architecture of what might be called the second renaissance, the second return to the classical past. The typical William and Mary baluster candlestick was gadrooned round the nozzle, round the knops and round the base. The tankards of the period had gadrooning round their domed lids and round their bases, and that curious punch-bowl of the period, the monteith, with its unexplained removable scalloped rim, usually had a fluted body and a gadrooned foot.

At this time there was a great influx of Huguenot craftsmen from France, whose influence on English silver was to be felt for almost a century. These were men who came to England to seek refuge

Fig. 3.6. Three silver-gilt, gadroon-decorated casters dated 1700

from political persecution following the Revocation of the Edict of Nantes by Louis XIV in 1685. The Huguenots were highly skilled craftsmen, and they flourished under the influence of the Age of Reason. The eighteenth century milord was a patron of the arts who believed that his age was a reincarnation of all that was good in ancient Rome. Huguenot silversmiths found him a generous patron, while his rigid classicism chastened their French ebullience. Adopting the baluster form, they expunged from it the fussy gadroons and produced the plain, stout, sensible silver of Queen Anne and the early Georges.

Many connoisseurs consider the silver produced by the Huguenot craftsmen and their English contemporaries during the first 35 years of the eighteenth century to be the finest of English silver, and it would certainly be hard to find anything more satisfying than their bold straight-sided coffee-pots (Fig. 3.7) and chocolate-pots, those elegant casters and trencher salts, plain candlesticks and caddies. Undecorated, except for the moulded wires strengthening foot and lip, unenriched with the mercurial gilding so popular earlier, they depended for their appeal on shape alone, and upon the charm of the soft grey silver highlighted by the flickering flames of candles.

Shapes changed as the century advanced. Straight-sided cylinders and octagons gave place to the pear-shape, the pyriform vessel (Fig. 3.8). A little more decoration crept in. Cast-chased lions' masks, palmer's shells and acanthus leaves appeared round the junctions of spouts and handles, while with the curved bodies needing the support of feet the silversmiths borrowed the baroque imagery of the furniture makers, employing their claws and spheres and their scrolls. But the bodies of their vessels still remained unadorned, essays in pure form.

Fig. 3.7. Straight-sided silver coffee-pot of the Queen Anne period, with handle at right angles to the spout

In the 1730s, however, the age of baroque gave way to the age of rococo. Plainness was replaced by a riot of decoration, symmetry gave way to asymmetry. This style came from France, and its chief exponent was a member of a refugee Huguenot family, Paul de Lamerie. There were great rococo silversmiths in Paris in the eighteenth century, but none of them was a greater exponent of the style than Lamerie, a fact reflected in the fantastic prices paid in the salerooms today for his work. He must be considered the greatest individual silversmith ever to have worked in this country. His control of rococo imagery was superb and, unlike some of the work of his contemporaries, his forms are never swamped by the riot of chasing, and despite the basic asymmetry of the style a Lamerie piece never looks lop-sided (Fig. 3.10). His repoussé-chasing and cast-chasing, whether depicting chinoiserie (a style

Fig. 3.8. Pear-shaped silver tea-pot of the Queen Anne period with spoon handle decoration on the lid and a hinged cover on the spout

which at this time had a brief revival), or the masses of shells, fruits, flowers, foliage and cartouches, of the true rococo, is un-failingly beautifully delineated and exquisite in detail.

The excavation at Pompeii and a Herculaneum in the middle years of the eighteenth century brought about yet another radical change of taste. The eighteenth century, as has been suggested, thought of itself as a reincarnation of the classical world. Up to the middle of the century it had seen this classical world through the eyes of the Italian Renaissance, which the eighteenth century gentleman had rediscovered on the Grand Tour. He had seen the architecture of Palladio, the paintings of Titian and Tintoretto and the statues of Michelangelo at first hand, and had brought back some of the art and the bric-à-brac of the Renaissance as souvenirs of his visit. He had then set the craftsmen of England to cast his

95

Fig. 3.9 (right). A simple bell made during the rococo period but showing no trace of rococo decoration. Made by Peter Archambo in 1739

Fig. 3.10 (below). A Paul de Lamerie silver-gilt cup and cover (1745), illustrating the asymmetrical decoration of the rococo style (by courtesy of Sotheby & Co.)

house, his statue-littered gardens and his household possessions, in a Renaissance mould. The art and architecture unearthed at Pompeii and Herculaneum came as a shock and a revelation. It transpired that the Italian Renaissance had been as wrong about Roman art as the Gothic revival of Victorian England was to be misguided about the Middle Ages.

The Adam brothers saw and seized their opportunity to found a new classical revival based on real Roman models. They employed artists to make drawings among the ruins dug up by the eighteenth

Fig. 3.11. Four drawings illustrating the change of style in the coffee-pot during the eighteenth century: 1—Queen Anne; 2—George II, the body now curved in at the base, and the lid much flatter; 3—the body now pear-shaped (1760); 4—influenced by the classical revival

century archaeologists, and armed with these drawings they descended from their native Scotland on to an England eager for something new. And so the age of Adam began.

Robert Adam, who dominated his age as he dominated his all-but-forgotten brothers, decorated everything with the motifs from the friezes of Pompeii and Herculaneum, not only the façades and the ceilings of his houses, but even the furniture, the carpets and the silver which he designed to go into them. The Romans, it seemed, were great lovers of the honeysuckle, the anthemium as they called it, and in every nook and cranny of such houses as Kenwood in Hampstead are found the stylised flowers of this climbing plant.

Robert Adam did not design a great deal of silver, but he focused the attention of the silversmiths of his day on the Roman style, and they produced vessels inspired by the slender curvaceous Roman

Fig. 3.12. An inkstand of 1794 influenced by the Adam style

vases newly unearthed, and they decorated their wares with the honeysuckle, the husks, the swags and ribbon bows that had once added beauty to Roman walls (Fig. 3.12).

The age of Adam, too, was the great age of piercing. The silver-smiths had rediscovered the piercing-saw earlier in the century. Prior to that, piercing had been done with punches. Now they ran riot with this new tool. Pierced dishes were produced in their hundreds, and the blue-glass liners of sugar basins and cruet holders peeped through the pierced sides.

The end of the eighteenth century was one of those periods of mixed styles. On the one hand silversmiths like Paul Storr were producing great dinner services in silver, completely plain except for the discreet decoration of a gadroon border (Fig. 3.13(a)), while at the same time these same craftsmen were producing exquisitely wrought monuments in silver, all-over chased so that not a square inch of the metal was left unadorned. The style was

Fig. 3.13(a). Paul Storr tureen—a relatively simple piece decorated with gadrooning and fluting once again in fashion

Fig. 3.13(b). Paul Storr tureen—a beautiful example in the baroque style

massively baroque, bold and heavy, a complete contrast to the delicate ornateness of Lamerie (3.13(b)).

It was this heavy baroque silver that heralded the styles of the nineteenth century. Like other material ages the nineteenth century worshipped the fanciful. The people of that age were incurably romantic and insisted on romanticising the past. To them the past was a fairyland of knights and gentle ladies living against a background of Gothic arches, Renaissance pillars and Byzantine domes (Fig. 3.14). In their applied art they mixed it all together and added

Fig. 3.14. Silver-gilt table centre designed by Prince Albert, and made in 1842 by Robert Garrard. In the collection of Her Majesty the Queen

the symbols of distant lands to the architecture of distant times. The camel and the elephant and the negro stand unabashed on a gothic temple. Seen now from a distance, nineteenth century revivalism has a charm of its own, and today there are many like John Betjeman who enthuse about it and would consider it as great a sin to tear down St Pancras station as once we thought it a sacrilege to replace Adam architecture with Shell-Mex House.

Silver of the Victorian period is often well made, the chasing and modelling beyond reproach. The smiths produced rich and worthy confections for a prosperous age. But perhaps this age is more important for the new type of silver and for the new imitations of silver which it produced for a new type of customer. In the past only the few had been able to afford silver, the rest having to be content with pewter. Now, however, a new middle class with money to spend was growing up and seeking to emulate those who had considered themselves their 'betters'. This rise of a new class (the *nouveau riche*) was the result of the industrial revolution, and it was the industrial revolution that supplied the means of satisfying the appetite of this new class for gracious possessions. In the new silver factories of Birmingham and Sheffield the thunder of the presses was replacing the steady tapping of hammers. The age of machine-made silver had begun.

The increasing use of the machine and the invention in the 1830s of electroplating brought silverware, and this new substitute looking exactly like silver, within the pockets of the many. The many wanted their machine-made silver and their plated ware to look as nearly like the craftsman-made silver bought by the rich as possible. The toolmakers of the period achieved prodigies of skill to this end. But if the buyer of machine-made silver could buy pieces nearly identical with the hand-raised silver of the day, he could not buy exclusiveness. A set of tools to make a tea-pot cost a lot of money, and a machine-made tea-pot would be cheap only if it were made by the hundred, and the price of the tools spread over hundreds of pots.

The necessity to make pieces that would sell in their hundreds soon led to the birth of the popular design, one aimed at the many who might have little or no taste, instead of to the man who had been brought up to appreciate the best of everything. It was this catering to the many, and the nineteenth century's romantic respect for the past, that led to the production in that age of so much that was pretentious and spiritless. It was this period which saw the birth of such designs as 'Celtic,' which had no more than a vaguely Celtic wire to justify its name, and the Queen Anne tea-sets which bore no resemblance whatsoever to the beautiful designs of the early eighteenth century. These pseudo-patterns are still with us to this day.

This has necessarily been but a brief summary of the styles of the past, and the reasons why these styles were born. The dividing lines between one period and another are not sharply defined. While the pioneers of a new style were exploring its possibilities, the more conservative craftsmen went on happily in the old way. Also the provinces tended to lag behind London. But the provinces also produced their own local variations on the fashions of the Metropolis, and they also catered for local tastes, making such pieces as the Scottish quaich and the Irish dish ring that were not made in London. Plain pieces have been made in every age. There were, for instance, little tumbler cups made in the seventeenth century. One also finds decorative pieces dating from plain periods—the two-handled cup and cover of the first quarter of the eighteenth century often had a wealth of cut-card, strap-work or spoon-handle decoration on body and lid, as well as very decorative handles. Nevertheless, most pieces of silver are true to their period, and to anyone familiar with the silver of a particular period there is something unmistakable about the proportions, the shape, and the detail, so that he has only to look at the hallmarks for confirmation of what he has already divined.

CHAPTER 4

Boxes of the Eighteenth and Nineteenth Centuries

The eighteenth century was the great age of boxmaking. This developed as a specialist craft in Paris, to cater for the demand for snuff-boxes from the snuff-takers at the French court. Then, as snuffing became a widespread fad throughout Europe, the craft of boxmaking flourished in the major cities, in London and Birmingham, in Amsterdam and Copenhagen, in Berlin and Dresden. Throughout the century, however, it was Paris that gave the lead and set the fashions.

The Paris boxmakers' workshops were located on or near the Quai des Orfèvres, and here were produced some of the most beautiful gold-wares produced at any time during the long history of the goldsmith's craft. Among the master craftsmen who produced these beautiful boxes was the Dutch émigré, Daniel Gours. Then there was Jean George, who fashioned boxes of exquisite simplicity known as 'georgettes' as well as sumptuous ones encrusted with diamonds like that in the collection of the Rijksmuseum in Amsterdam. Juste-Aurèle Meissonier, the Italian who launched the rococo fashion, produced chased gold boxes of complex form (Fig. 4.1), while from the workshops of Noël Hardvilliers and Jean-George Ducrollay came oval boxes decorated with superb examples of the enameller's art (Fig. 4.2). These and a score of other great makers supplied the French kings and the French court with thousands of snuff-boxes during the course of the century. Kings and courtiers collected snuff-boxes by the hundred. The Regent Philippe d'Orléans had a collection valued at a million livres when he died, and a number of people of rank were said to have a box for every day of the year.

The proprietors of the workshops in which these boxes were made are known to us from the records of the French Royal Mint, but in fact the boxes were seldom the work of a single craftsman. The Paris gold boxes resulted from the availability of many skilled specialists, most of them anonymous, who decorated the work of the boxmakers. These specialist craftsmen included men unequalled in their ability to chase complex patterns on the gold surfaces of a box with hammer

Fig. 4.1. Meissonier box (Paris, 1728) from the Ortiz–Patino collection, sold for a record 85,000 guineas at Christies in 1974 (by courtesy of Christies)

Fig. 4.2. Snuff-box by Jean Ducrollay, typical of the fine enamelled boxes made in Paris in the mid-eighteenth century (by courtesy of the Louvre, Paris)

and chisels, men who could paint in enamels with an amazing dexterity, and those who could build up intricate pictures from fragments of dyed mother-of-pearl.

Paris boxes of the great period are found mainly in museums today, or in a few famous private collections. When a collection comes up for sale, a single box perhaps no more than four inches across may fetch as much as £80,000. As snuff-taking spread, however, the demand for boxes of more modest pretensions, made in every conceivable material, increased. In fact eighteenth century snuff-boxes ranged from diplomatic boxes, made in Potsdam for Frederick the Great from apple-green chrysoprase sprinkled with diamonds, to boxes of papier-mâché and tin.

ALLEGORICAL CHASING

During the eighteenth century in Britain, Holland and Scandinavia, as well as in Paris, chased gold boxes of great beauty were produced for wealthy snuff-takers. The repoussé chasing used to decorate most of these boxes depicted classical or religious allegories, resembling those applied to the gold watch-cases of the period. Many of the best of the chasers were émigrés. In England, 'the first gold chaser in the Kingdom', according to Joshua Reynolds, was the Swiss, George Michael Moser, who had trained in Paris. In Holland refugee Huguenots from France, who settled in Amsterdam, were almost certainly responsible for the chasing on the most beautiful of the Dutch boxes, and that on the finest of the Scandinavian boxes also gives every appearance of Huguenot work, or at least of Paris training.

GERMAN BOXES

The German boxmakers copied French models in the first half of the eighteenth century, though they later developed their own styles of snuff-boxes, decorated with hardstone. These later German boxmakers exploited to the full the rich mineral deposits of Silesia and Idar Oberstein. The hardstone boxes they produced were of three types. There were gold-mounted carved hardstone boxes in the form of animals or human busts. There were boxes with hardstone panels to which were applied compositions of fruit, flowers and insects carved from various types of chalcedony (Fig. 4.3); the Hoffman family of Dresden were the finest exponents of this appliqué style. Lastly there were the zellenmosaik boxes. A zellenmosaik consisted of panels of small pieces of shaped hardstone set cloisonné in a gold frame. The style

Fig. 4.3. 'En cage' German box (Berlin or Dresden, c. 1750), with hardstone panels to which have been applied fruit motifs in carved gem material; gold mounts are set with diamonds (by courtesy of the Louvre, Paris)

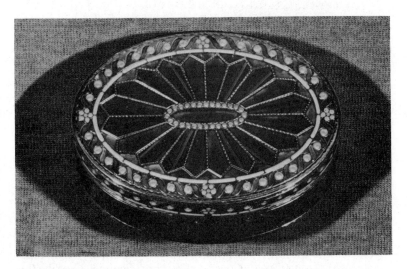

Fig. 4.4. Oval box in style popularised by Neuber (Dresden, c. 1770), set with green jasper and cornelians in star-shaped design; simulated pearl border with strips of white chalcedony (by courtesy of Sotheby & Co.)

was introduced by Heinrich Taddel, and was carried on and brought to perfection by his apprentice Johann Christian Neuber. Whereas Taddel's mosaics depicted landscapes and village vignettes, Neuber specialised in more formal geometric designs. The most famous of Neuber's boxes are his 'stein kabinetts' consisting of as many as a hundred different little pieces of stone arranged in geometric patterns. In the nineteenth century gold snuff-boxes generally deteriorated in quality and in inspiration throughout Europe, and to this period belong the Geneva boxes enamelled with sentimental landscapes, which Kenneth Snowman has aptly described as looking like picture postcards.

BOXES FOR THE PEOPLE

Boxes made of silver, painted enamel boxes, iron boxes, pewter boxes, papier-mâché boxes and wooden boxes were made throughout Europe during these two centuries. As few of these, even the silver

Fig. 4.5. Diaper-pattern silver snuff-box (English, 1798) by specialist smallworkers Phipps & Robinson

boxes, bear any marks betraying their origin, their provenance is often a matter of inspired guesswork. In Britain the first silver snuff-boxes were made in the late seventeenth century, though many of the capacious oval boxes from this period that are sometimes described as snuff-boxes were probably intended to contain smoking tobacco. Most of the eighteenth century silver snuff-boxes were lightly flat-chased or engraved, and only a few surviving examples are repoussé chased in imitation of the more expensive gold ones carried by the wealthy.

Another type of silver box popular in the eighteenth century had an agate set in the centre of the lid; others were set with mother-of-pearl panels or panels of ivory or tortoiseshell decorated with nail work known as piqué. Another popular type of snuff-box made during this century consisted of silver-mounted cowrie shells.

English silver snuff-boxes dating from the first threequarters of the century are, however, comparatively rare. Perhaps this was because the snuff-takers had so many alternatives to choose from. There were the boxes made from Christopher Pinchbeck's famous alloy simulating gold, and boxes made in Sheffield from the silver and copper sandwich invented in 1742 by Thomas Bolsover and now known as 'old Sheffield plate'. These boxes were usually made to resemble the fashionable gold and silver boxes that they simulated. If the numbers that survive are any guide, however, the most popular snuff-box of this period, beyond any question, was the painted enamel box. These boxes are often described as, and often believed by their owners to be, 'Battersea enamels'. In fact very few of them came from the ill-fated Battersea factory started by Stephen Theodore Jansen in 1753, which went bankrupt and closed down in 1755. By far the greater number of surviving boxes came from Bilston and Wednesbury, in south Staffordshire, or from Birmingham where John Taylor was producing them at least as early as 1755, paying a 'servant' a farthing each to paint them.

The technique by which these boxes were produced is a complex and interesting one. The bodies and lids of the boxes were made from paper-thin copper, originally bent up and seamed, but after 1770 stamped up. Powdered glass, mixed with metallic oxides to give it colour, was suspended in oil of lavender and applied all over the copper, and then the box was fired to fuse the enamel. The boxes, covered now with a layer of translucent white or tinted enamel, were then ready for painting in coloured enamels with romantic landscapes, flower pieces, crude copies of famous French paintings or portraits of the personalities of the day. These paintings were carried out laboriously by hand.

A cheaper method of decoration, invented at Battersea and later used in the Midland factories, was called 'printed enamelling'. This consisted of decoration applied to the enamel surface by means of an inked copper plate, the 'ink' being a stable compound that could be fired into the enamel. The production of these painted and printed enamel boxes went on well into the nineteenth century.

Snuff-boxes were also made from brass and from pewter. Sir Joshua

108

Fig. 4.6. Early English tortoiseshell box with silver mounts

Fig. 4.7. Very rare Bilston snuff-box; painted enamel on a lemon-yellow ground (by courtesy of Sotheby & Co.)

Reynolds had a pewter box described by Fanny Burney as of 'vile and shabby tin'. More popular were the japanned iron boxes made in the Midlands from the end of the seventeenth century onwards. From 1720 these were also produced in a factory at Pontypool in Wales, which became very famous, selling its production successfully in Holland as well as in England.

Japanned boxes owe their existence to the fashion during the late seventeenth century for lacquer wares imported from the East. The popularity of these wares led two Englishmen, John Stalker and George Parker, to study the work of the Japanese lacquerers, and in 1688 they published a *Treatise of Japanning, Varnishing and Gilding*. On the basis of this research an industry for producing japanned wares, including snuff-boxes, from iron covered with a glossy lacquer was developed.

Major John Hanbury, who ran the Pontypool factory, improved on the English boxes by dipping his iron boxes in tin before lacquering, which resulted in a more glossy lacquer. He also increased the colour range available to include red, blue, green and yellow boxes, as well as a plausible imitation of the fashionable tortoiseshell. The boxes from the Midlands were decorated with coloured designs, but the Pontypool factory restricted its decoration to painting in gold.

Yet another popular medium for producing snuff-boxes for the less well-to-do during the eighteenth century was papier-mâché, produced by mashing up paper in water and then moulding it. The dried box was then japanned and usually decorated by painting. Potato peel and even green vegetables were sometimes also mashed up and moulded to make snuff-boxes, being subsequently varnished.

In Scotland the snuff-takers used mulls, which were made both for the pocket and for the table. The smaller mulls were made from sheeps' horns mounted with a silver lid, usually set with a central stone, often a local agate or a cairngorm. The table mulls were made from cows' horns, and besides the silver lid they usually had silver feet. Commonly a little mallet to dislodge the snuff and a brush to sweep offending grains of snuff from round the nostrils were hung from the mulls on silver chains.

THE NINETEENTH CENTURY

The early years of the nineteenth century saw the snuff-taking habit at its height in England. The books of Fribourg and Treyer, who still sell snuff in London's Haymarket, reveal that the aristocracy of the early nineteenth century were avid snuffers, with the royal family and members of the aristocracy like Lord Petersham buying a vast variety of exotic snuffs suitable to be sniffed in winter or summer or specially blended for morning or evening use. In those days, where the aristocracy led the rest followed. As the demand for snuff grew so did the demand for snuff-boxes. The boxmakers found many new customers among the increasingly wealthy middle class, and the factories of Birmingham and London prospered, catering to this demand by producing gold and silver boxes.

The Birmingham makers evolved their own styles in the last quarter of the eighteenth century, and developed them in the early years of the new century. The classic box of the period was oblong with

Fig. 4.8. Nineteenth century Birmingham silver snuff-box

rounded corners. It had chased-up baroque wires standing proud round the top of the lid and round the base. The panels of these boxes were sometimes left plain, but were more often engine-turned, with patterns such as barley and fox-heads or with a repeat-dot design. The centre of the lid often had a chased cartouche containing the owner's initials. These boxes, however, were by no means the only type to be produced. There were oblong boxes with rounded edges, the body of the box bowed presumably to fit more snugly in the owner's pocket. Then there were boxes with repoussé-chased lids, or lids cast in high relief resembling repoussé. Some of these repoussé boxes were decorated with the classical allegories popular in the eighteenth century. Others were nineteenth century in feeling with flower designs, representations of field sports or vignettes of contemporary life depicted on them. The best known makers of such boxes were Joseph Taylor, the Linwoods, Nathaniel Mills and Samuel Pemberton. Taylor and Pemberton were also among those who produced perhaps the most charming of the silver snuff-boxes of the time, miniature boxes measuring an inch or less overall.

Later in the century Birmingham introduced the famous castle-top snuff-boxes. These boxes, made again by Mills and Taylor, but also by Joseph Willmore and Edward Smith among others, depicted on their lids in repoussé (or casting simulating repoussé) famous British castles or other famous buildings—cathedrals and abbeys, even town halls, and in 1850, inevitably, the Crystal Palace.

Form-boxes, in the shape of fox masks, were produced by Nathaniel Mills, and silver-mounted cowrie shells continued to be popular. Then the many new clubs and other convivial organisations that grew up during the century created a demand for large and pompous table snuff-boxes, usually with repoussé lids.

London produced many boxes too; usually the London boxes were more sophisticated and were produced in smaller numbers for a wealthier clientele. Gold snuff-boxes continued to be made during the nineteenth century, in both London and Birmingham; most of them were gold versions of the popular silver designs. Then the Lancashire watchmakers, hard hit by French competition, turned their skills to the production of brass snuff-boxes, often fitted with miniature combination locks. Wooden snuff-boxes, which had been produced all over Europe since the seventeenth century, were popular during the nineteenth century, too, particularly form-boxes made in the shape of animals, coffins (sometimes complete with tiny skeletons) or in the form of human heads and hands.

The boxmakers of the nineteenth century did not only make snuff-boxes; they had a thriving business producing vinaigrettes, the direct descendants of the segmented pomanders of the sixteenth century. These vinaigrettes had a pierced inner lid beneath which was a little sponge soaked in aromatic vinegar. They were used to dispel the 'vapours', a popular female affliction in the nineteenth century. These little boxes were made in the same styles as the snuff-boxes, castle tops being particularly popular. 'Calling' was another nineteenth-century institution, and the boxmakers made large shallow square silver boxes to hold the calling cards that people left with one another when they paid a formal call.

When cigarette- and cigar-smoking began replacing snuff-taking as a fashionable habit in the middle years of the nineteenth century the boxmakers turned to producing silver and gold cigarette and cigar cases and boxes. And to these were usually applied the classic engine-turned patterns that had originally been developed to decorate snuff-boxes.

CHAPTER 5

How Silverwares are Made

HOLLOWARES

The bodies of silver vessels can be made in three ways. They can be hand-raised, they can be spun, or they can be formed between dies in a press. Hand-raised silver is stronger, and most people contend that it is also more beautiful than silver produced either by spinning or by stamping. The hand-raising of silver is, however, an expensive process, for not only does it demand the skill of a highly trained craftsman, but it also takes a long time.

HAMMER BLOWS

The ancient skills of the silversmith have been handed down from generation to generation of craftsmen, and the tools as well as the methods of the hand-raiser go back as far as recorded history. The modern smith, like his predecessors in centuries past, uses a section of a tree trunk with shallow depressions sunk into it to start the shaping of the body of a vessel. He takes a disc of sheet silver which he has cut to size, places it over one of the depressions in the trunk and begins to hammer it with a ball-faced hammer. He hammers round and round the silver disc in courses, working gradually towards the centre. By the time he reaches the centre he has raised the flat disc to a saucer shape.

ANNEALING

The hammering changes the atomic structure of the metal, the silver becoming hard and brittle. When this happens the smith anneals his silver. He heats it with a torch until it glows a dull red, then he quenches it in water. By doing this he restores the malleability of the metal.

AT THE STAKE

When the smith starts raising the saucer shape to the shape of the body of a coffee-pot or a jug, he works over small anvils known as raising stakes. These are either firmly fixed in a tree-trunk, or more usually in a vice. With the saucer-shaped piece of silver supported on the stake he begins to hammer again, working this time from the centre outwards in the direction of the edge. Course by course he hammers, stopping to anneal when necessary, and the shape rises up under the hammer blows. It looks simple, just as the throwing of pottery looks simpler than it is. The silversmith's problems are indeed not greatly dissimilar from those of the potter. The silversmith's craft is slower and more painstaking; but both craftsmen are concerned to push their raw material in the way in which they want it to go, to get the walls of their vessel evenly thick, the shape true, and the strength where it is needed.

PLANISHING

At the end of a day of hard work the body of the vessel which the silversmith set out to make will be formed. It will, though, bear the marks of the hammer all over it, regular and even marks if the smith has done his work well, but too obtrusive to be acceptable. The next job, therefore, is to smooth out these hammer marks, which is done by more hammering. The smith goes over the whole surface with a flat-faced planishing hammer. This hammering also leaves its marks, but the regular pattern of small indentations left by the planishing hammer is one of the things which gives hand-raised silver its character.

WIRES

Wires are often used to strengthen the lip of a vessel. Standard pattern wires can today be bought from the bullion dealers, but many silversmiths still make their own. Judith Banister, in her book *Old English Silver*, describes the process of wire-drawing as having: 'a ring of the medieval torture chamber about it'. Certainly the machine, the draw-bench, used to draw wire looks not unlike one of those racks on which prisoners were stretched to loosen their tongues. Wire-drawing is, in fact, a stretching process. A length of silver rod, which has been reduced in diameter by passing it back and forth between grooved rolls, is drawn through the progressively smaller holes that have been drilled in a draw-plate. The rod gets thinner and longer as it is drawn through ever smaller holes, and so becomes wire of the required diameter. Fancy wires are made either by casting or by rolling.

CASTING

Not only wires, but also decorative details such as those placed around spout and handle junctions, and also the feet and finials of vessels, are made by casting. A wooden or metal model of the part to be cast is first made. Then the two halves of a metal box, with a pouring hole at one end, are filled with oiled sand. The model is placed in one half of the box, both surfaces of the sand are dusted with charcoal so that they will part easily, and then the top and bottom of the box are brought together and the sand is dried. The two halves of the box are now parted, and the model removed. A channel is formed in the sand to connect the impression left by the model with the mouth of the metal box. The two halves of the box are next brought together again and clamped. Molten silver is now poured into the mouth of the box and flows into the mould in the sand.

The metal is allowed to cool and the casting box is opened again and the silver impression of the model taken out. Any flash, as the metal straying round the edges of the impression is called, is removed and so is the sprue, the tang of metal that sets in the pouring channel. The casting is then brightened up by chasing. Increasingly, nowadays, silver components are lost-wax cast, however (see page 204).

CHASING

Hand-raised silver is decorated either by flat-chasing, cast-chasing, repoussé-chasing, engraving, texturing, piercing or enamelling.

Chasing is the name given to the process of decorating silver with a hammer and punches. To flat-chase the walls of a vessel, it has to be supported either by resting it on a bed of pitch or more often by actually filling the vessel with pitch, and placing it on a sand-filled leather bag. The pattern is marked out on the silver. Usually it is outlined with a fine punch. Then the chaser begins to fill in the

Fig. 5.1. The chaser at work. The chasing of one life-sized model of a pheasant takes 175 hours

Fig. 5.2. The chaser painstakingly follows, a fraction of an inch at a time, the pattern drawn on to the body of the vessel

detail. He chooses the right punch from the hundreds or even thousands standing in round tins on his bench. He places the punch on the silver and gives it a deft blow with the hammer. The punch pushes the metal aside and forms a small indentation in the surface. The chaser moves his punch, deals it another blow and so he creates

Fig. 5.3. Cup with repoussé-chasing and cast-chased handles. This piece dates from 1658

a channel. Patiently, blow by blow, he builds up a pattern of lines. One of the best known chasers in the trade has a collection of 6000 punches, some of them dating back to the reign of William and Mary. His hammer is 170 years old, and some idea of the work entailed in chasing may be gained from the fact that it takes him 175 hours to chase a life-sized model of a pheasant (Fig. 5.1).

Not only can the chaser create channels in the silver but he can also, by the use of special matting punches, texture the metal between the lines.

Cast-chased decoration is the application of chased-up castings to a piece of silver. Repoussé-chasing is relief decoration that has subsequently been chased up (Fig. 5.3). The relief pattern is first hammered up from inside. To do this on an enclosed vessel such as a tea-pot, a special tool called a snarling-iron has to be used. This is a Z-shaped piece of steel one end of which is domed. The non-domed end is secured in a vice, and the vessel is put over the domed end. By hitting the arm of the iron the craftsman drives the dome against the inside of the silver and bows it outwards. It can be imagined what skill was required to create one of those deeply embossed patterns of fruit and flowers on a Caroline jug, working by remote control with a snarling-iron. Once the repoussé pattern has been raised on the silver, the chaser then puts in the detail, in the same way as he does his flat-chasing.

ENGRAVING

Although superficially it resembles chasing, engraving is carried out in quite a different way. It is done with a graver, a pointed piece of steel rod fitted into a handle. The engraver cuts away metal with this tool, whereas the chaser pushes metal aside with his punch. The engraver cuts his line with a single rapid stroke, as one draws a line with a pencil. The chaser has to create his line laboriously, blow by blow, advancing perhaps a tenth of an inch each time he moves his punch.

The character of these two kinds of decoration is implicit in the way in which they are carried out. Engraving is sharp and free and

Fig. 5.4. An engraving on a piece dating from the reign of Charles II shows the free-flowing nature of this decoration (by courtesy of Sotheby & Co.)

flowing at its best (Fig. 5.4); chasing is a softer and stiffer form of decoration. But chasing is more varied in its texture because the chaser by changing punches can easily change the weight of his lines.

TEXTURING

Modern hand-raised silverwares are sometimes decorated with texturing. The texturing is applied with specially made hammers with indented faces.

SAW-PIERCING

Saw-piercing is a very ancient craft, but was not used by the English silversmiths until the eighteenth century, and not extensively as a method of decoration until the second half of that century. Saw-piercing is reserved for fruit dishes, for the covers of rose bowls, for the tops of casters, and so on. The piercing-saw is like a fret-saw, and the technique is the same as fretwork. After the design has been marked out—usually by powdering a pricked paper pattern with

Fig. 5.5. Saw-piercing. The handles and border on this piece were cast and then chased up

chalk—the piercer drills a hole in the silver, inserts his saw-blade and begins to follow the intricate curves of the design (Fig. 5.5).

ENAMEL

Enamel is glass containing small quantities of metallic salts to give the different colours. The presence of iron oxide gives the glass a green colour, gold chloride gives a red, and so on. These metallic oxides give transparent colours, the addition of others, such as tin oxide, give opaque colour. To create the enamel the glass is powdered and mixed with the powdered oxide. The mixture is suspended in water and painted on to the silver. It is then fused in an oven and finally polished with pumice. A number of coats of enamel are usually given, each one being separately fired.

Enamelling is a very old craft, and different forms of enamel decoration have been used at different periods. Those ancient Celtic brooches seen in museums are decorated with cloisonné enamel. In this process raised pattern was created by the soldering of metal strip on to the surface of the article to create little cells called cloisons, and these cloisons were then filled with enamel of different colours. Many sixteenth century watch dials were decorated by a somewhat different type of enamel work, known as champlevé enamelling. Here, metal was gouged away to create a recessed design, and the recessed areas were then filled with enamel.

One sometimes also comes across other types of enamelling referred to in books and in saleroom catalogues, such as basse-taille, plique-à-jour and grisaille. Basse-taille is a form of champlevé enamelling, but the metal is cut away to different depths to produce a shaded effect. Plique-à-jour is like cloisonné, but the cloisons have no backs, so that a stained-glass-window effect is produced. Grisaille enamelling is painted enamelling, but only shades of grey are used to delineate the design.

The seventeenth century saw the great flowering of the art of painting in enamels, a craft still used today to decorate watch cases, brush-sets and compacts. A matt white enamel was laid over the surface and then allegorical pictures and flower sprays painted over this. One colour at a time was laid, each colour having to be fired separately, so that a painted enamel may require ten or more firings.

IN THE FACTORY

Reference has already been made to the development of mass production in the silver trade in the nineteenth century, and today most of the silverwares, and all the silver-plated wares sold by the retail jeweller, are made in the factory rather than in the craft workshop. They are formed between dies in the press and not hand-raised under the hammer. The bodies of vessels are produced by three or four blows of the force of the press, instead of by thousands of hammer blows, and so the process takes a matter of minutes.

If, however, the making of the vessel itself is today a rapid and a not particularly skilled operation, the making of the dies is a highly skilled, a lengthy and a very expensive business. The diesinker works in toughened steel, tough enough to stand up to heavy and repeated blows. He works from a copper model of the vessel that his dies will eventually reproduce. First of all he squares up a pair of steel blocks, mills the surfaces to very exacting tolerances, and polishes the blocks to a high finish. Taking his measurements from the copper model, he cuts out, or 'sinks', an impression of the outside form of his vessel into one of the blocks, carving away the steel and then polishing the inner surfaces. This recessed tool is called the female half of the tool and is concave. The male half of the tool is convex and reproduces the inside form of the vessel. The female half is fixed into the bed of the press, and the male tool is fixed into the force of the press—into the weighted hammer that descends with a great crash when the press is operated. If a circle of silver sheet covers the female tool it will be forced by the male tool to take the shape of the original copper model from which the tools were made. The force of the press will 'draw' the body of the vessel. If the vessel is a deep shape, and has to be deep-drawn, it will not be possible to form it in one operation between one pair of tools. It may have to be drawn by a succession of blows in the press between a succession of progressively deeper tools. If the vessel is of a complicated shape it may be necessary to stamp the body in two halves, and then to solder the two halves together.

SPINNING

This is the third method of making the body of a silver vessel and stands halfway between hand-raising and stamping. Spinning consists of forcing the silver over a chuck in a lathe. It is a skilled craft, but is much quicker than hand-raising. Spinning does not strengthen the metal as does hammering, but it is possible by this technique to produce flowing curves that have a beauty of their own. The spinner first makes a chuck in wood. This chuck represents the inside shape of the vessel to be spun. It is mounted in a spinning lathe, and a disc of silver sheet is placed against it. The spinner now pushes the silver sheet over the revolving chuck using a tool that consists of a chisel-like burnisher fixed in a long wooden handle. The long handle fits under the spinner's arm and gives him the necessary leverage to force the metal over the chuck. Split chucks are used for vessels of an enclosed form, so that they can be withdrawn through a narrow neck.

DECORATION FROM THE TOOLS

Silverwares made by spinning, and those which are formed in the press, may be decorated in exactly the same ways as hand-raised silverwares, but decoration can alternatively be put on in the course of the pressing operations. It is possible to simulate chasing by using tools that have a pattern raised on the female half of the tool and the same pattern recessed on the other half. Similarly, saw-piercing can be simulated by using dies. Imitation chased decoration or imitation saw-piercing is, however, rather lifeless when compared with the real thing. It is too regular, lacking human variation, but of course it is very much cheaper to produce. Because decorative silver has been out of fashion in recent years, and because the silver trade is shrinking, only a handful of craftsmen remain today who can carry out the decorative processes by hand. In the foreseeable future, therefore, more and more machine-applied decoration may have to be accepted.

The decorative wires used on such patterns as Celtic are produced by rolling silver between hardened steel rollers on which the pattern of the wire has been cut out in bas-relief just as a female tool is cut out.

SMALL WARES

Silver cigarette boxes, compacts, and silver-backed brushes, can also be made either by hand or in the press, the former having the advantage of greater strength and beauty, and the disadvantage of greater price. The strength of these wares is again the result of hand-hammering. A cigarette box that has been flat-hammered by hand is much less likely to bow or dent than one stamped out in the press, but this hand-hammering is a long, skilful and therefore expensive, process. Usually much more care is given to the details when making hand-made wares. Often, for instance, hand-made boxes have beautifully made flush hinges that are all but imperceptible when the box is closed. It is by pointing out such details as this, as well as the greater strength of the article, that the salesman can justify the considerably higher price of the hand-made over the machine-made product.

ENGINE-TURNING

This is a type of decoration usually reserved for boxes and brush-sets. To carry out this operation the part to be decorated is fixed with pitch to a block which is then clamped on the carriage of the engine-turning machine. The cutting tool of the machine is not unlike a graver, and indeed this is an engraving operation, for the tool cuts away the silver. The tool is brought to the work by the engine-turner, and the work is moved against the tool. For straight-line engine-turning the piece simply moves up and down against the tool, and when each cut has been completed the work is moved sideways, so that a row of furrows is cut right across, say, the back of a cigarette case. To create the wavy lines of the well-known barley pattern the work is vibrated as it moves against the tool. The use of concentric and eccentric cams makes it possible to create these wavy patterns.

Sometimes engine-turned wares have layers of transparent enamel applied over the pattern.

FINISHING

Once the component parts of a silverware have been produced they have to be soldered together. Silver solders, which are up to the sterling standard, are bought from the refiners, and solders that melt at different temperatures are available so that a second joint can be soldered close to one that has been soldered previously, without the risk of melting the first joint again. Now the silverware is ready to be sent to the assay office.

Back from the assay office a silverware still has to have one very important operation carried out upon it—polishing. At this stage it will be milky-white in colour and non-reflective. If a piece is badly scratched it may have to be given a preliminary finish against a grinding wheel, but usually the first polishing operation consists of mopping, or buffing. A mixture of oil and sand is thrown on to the piece as a polishing medium and the piece is then held against a rotating leather mop. Even this, however, is a rather too abrasive form of polishing for hand-raised silver. It would almost certainly remove the desirable patina produced by the planishing marks. Usually, therefore, the first polishing operation on hand-raised silver is done on a calico mop, using Tripoli powder as a medium. The matt finishes which are becoming increasingly popular are produced by using special mops.

A felt mop and jewellers' rouge, which is powdered hematite, is used to give the silver its final brilliant polish. A very high finish is sometimes imparted to small articles by a process known as burnishing, which consists of rubbing the silver with a small steel chisel. Brown ale is commonly used as a polishing medium in this process.

Machine-made silverwares vary considerably in quality. At their best they are but little inferior to hand-raised silverwares. At their worst they can be frightful, made from the thinnest gauge silver, decorated with shoddy imitation chasing or crude repetitive pierced scroll patterns thumped out in the press. Solder joints are sometimes rough, and the bright finish which is imparted by the polishing fails to hide the unevenness of the surfaces. The decorative wires and crude cast feet produced from bad models are poorly finished.

ELECTROFORMING

The technique of electroforming has been used by some silversmiths in recent years to produce decorative silverwares. Electroforming is not

Fig. 5.6. Pattern and two dishes produced by electroforming (by courtesy of The Worshipful Company of Goldsmiths)

a new technique. It has been used by museums over the years to reproduce models of antiques, but its use by silversmiths as a production technique is a more recent development. The technique consists of first making a non-metallic mould, nowadays usually of an epoxy resin. This is then placed in an electroplating bath where the metal is deposited on the mould, reproducing every surface detail. The process therefore avoids the production of expensive dies, or such labour-intensive operations as chasing or engraving. A famous example of the use of this process was the production by Louis Osman of the 24 carat gold crown used for the investiture of Prince Charles as Prince of Wales in 1969. Figure 5.6 shows an epoxy mould, together with two complicated dishes produced from it by electroforming. It clearly demonstrates the saving involved, compared with producing such dishes by more conventional techniques.

FLATWARE AND CUTLERY

Flatware, the tools used for eating that do not cut, can be made by handcraft methods, but today only a tiny fraction of the total annual production of spoons and forks are hand-forged.

HAND-FORGING

This is the traditional method of making silver flatware. The craftsman who sets out to hand-forge a silver spoon or fork takes a piece of silver bar and beats it over an anvil with a hammer. It is this hammering which gives the hand-forged spoon or fork its strength, in the same way that the hammer blows used to raise hollowares, or the flat-hammering of a silver tray, give these strength. You can drive the tines of a hand-forged fork into a plank without bending them, a test of strength that few mass-produced forks would withstand.

When the smith has flattened out the silver bar, he roughly shapes the piece by hammering it over a recessed die known as a swaging block. He raises the bowl of a spoon in much the same way that a smith begins to raise the body of a tea-pot over a recess in a tree-trunk, but using in this case a concave metal block. This process gives the spoon-bowl a distinctive thick edge, which is a sure indication that a spoon has been hand-forged (Fig. 5.7).

The next process is to impart the pattern to the handle of the piece, and to give it its final shape by die-stamping it in a drop-forge (Fig. 5.8). This, too, is really a hammering process. The hammer is the heavy 'monkey', the descending weight of the drop-forge.

The hand-forging of flatware survives only to cater for special orders from a handful of customers to whom price is no object. But it makes it possible to perpetuate some of the beautiful old patterns, such as chased-vine, for which the demand is so small that it would be impossible to recover the cost of producing a set of press tools.

126

Fig. 5.7(a). Hand-forged spoon—stages in the forming

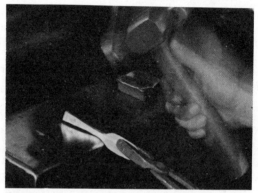

Fig. 5.7(b). The spoon beginning to take shape under the hammer

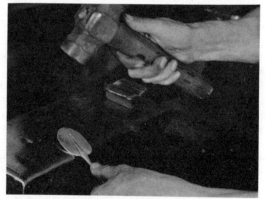

Fig. 5.7(c). The craftsman spreading out the silver with his hammer to form the bowl of the spoon

Fig. 5.8 Pattern being struck on to the handle end of a blank in a drop-forge

FLATWARE FROM THE FACTORY

In a flatware factory, silver flatware is produced from silver sheet, e.p.n.s. flatware from nickel silver sheet, and stainless-steel flatware from the appropriate grade of stainless-steel sheet, usually 18/8. From the sheet the blanks are cut in the first of a series of stamping operations. The shape of the blank already suggests the form of the final product, but the metal is the same thickness all over. The next operation is to cross-roll the part of the spoon which will become the bowl and that part of the fork which will become the tines (Figs 5.9(a)–(c)). Heavy rollers spread out the metal and reduce it to the right thickness. After that the spoon is bowled and the prongs, or tines, of the fork are cut out in a press (Fig. 5.9(b)). Further press operations impart the patterns to the handles, and the curves to the profiles of the pieces. Between these operations the blanks have had, of course, to be annealed regularly to restore ductility to the work-hardened metal.

Fig. 5.9(a). Production of forks and spoons by mass-production techniques—stages in the process

After these various forming operations there follow a complicated series of finishing operations. The edges of the pieces are smoothed off against grinding wheels, and the spaces between the tines are cleaned out (Fig. 5.10). Increasingly these days these operations are carried out mechanically. Next, the pieces are polished with a mixture of sand and oil on revolving leather mops. The famous women, the 'buffers', who have done this work in the factories of Sheffield, are a dying race, as no young girls care to take up this work (Fig. 5.11(a)). For this reason, also for speed and economy, more and more flatware is nowadays being polished on automatic machines. The pieces are clamped in long racks and positioned against a battery of revolving mops. After one end of the flatware has been polished the pieces are turned round in the racks and presented to the mops again. The pieces are finally mopped with felt mops on other machines. Few people would deny that the buffers

Fig. 5.9(b). *Male and female dies used to form spoons and forks in the power presses of a modern flatware factory*

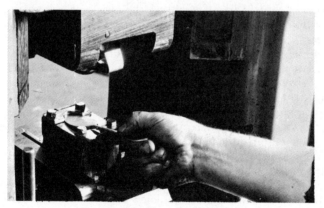

Fig. 5.9(c). *Bowling a spoon in the press*

do a better job than the machine, but there seems to be no alternative to accepting a slightly lower standard of polishing in the future (Fig. 5.11(b)).

After polishing, nickel-silver spoons and forks go to the plating shop, where their coating of silver is electrolytically deposited on to them. In modern factories this process too has been mechanised

Fig. 5.10. One of a series of grinding processes to smooth the edges of the pieces and to clean between the tines of the forks

(Fig. 5.12). The spoons and forks are loaded on jigs, and on these they travel automatically from bath to bath. First they go through a series of degreasing and washing processes to ensure that they are absolutely clean. Dirt or grease on the article would prevent the silver from adhering properly to the base metal core. When the articles have passed through the cleaning baths they arrive at the plating bath. Control of the current density and of the time-cycle of the automatic plating plant makes certain that a controlled thickness of silver is plated on each piece, and regular tests are made to ensure that the plating is of the desired thickness and that the adhesion is good. There is still, however, as mentioned in an earlier chapter, no generally adhered-to standard, and the A.1 symbol seen on most good-quality e.p.n.s. is therefore meaningless.

After plating, the racks with their burden of flatware continue their journey on the electrically-powered roundabout, which dips them into cleaning baths and into rinsing baths, until finally they reach the end of their journey. They are then dried in sawdust, given a final brilliant polish with jewellers' rouge and packed.

KNIVES

The domestic knife was revolutionised by the discovery in 1914, by Harry Brearley, of stainless steel. This new metal presented some initial problems of working, but before long it had entirely replaced

131

Fig. 5.10(a). A 'buffer' hand-polishing flatware in a Sheffield factory

Fig. 5.10(b). Mechanised polishing of flatware

carbon steel as the raw material of the domestic blade. The knife blade is fashioned from a length of stainless-steel rod, which is die-stamped in a drop-forge, after being brought to red heat (Figs 5.13 (a) and (b)). In this operation the tang and the bolster are formed. The tang is the rod which will eventually fit into a hole in the knife handle and secure the two together; the bolster is the collar separating the blade from the handle. After these have been formed the metal is reheated and the blade rolled out. Then it is given its final shape with blanking tools in a press.

Fig. 5.12. Mechanised plating—the blanks are loaded on jigs

The blade now has to be turned into a cutting tool—it has to be forged, or hardened, so that it will take and hold an edge. Formerly this was done by hand, but today mechanical hammers are increasingly replacing hand-hammering for this work. Hammering, as has been seen, makes metal brittle, and a brittle blade would be of no use. So the brittleness must now be taken out of the metal by a process known as tempering. The blade is heated in a furnace to a high temperature and cooled, usually in a blast of air. It will now bend without fear of cracking. It is, however, possible to buy cheap knives the blades of which have not been properly tempered, or not tempered at all, that can be snapped in two just by pressing them firmly on a table.

A variety of handles are used for domestic knives today. The old celluloid handles, called Xylonite, that imitate ivory, are still

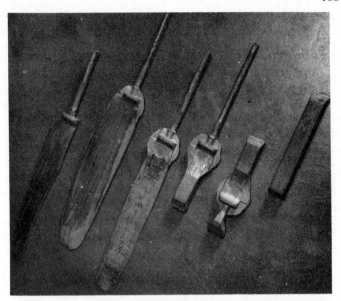

Fig. 5.13(a). Knife-making—stages in the making from stainless-steel rod

Fig. 5.13(b). Knife-making—die-stamping in a drop-forge after
heating red-hot

popular, but are being replaced by nylon. Laminated wooden handles bonded with water-resistant synthetic resin glues are used, and so occasionally are ceramic handles. All these handles, however, have one fault in common. The adhesion of handle and blade depends on the 'cement' used to glue them together, though modern adhesives and modern techniques have made it much more likely than in earlier days that these knives will stand up to domestic abuse.

It is, however, expecting much of any bonding agent to withstand regular immersion in boiling water, while the washing-up machine represents a new threat to this bond. It can be appreciated therefore why the one-piece knife and the hollow-handled knife, which is hard-soldered to the blade, are becoming more and more popular.

The one-piece knife is made all of a piece, the handle being hot forged from the bar before the blade is rolled out. Hollow handles are made from two stampings struck with the pattern of the flatware they are made to match. These are then soldered together and hard-soldered on to the blade.

WORKING IN STAINLESS STEEL

Most of what has been written about silver and e.p.n.s. flatware applies equally to stainless-steel flatware. The only difference is that stainless steel, being a much harder metal than the other two, is much harder on the tools. It is much more difficult, too, though not impossible with very heavy presses, to draw very deep shapes in stainless steel. One notices that there is a tendency for the bowls of stainless-steel spoons to be much shallower than those of silver or e.p.n.s. patterns. They were made in this way to begin with because it was easier and cheaper, but now shallow bowls have become fashionable, an interesting example of economic considerations starting a fashion.

When it comes to forming deep-bodied hollowares in stainless steel the problem is, of course, much greater. Experiments have been made to form these by other means than between dies in a huge press. One of these new methods is explosive forming. The explosion of a small charge has been used to drive liquid inside a cup of stainless steel with great force, persuading it to take the shape of a female die. It seems likely that we may see forming of this type becoming more common in factories producing stainless-steel hollowares in the future.

WORKING IN PEWTER

The best pewterwares are cast. The pewter is melted and poured into gun-metal moulds, and many of the moulds used today date back to the times, a hundred years ago and more, when pewterware was used in every home in the land. Pewter can also be spun or stamped in the press. Pewter stamping is no different from stamping silver or nickel silver. But pewter spinning differs from silver or nickel-silver spinning—the craftsman usually does not use chucks. He 'spins on the wind' as they say. The reason why cast pewter is better than either spun or stamped pewter is that the rolling out of the metal into sheet form, as the necessary preparation for either of these processes, breaks up the atomic structure of the metal. This results in a softer weaker vessel than one made by casting.

CHAPTER 6

Hallmarks on Gold, Silver and Platinum*

HALLMARKING

In the Middle Ages crafts were controlled by craft guilds who fixed prices and wages, insisted on reasonable working conditions, and looked after the sick and needy members of the craft. They also ensured that a journeyman was skilled in his craft before they would allow him to practise it, and they demanded that everything made by any member of the guild was up to standard. They maintained that bad workmanship or the use of poor materials by the individual could undermine the reputation of the whole craft.

IN LONDON

The Goldsmiths' Guild of London was one of the earliest of the guilds to be formed. This was already in existence in Norman times, and by the thirteenth century it was 'a numerous and powerful body'. But not powerful enough, it would seem, or not sufficiently jealous of its reputation, to exercise sufficient control over its members. Nothing, of course, could have been easier in those days than to defraud the public by adulterating gold and silver with too much alloy, and the temptation proved much too great for some of the members of the guild to resist. By 1238, things were getting serious, and 'as a result of numerous frauds perpetrated by some of the members of the craft', Henry III made an Order in Council, in which he commanded the Mayor and Aldermen of the City to choose six 'discreet goldsmiths' to superintend the craft. It was the successors of these six discreet members of the guild who were, in 1300, recognised by Edward I as the guardians of the craft, and entrusted with the job of assaying 'every manner of vessel

* The author is indebted to John Forbes (Deputy Warden of the Assay Office, Goldsmiths' Hall) for amending this chapter in the light of the new legislation.

of silver' before it was offered for sale. To show that they had carried out this assay, a word which derived from the French word *assai*, meaning to essay or to try, the guardians marked the pieces that had been through their hands, with a punch showing a leopard's head. They were also required to assay wares of gold to see that they were of the required standard.

The standard demanded for silver, under the Act of Edward I, which gave these powers to the guardians of the craft, was 'of the sterling allay or better, at the pleasure of him to whom the work

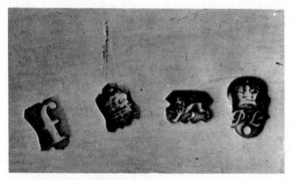

Fig. 6.1. Set of marks on a valuable piece of antique silver, sent to the London Assay Office in 1741 by Paul de Lamerie

belongeth'. Those who worked in gold had to 'work no worse gold than of the Touch of Paris', which was $19\frac{1}{5}$ carat.

This then was the beginning of the practice of assaying and hall-marking. The old guild became the Worshipful Company of Gold-smiths, receiving its first Royal Charter from Edward III in 1327, and this body is still to this day responsible for hallmarking in London.

Under an Act of 1363 every master goldsmith had been required to stamp with his own mark each piece of gold and silver that he made, and from that date London-made silverwares began to bear two of the four marks found on modern pieces. One of these was the Warden's mark, the leopard's head, sometimes called the King's mark, the other the maker's mark. To begin with, makers' marks were usually in the form of heraldic devices, probably taken from the creaking signs that hung above the goldsmiths' shops. Only later, at the end of the seventeenth century, did it become customary to use letters. First of all, under a statute of William III of 1696, the first two letters of the goldsmith's surname were used. Then from 1720 the goldsmith's initials were used, and this is the type of maker's mark used to this day (Fig. 6.1).

The practice of punching silver- or goldwares with a separate mark in the form of a letter of the alphabet, to show in which year they were submitted for assay, began in 1478. Since the research carried out into the date letter system by Octavius Morgan in the 1850s, the existence of these date letters has been an invaluable aid to collectors and dealers in antique plate, as they make it possible to ascertain at a glance exactly when a piece of plate was made.

The last of the four marks that we find on London silverwares made its first appearance in 1544. This is the quality, or standard, mark. It took the form of a lion standing sideways in a shield with its head turned to the left, the lion passant guardant of heraldry, and it was probably borrowed with royal sanction from the Tudor arms.

OUTSIDE LONDON

London was not, of course, the only city in medieval England where gold- and silverwares were made. In law, the London guild had jurisdiction over all the provincial goldsmiths, but in practice the local guilds exercised control locally, 'touching' and marking the plate made by their members. That section of the Act of 1300 that read 'and that all the good towns of England, where any goldsmith be dwelling, shall be ordered according to this statute as they of London be; and that one shall come from every good town for all the residue that be dwelling in the same unto London, for to be ascertained of their touch', was somewhat unrealistic in an age when lumbering carriers' waggons might take days to cover a few miles of mired tracks. A statute of 1378, in fact, placed the onus on 'the Mayors and Governors of the cities and boroughs' to carry out the 'assay of the Touch'. In 1423, the Statute of Henry VI appointed York, Newcastle-upon-Tyne, Lincoln, Norwich, Bristol, Salisbury and Coventry to have 'divers touches'. Many other towns, without this express permission from the Crown, marked the plate made by local craftsmen. One comes across silverwares marked in Taunton and Exeter, King's Lynn and Leeds, Leicester and Lewes, Hull and Barnstaple, to name only a few of the towns where at one time or another goldsmiths have worked.

By the middle of the eighteenth century many of the old towns of England had lost their former importance. There was little work for the silversmiths and the craft died out. At the same time in two newly important and growing towns, Birmingham and Sheffield, manufacturing silversmiths were opening factories and prospering.

139

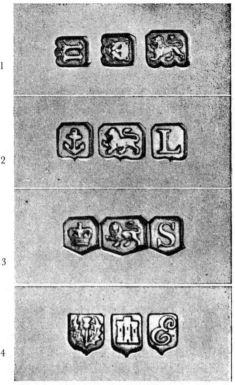

*Fig. 4.2. Marks found on modern silver: 1—London;
2—Birmingham; 3—Sheffield; 4—Edinburgh*

*Fig. 4.3. 1935–36 marks of assay offices now closed:
1—Chester; 2—Glasgow*

They soon found, these Birmingham and Sheffield smiths, that having no assaying and marking facilities locally made life very difficult. The nearest assay offices were those at London and Chester, and it took a long time for goods to travel to and from either of these offices in those days. The silversmiths of Sheffield, the more important silver town of the two, were said to be 'under great difficulties and hardships in the exercise of their trades for want of assayers in a convenient place . . .'. In Birmingham, the great Matthew Boulton was equally concerned. In 1771, a piece of plate commissioned from him by the Earl of Sherbourne had not only been delayed on the 70-mile journey from Chester, but what was worse, 'the chasing was entirely destroyed by the wilful and careless packing of them at Chester'. This delay and damage, which led to the upsetting of an important customer, was the last straw for Boulton. He drew up and submitted a petition to Parliament on behalf of himself and the other silversmiths of Birmingham. He wanted, he said, to become a great silversmith, but it was useless 'unless the powers can be obtained to have a marking hall at Birmingham'.

Birmingham and Sheffield got their assay offices under an Act of 1773, despite opposition from the silversmiths in London and the Goldsmiths' Company of London, inspired either by fear for their own trade or concern lest the new provincial offices might not maintain standards. Soon the new offices were working on one or two days a week. The Birmingham Assay Master presided over four or five helpers in the King's Head public house once a week.

Of all the marking halls that have existed at one time or another during the past six and a half centuries, only three now remain in England. These are the offices in London, Birmingham and Sheffield. Scotland has only one assay office now, in Edinburgh (Fig. 6.2). The last two offices to close down were Chester, in 1962, and Glasgow, in 1964 (Fig. 6.3).

THE DUTY ON SILVER

Besides the four marks to be found on most silverwares made later than the middle of the sixteenth century, a fifth was used between 1784 and 1890 (Fig. 6.4). This mark, in the form of a portrait of the reigning sovereign in profile, was struck to indicate that the duty payable under the Act of 1784, which was collectable by the assay offices on behalf of the Excise, had in fact been paid.

At an earlier date, between 1720 and 1758 a duty of 6d. an ounce had been applied to silverwares, but was avoided by many silversmiths. It was this duty-dodging which led, when the tax was reintroduced, to the use of a duty mark being made statutory. It was felt that this mark would make it easier for authority to check up on the duty dodgers but, as will be seen, a new way was soon discovered of avoiding payment of this unpopular duty at least on important pieces.

Fig. 6.4. Duty marks showing the head of the reigning sovereign in profile. Found on silver made between 1784 and 1890

Fig. 6.5. The Jubilee mark showing the heads of King George V and Queen Mary, added to the Chester marks for 1935

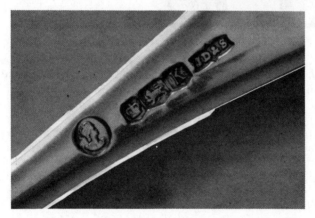

Fig. 6.6 Mark struck at the Sheffield Assay Office (1953) to celebrate the Coronation of Queen Elizabeth II

The reigning sovereign's head in profile has appeared on silver twice since the repeal of the duty in 1890. The first time was when George V and Queen Mary were celebrating the twenty-fifth anniversary of their accession to the throne (Fig. 6.5). To mark this occasion, silverwares were, between 1933 and 1935, stamped with a mark showing the King and Queen in profile. Then between 1952 and 1954, gold- and silverwares were stamped with a Coronation mark showing the profile of Queen Elizabeth II (Fig. 6.6).

THE BRITANNIA STANDARD

Sterling silver (silver being 925 parts in 1000 pure) has remained, with the exception of a period of 23 years, the minimum standard which it is legal to offer for sale in this country, since 1300.

As was mentioned when discussing coinage in a previous chapter, the great demand for silverwares from the Court of Charles II and the Cavalier squires who returned from France and the Low Countries after the Restoration, led many silversmiths to clip the silver shillings of the period, and even to melt them down in order to obtain enough raw material to carry out their commissions.

Fig. 6.7. Marks which indicate Britannia standard silver

This soon began to have serious repercussions. There was the unofficial devaluation of the shilling which increased the value of a guinea from 20*s.* to 21*s.*, and there was soon a great shortage of silver coins. Charles did nothing. James did nothing. Eventually, in 1697, Dutch William took action. He decided that the melting and the 'wicked and pernicious crime of clipping' had to stop. To discourage these practices he raised the minimum standard for silver plate so that it was higher than the standard for the silver coinage. In future, if the silversmiths continued to clip and melt shillings, they would be put to the considerable trouble of refining their ill-gotten silver if their wares were to pass an assay.

The new minimum standard, set by William III, was called the Britannia standard. Silverwares had to be 958·4 parts in 1000 pure. At the London Assay Office this new standard was marked with a lion's head erased (see Fig. 6.7) and a seated figure of Britannia. The wares also bore, of course, the usual maker's mark (consisting of the first two letters of his surname) and the date letter.

The sterling standard was restored as the minimum standard in 1720, but even after that date a few pieces were made to the Britannia standard, and occasionally even today a silversmith will make a special piece in the higher standard and have it marked accordingly.

UNMARKED PLATE

Not all goldsmiths and silversmiths who have worked in England during the past six and a half centuries have been honest men. Some avoided the charges for assaying and marking, some evaded the duty, and some were fakers and forgers. And so we meet silver with no marks, and silver bearing marks that are not what they purport to be, or do not belong to the piece to which they are attached.

A lot of silver made during the sixteenth and seventeenth centuries bears no marks at all, or just a maker's mark. The reason is probably that the silversmiths misunderstood, or took advantage of, that part of the Statute of 1575 referring to silver being assayed and marked before being offered for sale. They assumed that this meant that commissioned work was exempted. By 1643 there was so much unmarked plate in the country that it was given an official price of 8d. an ounce lower than that for marked plate.

FALSE MARKS

A number of different types of false mark are to be found on silver, among them being those applied by the duty evaders. With the introduction of a duty, in 1719, quite a number of silversmiths seem to have hit on the idea, when producing a big piece, of sending off a little piece, weighing only a few ounces, to the assay office. They paid the small amount of duty and, after 1784, got back the piece complete with the duty mark. They then proceeded to cut out the marks from the small piece and apply them to the big piece, so saving the duty on perhaps a few hundred ounces of silver.

Then there are the marks on faked pieces. Fakes are sometimes made by casting, or electrotyping, from a genuine piece. When this is done the marks are transferred to the fake by the same method used to reproduce the form and decoration of the original. Other fakes are made by more traditional methods, being raised exactly as the piece being imitated would have been raised. If pieces are made in this way, the faker has a choice of two methods of producing a spurious set of hallmarks for his spurious ware. He can make a fake set of punches, or he can take genuine hallmarks from a damaged piece or from a piece of little value of the right date. Forging or transposing hallmarks in this way are, of course, really serious offences. They render the perpetrator liable to a maximum penalty of 10 years' imprisonment.

It is equally illegal to sell fakes, forged pieces, or pieces with transferred marks. It is also illegal to sell hallmarked articles that have been altered and not regularised by an assay office. Therefore, anyone selling silverwares must be on the lookout for anything suspicious. One thing that reveals a fake to the expert is decoration that is wrong for the period indicated by the mark. This is more common than one might expect, as few fakers it would seem have any historical sense. Then there are the technical clues such as signs of soldering round a hallmark that can often be brought out by breathing on the silver. Blow-holes near marks suggest casting. An exact similarity of the placing of marks on a pair of spoons or casters suggests that one or both are cast or electrotype copies. Silver was usually marked with four punches individually applied, and so the chance of an exact repetition of the relative positioning of the marks is most unlikely.

In addition to the true fakes there have been many attempts to deceive the public into believing that they were buying silver when they were not. In writing about pewter it was mentioned that the Goldsmiths' Company were forced to take out an injunction preventing the pewterers from simulating hallmarks on their wares. There have been a number of attempts by manufacturers of electroplate to get away with marks looking at first glance exactly like a set of silver marks, while not infrequently American firms have blatantly copied English hallmarks.

HALLMARKS AND THE LAW

Lawyers faced with the various Acts that used to regulate assaying and hallmarking have been known to describe them as 'complicated', 'confusing' and 'archaic'. A new Act, the Hallmarking Act of 1973, which came into force on January 1, 1975, has however simplified the situation. This Act has repealed the previous Acts, and removed most of the anomalies.

The new legislation has no effect, of course, on the validity of the marks struck in the past, and anyone working in the jewellery trade, who will be dealing both with current production and with jewellery and silverwares produced before January 1, 1975, has to be familiar both with the modern and the older legislation. The retail jeweller need not, however, concern himself with all the intricacies of the law. He must, however, avoid any breach of that section of the law that reads: 'Any person who in the course of a trade or business (*a*) applies to an unhallmarked article a description indicating that it is wholly or partly made of gold, silver or platinum, or (*b*) supplies or offers to supply an unhallmarked article to which such a description is applied, shall be guilty of an offence.' The law does not require every gold- and silverware to be hallmarked. Certain wares are specifically exempted under the new Act, though the list of exemptions under this Act is somewhat different from that in force prior to its introduction. The details of the current exemptions are listed in Appendix 2, page 300.

Today, many manufacturers ignore these exemptions, because they find it to their advantage to have such wares voluntarily assayed and marked, so they can be advertised as hallmarked.

The main tenets of the new Act are that:

1. Platinum, which previously did not have to be hallmarked, now comes within the hallmarking legislation. The legal standard for platinum is 950 parts in 1000.
2. Wares of gold and silver below the legal standard or unhallmarked wares, which under the previous legislation could not be offered for sale, may now be legally sold provided they are not described as 'gold' or 'silver'.
3. Changes have been made in the list of exemptions from hallmarking.
4. A Hallmarking Council has been set up, whose principal job is to keep the law continuously under review, and recommend such changes as are desirable.

It is important for the jeweller in dealing with customers' possessions to bear in mind the wording of the law, that the offence is not to possess but to sell or offer for sale in the course of a trade or business. There is no reason why the customers should not continue to enjoy the use of unmarked wares that they may have inherited or acquired from abroad. If a dealer wished to sell unmarked wares as gold, silver or platinum they would, of course, have first to be submitted for assay and marking (unless they were in an exempt category). There is the possibility with foreign wares that they might not pass the stringent tests of a modern British assay office. This would not mean, however, as many people believe, that they would be destroyed. Substandard articles that are not new are not 'broken' by the assay office but are returned to their owner unmarked.

Only if the piece bears counterfeit hallmarks is the mere possession of the piece an offence against the law. It is illegal to deface marks without the consent of an assay office. Nor may the character of wares be changed, or additions made, without the prior approval of an assay office. It is also an offence to deal in wares that have been altered without the consent of an assay office.

THE MARKS ON GOLD, SILVER AND PLATINUM

THE QUALITY MARK ON STERLING SILVER

The leopard's head was used originally to denote that both silver and gold were up to standard, and was sometimes called the King's mark. In an indictment of 1597, however, we find the lion passant guardant described as Her Majesty's Lion, and for many years now all the English assay offices have used either the lion passant or the lion passant guardant to denote that a piece of silver has been assayed and found to be up to the sterling standard. At first the lion passant guardant, which the London office used, was crowned, but the crown disappeared in 1550. From 1821 the London lion no longer looked to the left. It became simply a lion passant.

The shape of the shield containing the lion has changed through the ages, as indeed have the shapes of the shields containing all the assay marks, as reference to *Bradbury's Book of Hallmarks* will show. This is a useful aid when dating pieces with worn marks.

Birmingham used a lion passant guardant as the quality mark on sterling from the opening of the office in 1773 until 1875, and then changed to the lion passant. Sheffield used the lion passant guardant until 1975, and so did Chester until the office there closed, though some early Chester pieces are found with the word 'sterling' in a shield, and up to 1839 the lion passant guardant was accompanied by a leopard's head crowned.

The Scottish offices used their own standard marks. Edinburgh used a thistle from 1759 to 1975, but has now adopted a lion rampant; when the Glasgow office closed, a thistle and a lion rampant had been used since 1914. Before that a lion rampant only had been used, and earlier still, before 1800, there had been no separate quality mark at all.

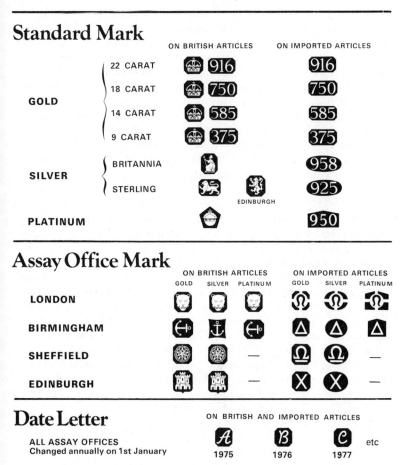

Fig. 6.8. British system of standard marks, assay office marks and date letters used since January 1975

THE TOWN MARK

The leopard's head has been used by London as its office mark since it ceased to do double duty as an office mark and quality mark in the sixteenth century. At first the leopard was a noble beast bearing a crown, but he lost his crown in 1821 and since then onwards has looked more like a teddy bear than a beast of the jungle.

Birmingham has used an anchor as its office mark since its establishment. Sheffield had always used a crown until 1975, but has now adopted the York rose previously used only on goldwares. Chester used the arms of the city, a shield bearing three wheat sheaves, and until 1839 a leopard's head was also punched into sterling silver marked at this office—a crowned leopard until 1822, and thereafter uncrowned.

Edinburgh uses a castle as its office mark and has always done so. The distinctive three-turreted castle was introduced in 1617 and has appeared in slightly different forms ever since. Glasgow used its City Arms, a most complicated heraldic device consisting of a tree, a bird, a bell, a fish, and a ring.

THE DATE LETTER

The date letter system, while it provides a unique method of dating antiques, was complicated in the past by three facts. First, rarely were all the letters of the alphabet used, and the various offices were not consistent about which ones they omitted. Then the different offices started the cycles of letters in different years, and introduced their new date letter at differing times of the year. They also used their own styles of lettering in their own styles of shield. The only hope for anyone, without a photographic memory, to find his way around in this gloriously inconsistent world of the date letter on pieces made prior to 1975 is to look up Bradbury, or the tables in Jackson's *English Goldsmiths and Their Marks*. In doing this, care must be taken to check the office mark first, and to see that the letter and the shield really do agree with those in the tables; positive identification can be difficult if the marks on a piece are badly worn.

It is, none the less, perhaps well for those employed in the trade to understand the way in which the various offices organised their date marks system. The following is a simple guide.

London used 20 letters, A to U, omitting the J which in some alphabets could easily be confused with an I. Formerly, London changed from one date letter to another on May 19, the day of St Dunstan, the patron saint of the goldsmiths. In 1660 it was decided to mark the triumphal return of Charles II to London after his exile by changing the date letter on May 29.

Birmingham generally ran a 25-year cycle of letters, starting with A and going right through to Z, but omitting I or J. Sheffield did the same, but though the two offices began marking in the same year the cycles did not coincide. Sheffield's system went haywire for some reason at the start. For example, in 1797 an X followed Z, and then came V, E, N, H, and so on. Chester also had a 25-year cycle and always omitted J.

Edinburgh, except for two periods, used a 25-year cycle from 1681, also leaving out J. Between 1806 and 1832, however, Edinburgh used a 26-letter alphabet, and in the period from 1882 to 1906 a 24-letter alphabet was used, with U as well as J being omitted in that series. Glasgow used all 26 letters of the alphabet from 1819 onwards. Its earlier system is very difficult to follow as the office in those days seems to have been particularly addicted to the letter S, using it sometimes in different forms year after year. At the time this office closed it was using a Celtic alphabet with only 18 capital letters. This cycle had started in 1949.

London, as already stated, changed its letter in May. Birmingham's letter was altered on July 1, as was Chester's when that office was open. Sheffield changed its letter on the day following the office's annual general meeting, which is held in July. Edinburgh introduced the new letter on the day following the third Thursday in October, and Glasgow used to make the change on the first Monday in July.

As from January 1975 this chaotic situation has been rationalised, with all the offices using the same letter in the same year and changing the letter on January 1 each year. The offices all began a new cycle in 1975 using a script capital alphabet (see Fig. 6.8).

THE SPONSOR'S (MAKER'S) MARK

As a glance through Jackson's invaluable guide shows, the goldsmiths in the early days of marking put some very attractive marks on their wares before sending them to the Hall to be assayed. But nowadays the maker's mark, renamed the sponsor's mark under the new legislation, is more mundane. Gone are the crossbows and the fish, the lambs' heads and the eagles. Today, initial letters are used—those of the firm's name, or those of the individual smith submitting the ware.

The sponsor's mark is registered with the office, being stamped on a plate by the 'maker' so that the office can check who has sent in a particular piece.

The term 'maker's mark' was obviously a misnomer. Anyone can register a mark, and wholesalers and retailers often have wares that have been made for them marked by the manufacturer with their own mark. It is not unusual for a firm of manufacturing silversmiths to put its own name on only 50 per cent of the silver it produces, while putting the marks of its customers on the rest.

THE MARKS ON BRITANNIA SILVER

The Britannia standard, the higher standard introduced to discourage the clipping and melting of the silver coinage, was the minimum legal standard from 1697 until 1720. After 1720 Britain reverted to sterling as the legal minimum, but silver to the higher standard continued to be made, and indeed is still made to this day. Silversmiths, when they are making a reproduction of a Queen Anne piece, for instance, sometimes use Britannia silver so that the marks, except for the date letter, will be similar to those on the original.

It was necessary from the beginning to differentiate between Britannia standard and sterling standard silver by the punching of distinguishing marks. So, in 1697, a new mark, one showing the seated figure of Britannia with her shield and her spear, was struck on English silver for the first time and has been used ever since by the London Assay Office to indicate that silver has been assayed and found to be at least 95·84 per cent pure. When offices were opened in Birmingham and Sheffield they also adopted the Britannia mark as a quality mark for the higher standard, and so did Chester up to the time the office closed. Edinburgh added the Britannia to its usual marks as did Glasgow when that office was operating.

To further distinguish Britannia from sterling, London used a different town mark for Britannia, substituting for the leopard's head what in heraldry is called a lion's head erased, that is to say a lion with a ragged neck. Chester used the lion's head erased and the Britannia mark, but retained its normal town mark, the wheat sheaves on a shield.

As from January 1975 the seated Britannia is used as the standard mark by all assay offices, and each uses its normal town mark (Fig. 6.8). The lion's head erased mark, formerly used by the London office, has been dropped.

THE DUTY MARK

Most gold- and silverwares made between 1784 and 1890 should bear as a mark a portrait in profile of the head of reigning sovereigns. The presence of the profile of George III, George IV, William IV or Queen Victoria, indicates that the duty payable under the Act of 1784 had been paid. Edinburgh put no duty mark on goldwares below the 18 carat standard.

There exist some pieces marked in Sheffield bearing two portraits instead of one. This was because when the duty was raised, those in charge of that assay office decided, for a six-month period in 1797, to use a double mark to show that the higher duty had been paid. After this little burst of Sheffield individualism the office reverted once more to normal practice.

THE MARKS ON GOLD

The hallmarking of goldwares is complicated because today there are four standards, 9, 14, 18 and 22 carat gold (Figs 6.9, 6.10, 6.11). The two higher standards were marked until 1975 in a different way from the lower. The 18 and 22 carat goldwares assayed and found to be up to standard were marked with a number indicating the carat quality and with an additional mark. The English offices used a crown with the figures 18 or 22, the crowns used by the various offices being slightly different in detail one from another. The Scottish offices did not use a crown. Edinburgh used a thistle, and Glasgow used a thistle together with a lion rampant. The use of the standard mark for 18 carat was authorised by an Act of 1798, and for 22 carat by an Act of 1844. To these marks the assay offices added the usual date letter and town mark, and of course the maker had to stamp his mark on the piece before submitting it.

The Sheffield Assay Office, which started to mark gold only in 1904, realised that the use of its normal town mark, a crown, on

LONDON   BIRMINGHAM   SHEFFIELD

CHESTER   EDINBURGH   GLASGOW

Fig. 6.9. Standard marks used by various assay offices for 22 carat gold before 1975

Fig. 6.10. Standard marks used by all assay offices for 14 and 9 carat gold before 1975

Fig. 6.11. Marks of the discontinued 15 and 12 carat standards

Fig. 6.12. The rose, the alternative Sheffield town mark used on goldwares only, before 1975

goldwares would be confused with the quality mark, so it used the Yorkshire rose as a town mark on gold (Fig. 6.12).

The lower standards of gold were also marked with two quality marks—a figure in a shield denoting the standard of the gold, and a second shield bearing a set of figures indicating the percentage of gold in the alloy. The figures ·585 appear on 14 carat gold, and the figures ·375 on 9 carat gold.

At varying periods gold of other standards has been legal. From 1854 to 1932, for instance, both 12 and 15 carat were legal. They were marked as 14 and 9 carat were marked before 1975, but with the appropriate carat and percentage figures in the two shields.

From 1477 to 1576 the minimum legal standard was 18 carat. Then for 222 years to 1798 it was 22 carat. From 1798 to 1854 the minimum standard was lowered to 18 carat again.

 Fig. 6.13. Mark (not strictly a hallmark) used during the war years on 9 carat plain wedding rings weighing not more than 2 dwt

It was in 1854, because of a growing demand from the jewellery trade, that gold of a standard lower than 18 carat was first allowed. That year saw the introduction of 9 carat as the minimum standard for goldwares permissible in this country. Since that date it has been legal to sell 9 carat goldwares but until 1975 it was illegal to sell goldwares of a quality lower than 9 carat, whether described as gold or not.

Under the new legislation all the offices now use the same two standard marks on goldwares—a crown in a square with cut corners, and a set of figures in an oblong with cut corners denoting the gold content of the piece in parts per thousand (see Fig. 6.8).

THE MARKS ON PLATINUM

With the advent of platinum hallmarking a new quality mark had to be devised, and this mark depicts an orb (see Fig. 6.14). The mark is punched by the various offices together with the office mark, the date letter and the sponsor's mark.

Fig. 6.14. Marks used on platinum by the London assay office in 1975

MARKS STAMPED ON IMPORTED WARES

All platinum-, gold- and silverwares imported into Britain are subject to the same legal requirements as British-made articles. Hallmarking of foreign articles began in 1842. From 1883 until 1904 the letter 'F'

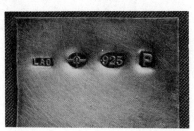

Fig. 6.15. Mark struck by the London Assay Office on a piece of imported sterling silver

for foreign was added in an oval. Following the passing of the Foreign Plate Act of 1904, the various offices began to use their own special marks for foreign wares (see Fig. 6.8). These are placed in different-shaped surrounds depending on the metal to be marked. Gold is marked with an oblong shield with cut corners, silver with an oval, and platinum with a pentagonal surround shaped like the façade of a building.

At first London used a Phoebus, Sheffield two arrows crossed and Glasgow a bishop's mitre, but after two years London and Sheffield adopted their present marks. Today, London uses the sign of the constellation of Leo, Sheffield the constellation of Libra, Birmingham an equilateral triangle and Edinburgh the Cross of St. Andrew. Glasgow used two letter 'F's on top of each other, and Chester used an acorn and oak leaves.

The quality marks placed on foreign wares consist of figures indicating the various standards of gold and silver (see Fig. 6.8).

To these two marks is added the date letter.

IRISH MARKS

The Dublin Assay Office was set up in 1637 as a result of a Royal Charter of Charles I. In 1637 a crowned lamp was added by this office to the maker's mark, and in 1638 a voluntary date letter was introduced. After the passing of the Tillage Act of 1729 the Hibernia mark (Fig. 6.16), not dissimilar from the Britannia mark on English silver, was used to denote that the duty levied under the Act had been paid. From 1807 the English practice of using a profile of

Fig. 6.16. The Hibernia mark

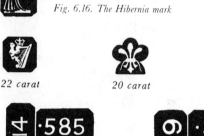

22 carat   20 carat   18 carat

Fig. 6.17. Marks struck by the Dublin Assay Office on 22, 20, 18, 14 and 9 carat gold

the reigning sovereign was followed in Dublin, but the Hibernia mark was retained as a town mark.

Before 1784, 22 carat was the legal gold standard in Ireland, and was marked with the crowned harp. From 1784, 20 carat and 18 carat gold became legal; the former was marked with a plume of three feathers and the latter with a unicorn's head erased. In 1854, 15, 12 and 9 carat gold were permitted, and were marked by the maker with a number to indicate the carat standard of his wares (Fig. 6.17). From 1935 the 15 and 12 carat standards were replaced by the 14 carat standard, leaving the Republic of Ireland with five standards for gold—22, 20, 18, 14 and 9.

The Irish Free State Order of 1923 ordained that 'plate manufactured in the Irish Free State should not be deemed to be British wrought plate within the meaning of the Customs Acts'. And so Irish plate entering Britain has to be marked just as other imported plate. Also British plate entering Southern Ireland has to be submitted to the Dublin Assay Office for assay and marking.

One sometimes finds Irish silver with marks other than those punched by the Dublin office. Cork, Galway, Limerick and Youghal marked their own plate in the seventeenth century.

HALLMARKS OF THE OTHER COMMON MARKET COUNTRIES

The following is a brief summary of the hallmarking systems of France, Belgium, Germany, Holland, Italy and Denmark.

FRANCE

Among the Common Market countries, France has the oldest and most complicated system of hallmarking. The French guilds started marking gold and silver in the thirteenth century. Every town had its own marks, and the mint master responsible for marking stamped his initials in the town marks and these are often quoted in sales catalogues. In the reign of Louis XIV a system of tax marks was introduced. There were two tax marks, the charge mark stamped on the piece in its unfinished state by the Warden of the Guild, and the decharge mark stamped into the finished piece by the tax collector to show that the duty had been paid.

Current Marks on Gold

The French mark three qualities of gold: 900/1000, 840/1000, 750/1000. Since 1919 an eagle's head is used for all qualities, but the shape of the shield varies and the figures 1, 2 or 3 within the shield identify the quality of the gold. Wares which are not tested by cupellation but by the touchstone are marked with an eagle's head with no surrounding shield and no quality number. Goldwares are also stamped with a maker's mark. French manufacturers stamp their wares with their initials within a diamond. Imported wares have the importer's initials within an oval. Wares below the French standard intended for export are stamped with an obus, which looks like a space capsule.

Chains

What complicates the system is that some types of goldware bear different marks from those above. The system used to mark chain necklaces and bracelets is almost incomprehensible to anyone but a French bureaucrat. The idea is to indicate the weight of the chain. The eagle's head is used in combination with the head of a rhinoceros. By their position on the clasp or on the outer link of the chain it is possible to determine what the weight of the chain should be, and, subsequently, whether some of the links have been removed.

Imports and Exports

On imported wares which conform to the French standard, including chains, a weevil in an oval replaces the eagle's head. An owl in an oval is stamped on all imported watches and on wares which come from countries whose legal standards are not the same as the French ones. French gold intended for export is stamped with the head of Mercury with a figure indicating the quality. Such a piece can only be sold in France if it is stamped with a return mark in the form of a hare's head to show that tax has been paid on it. A system of counter-marking exists in France to make forgery more difficult; pieces are marked over an anvil covered with bands of insects that indent the metal on the opposite side to the hallmark.

Current Marks on Silver

The French have two standards for silver, 950/1000 and 800/1000, which they mark with the head of Minerva in an octagonal shield and with a crab mark, respectively. The Mercury mark in a six-sided shield is used for exports and the weevil in an oblong for imports.

Marks on Platinum

In France, platinum of the standard 950/1000 is marked with the head of a dog. Platinum wares intended for export bear the head of a girl and imports the head of a bearded man.

Office Marks

All the different French offices have distinguishing marks. Some like Marseilles use a letter, in this case an 'M', others like Amiens use a symbol, in this case a star.

BELGIUM

Hallmarks were first used in the thirteenth century when this area was under French rule, and the various towns continued to strike their guild marks on gold- and silverwares as they did in France. Then, with the unification of the Netherlands in the sixteenth century, a unified system was introduced. This lasted until the French restored their system again in 1795 when they occupied the Netherlands. After the French withdrawal in 1814 the Netherlands again had their own system.

Current Marks

Hallmarking has been voluntary in Belgium since 1869, and in that year new marks were introduced to show the standard. For gold of the standards 800/1000 and 750/1000, two different devices, both containing stars, are used, the first also containing the figure 1, and the second the figure 2.

For silver, for which there are also two standards, 925/1000 and 835/1000, rose marks are used. The higher standard is marked with a rose within an octagon containing the figure 1. The lower standard is marked with a rose within an octagon containing a Roman two. Platinum is marked with a crown mark.

If the maker or importer chooses not to have his wares officially marked, he must still place his own mark in a barrel-shaped shield on the pieces together with a standard mark (see Fig. 6.18).

GERMANY

There is no hallmarking system in Germany. Government inspection is used to ensure that manufacturers' wares are of the standard stamped on them. The minimum accepted standard for gold jewellery is 8 carat and for silverwares the standard is 800/1000.

HOLLAND

Makers' marks were stamped into Dutch gold- and silverwares as early as 1386, but no hallmarking system proper existed until the formation of the Republic of the Seven Provinces, which passed hallmarking laws in 1663, but as with Belgium the French imposed their system between 1795 and 1814.

Current Gold Marks

The current system has been in force since 1953. The Dutch now recognise three standards of gold: 833/1000, marked with a rampant lion in an octagon; 750/1000, marked with a lion passant in an octagon holding a sword; and 585/1000, marked with a leaf in an oval. On smaller goldwares different stamps are used for the two higher standards (see Fig. 6.18). The assay offices also stamp goldwares with the head of a lion in a circle with a capital letter to indicate the office. Holland also has a date-letter system which changes every year.

Current Silver Marks

Since 1953 two standards of silver are permitted in Holland; 925/1000, marked with a rampant lion in a shield and the figure 1, and 835/1000, a lion passant in a six-sided surround accompanied by the figure II. The assay office's mark for silver is a helmeted head.

Platinum

Platinum is marked with a standard mark indicating the 950/1000 official standard. There are also special import marks which are obligatory.

ITALY

Italy, like Germany, consisted of a collection of city states, each of which had its own system of marking. In Naples, gold and silver was marked as early as the fifteenth century. Parts of Italy came under French domination during the nineteenth century and were subject to French hallmarking regulations. In 1934, hallmarking became compulsory throughout the country. After a period of grace of four years, during which time goods in stock were marked with a single mark consisting of a radiating star, all goods had to bear two marks, a maker's mark consisting of a three-digit number assigned to the maker, followed by the initials of the province in which the goods were made. Before 1946 this mark also bore the old roman fasces symbol, a bunch of twigs surrounding an axe. The second mark consisted of a standard mark expressing the quality of the metal in thousandths.

Current Marks

From 1968 the form of the maker's mark was changed and a five-point star incorporated in it. A third mark was also added, a Perseus mark applied to works optionally assayed at the request of the manufacturer. Otherwise, marks are applied by the manufacturer and are subject to checking by the state. The standards current in Italy for goldwares are 750/1000, 585/1000, 500/1000 and 333/1000. A standard of 753/1000 is also permitted for goldwares made by lost-wax casting. There are three standards for silver,

925/1000, 835/1000 and 800/1000, and a single standard for platinum of 950/1000.

DENMARK

Wares made from precious metals have been hallmarked in Denmark since the beginning of the seventeenth century. The first mark to be used was a town mark, like the three towers used by Copenhagen. After 1679 the assay master also stamped his initials on the wares.

Current Marks

The present voluntary system was introduced in 1893 and modified in 1961. Two standards are recognised for silver, 830/1000 and 925/1000, with a tolerance of 2 parts per thousand. The minimum quality for gold is 585/1000, or 14 carat, and imported wares must be of a minimum standard of 15 carat. A standard of 950/1000 is laid down for platinum. If a ware is submitted for assay and marking it is stamped with the old three towers mark of Copenhagen, otherwise all articles of gold, silver or platinum must bear a maker's mark registered by the State and the quality of the metal expressed in parts per thousand. From the annual total of 600,000 to 900,000 wares produced in, or imported into, Denmark government inspectors check the high proportion of 12,000 to 14,000 to discourage abuse of the regulations.

INTERNATIONAL AGREEMENT

It has been recognised for some time that a common marking system would be of benefit to international trade. The first steps were taken in 1972 to produce a system of assaying and hallmarking that would be generally acceptable internationally. The former E.F.T.A. countries signed an agreement in that year known as 'The Convention on the Control of Articles of Precious Metals'. The Convention is open to any country to join provided it has the necessary assay office facilities. The Convention has been ratified by Austria, Finland, Sweden, Switzerland and the United Kingdom. Under the Convention, an article bearing certain specified marks (namely a sponsor's mark, fineness mark, common control mark and assay office mark) is accepted

160

France

1

2

3

4

5

6

7

8

Belgium

1

2

3

4

Holland

1

2

3

4

Italy

1

2

3

Denmark

Fig. 6.18. Common Market hallmarks

FRANCE

1. Early Paris town mark incorporating the mint master's initials.
2. Charge and decharge marks used in Toulouse from 1780 to 1789.
3. Current standard marks for goldwares. *Left:* the number 1 incorporated in this mark indicates the highest standard of 900 parts per 1000. *Right:* The head without a number indicates that the piece was tested by the touchstone only.
4. Marks used on imported wares. The weevil in an oval is used for gold. For silver the weevil is contained in an oblong.
5. The head of Mercury used on goldwares produced for export.
6. The mark used on exported watch cases.
7. The current silver marks. The Minerva's head incorporates a number indicating the standard. The crab is used on wares tested only by the touchstone method.
8. Marks used on platinum. The dog is used on wares designed for home consumption. The girl's head is used on wares designed for export.

BELGIUM

1. Old town marks of Antwerp.
2. State marks. *Left:* gold of the 800/1000 quality. *Right:* 750/1000 quality.
3. State marks on silver. *Left:* 925 silver. *Right:* 835/1000 silver.
4. State mark for platinum.

HOLLAND

1. The three marks indicating the three legal standards for goldwares.
2. Marks used on small goldwares of the two higher standards.
3. Marks used to indicate the two legal standards for silver.
4. The current assay office marks: *left*, gold; *right*, silver. The letter indicates the town where the wares were marked. K indicates the Hertogenbosch office.

ITALY

1. *Left:* makers' mark used from 1934 to 1938. The three zeros represent the three-letter number allocated by the state to the manufacturer. *Right:* after 1938 the fasces was removed.
2. The current maker's mark.
3. The optional state mark.

DENMARK

The optional official guarantee mark is the historical three tower mark, once the town mark of Copenhagen. The date is incorporated in the mark, the last two figures of the year being used. The mark shown would have been stamped on pieces assayed in 1929.

in any of the above countries without any further assay or marking. The common control mark and assay office marks must be applied at an authorised assay office under agreed rules.

The standards recognised under the Convention are for gold 750 (18 carat), 585 (14 carat) and 375 (9 carat), for silver 925, 830 and 800, and for platinum 950. However, since the 830 and 800 standards for silver are not legal in the United Kingdom, Convention marks of these standards are not approved hallmarks and articles bearing such marks must not be sold in the course of trade.

Examples of the new common control marks which will be used under the Convention are as follows:

On the left is the mark for 18 carat goldwares; right, for sterling silver articles; and centre, for platinum wares. The marks will be applied by authorised assay offices only, and countries may refuse to import articles which are of a lower fineness than its national minimum standards.

Figure 6.19 shows the assay office marks that are used under the Convention by other signatory countries. In the U.K. the normal assay office marks are used on articles of the legal standards.

ASSAY OFFICE PROCEDURE

The assay was previously known as the 'touch', which was the method of testing gold and silver by rubbing it on a touchstone—a black siliceous stone or an earthenware block. The streak left by rubbing the metal on the stone was compared with the streak made by gold or silver of known standard. (See Appendix 4, pp. 309–312, for details of the touchstone method.) This method is still used by most Continental assay offices, and though it is a surprisingly accurate technique when used by an expert, it is far less accurate than the cupellation method for gold, and the titration method for silver, used by British assay offices.

The London Assay Office abandoned the touchstone method at a very early date, though the term 'touch' continued in use for some

AUSTRIA

FINLAND

SWEDEN

SWITZERLAND

750	585	375
Gold "Helvetia"	"Ecureuil"	"Morgenstern"

925	950
Silver "Canard"	**Platinum** "Bouquetin"

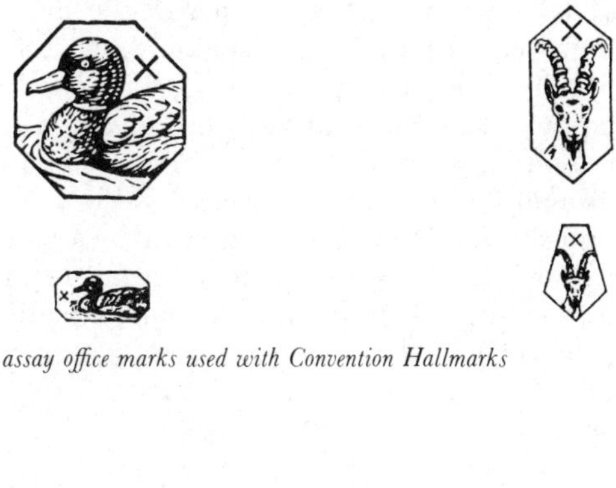

Fig. 6.19. Foreign assay office marks used with Convention Hallmarks

time. In an entry in his diary for May 19, 1669 Samuel Pepys described a visit to the Royal Mint. He recalls how he 'after dinner went to the Assay Office and there saw the manner of assaying gold and silver'. The technique of assaying gold which he witnessed and described differs little from that used to this day. He wrote that the method '. . . if it be for gold is by taking an equal weight of that and of silver . . . this they do wrap up in within lead.' Then they put the samples 'into little earthenware cups made of stuff like tobacco pipes and put them into a burning hot furnace, where after a while, the whole body is melted, and at last the whole body of the lead . . . is sunk into the body of the cup, which carries away all the copper and the dross with it, and left the pure gold and silver embodied together. . . .' The silver was then dissolved in acid leaving pure gold.

If, however, the method used is basically the same as that of Pepys' day, the modern assay office is a very different place from the one which he visited and described. It is a combination of well-equipped laboratory and workshop. When wares are delivered they are weighed; the accurate weighing of wares sent in for testing and marking ensures that the correct amount of gold or silver submitted by the manufacturer or retailer is returned to him—an important consideration when precious metals are concerned.

After weighing, the wares go to the drawing department, where the drawer takes scrapings from different parts of each piece. If he is sampling a coffee-pot, for instance, he takes drawings from the body, the spout, the handle fitting and the lid, to make sure that all the silver and all the solder used are up to the sterling standard.

This drawing is a highly skilled operation. For one thing the drawer has to be careful not to mar the work. If he is sampling a piece of Continental manufacture, which has been submitted in the finished state, it may not only be delicate, but also highly finished or expensively textured. So skilled are most drawers that they can not only sample delicate wares without damage, but they can often spot base metal or substandard metal just by the feel of it under the scraper. This feel for metal is perhaps understandable when it is realised just how much work passes across the drawer's bench in the course of a year. In 1975, the London Assay Office tested and marked 5,610,700 gold articles.

After sampling, the samples are weighed so that a known amount of metal is sent forward for testing. The scrapings of gold are wrapped in small sheets of lead with pieces of fine silver and placed in cupels, cup-shaped depressions in a refractory block. This block is then put in a furnace, where, at a temperature of 1100°C, and in a current of air, the lead and the base metal oxidises. The oxides are absorbed in the pores of the refractory material. After removal from the furnace, an alloy of gold and silver in the form of little beads remains in the depressions in the block. Each bead is flattened, annealed, rolled into a thin strip and placed in a small platinum cup; nitric acid is added and brought to the boil. The silver dissolves in the nitric acid and the liquid is poured off leaving pure gold behind in an amorphous state. The amorphous gold is then annealed and weighed. The weight of the pure gold is compared with the weight of the sample scrapings, and the percentage of pure gold in the sample can then be calculated.

Silver is tested in quite a different way—by the titration technique, which varies slightly in detail between office and office (Fig. 6.20).

Fig. 6.20. Silver assayed by the titration method

At the Birmingham and Sheffield Assay Offices the silver is first dissolved in nitric acid and an iron nitrate indicator added. An exact quantity of ammonium thiocyanate is titrated, and results in the formation of a silver salt, silver thiocyanate, which sinks to the bottom of the jar in which the test is carried out. A known amount of ammonium thiocyanate solution added will combine with a known amount of silver. It is now possible by comparing the solution with a standard sample to discover if there is too much pure silver, or too little, for the ammonium thiocyanate. If the liquid is lighter brown in colour than the known sample the silver being tested is above the standard, if it is darker it is substandard. By adding thiocyanate solution, or silver solution of known strength, until the sample matches the colour of the standard sample, the exact percentage of silver in the sample from the piece being assayed can be calculated.

After testing, the wares that have passed the assay are marked. If they are wares made in series, such as gold lockets, they are marked in a press with tools made specially for the job. Individual pieces are marked by hand, the punches being struck with a hammer to drive them into the metal. The assay offices have hundreds of

Fig. 6.21. Beds used by the Birmingham Assay Office to support pieces when they are being struck with the marks

shaped beds on which to rest the wares so that they will not be damaged, and recently the use of plastic beds that can be formed to the exact contours of the piece means that it is possible to mark almost any silver- or goldware, no matter how small or thin, without damage (Fig. 6.21).

In addition to the day-to-day work of assaying and marking, the assay offices also do valuable research work. Experiments carried out to discover the best way to assay platinum in anticipation of any future legislation resulted in the development of the technique now used daily. Spectrographic analysis has been used at the London Assay Office to test antique silver. Apparently silver alloys have varied down the ages, and it is possible to date an alloy by analysing its constituents.

This confirms that the silver used and the marks on a piece belong to the same period. The technique has been of great assistance to the Goldsmiths' Company's Antique Plate Committee, an advisory committee of experts, who, over the past 20 years, have examined 17,000 pieces of plate submitted to them because its authenticity was in question.

ASSAYING PLATINUM

The new hallmarking legislation in force since January 1975 made it necessary for the assay offices to evolve a technique for assaying platinum. The technique that they use is called atomic absorption spectrometry. Scrapings are taken from the platinum jewellery submitted for assaying and marking in the same way as for gold- or silverwares, but much smaller samples are taken of the platinum, only 10 milligrams as compared with 100–250 milligrams for goldwares. An electronic microbalance is employed for weighing the sample.

The scrapings after weighing are dissolved in *aqua regia* (a mixture of hydrochloric acid and nitric acid). The solution is diluted to 100 ml and introduced into an air/acetylene flame in the atomic absorption apparatus. The platinum is converted into free atoms in the flame. Radiation from a special lamp having a platinum cathode is passed through the flame and part of this radiation is absorbed by the platinum atoms in proportion to their number. The intensity of the incident radiation is measured and recorded, and from this measurement the platinum content of the sample can be calculated.

CHAPTER 7

Jewellery of the Past

In the normal course of business the retail jeweller and his staff are not likely to come across much, if any, jewellery made before the eighteenth century. Because during the nineteenth century the designers of jewellery so frequently harked back to the past, however, it will be useful to the jeweller to have some knowledge of the styles of earlier periods, if only to understand better this later revivalism. Also the tremendous public interest in the jewellery of the past, fostered by a number of major London exhibitions, notably that of the treasures of Tutankhamun, makes it desirable for those engaged in the jewellery trade to have some knowledge of the jewellery of earlier times.

It is true that the jewellery of the past has been subject to the same influences as architecture, furniture and silverwares. In broad terms, it was gothic during the Middle Ages, baroque during the Renaissance, rococo during the middle years of the eighteenth century, and a little of everything during the nineteenth century. It was Eastern in derivation during those periods when the mysterious East was in fashion, and at times when people were looking back to the Middle Ages with a nostalgic longing for the good old days, the jeweller produced gothic revival jewellery to cater for customers who lived in houses vaguely resembling castles. But the jeweller has always been very much of an individualist, often making a piece with a particular customer in mind, and trying to surprise that customer with his ingenuity. A classic example of such a jeweller was Carl Fabergé. Every year he produced his famous Easter eggs for Alexander III and Nicholas II of Russia, and apart from the different surprise contained in each egg, the style of each new egg was different from the one made the previous year.

It has always been the task of leading jewellers in every age to please princes and wealthy patrons by a display of their skills and their imagination, and the jeweller has never been hampered by considerations of utility. An architect has to create a house that can be lived in. A coffee-pot is a utensil and must function as such. A chair must be comfortable. To some extent the famous Bauhaus dictum that 'form must follow function' has always applied. But jewellery has no function in this sense. It is pure adornment, and in the past it was always accepted as such. People didn't ever expect it to be

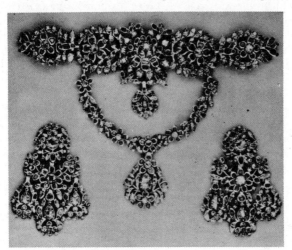

Fig. 7.1. Early seventeenth century jewellery

practical. No king would ever have worn a hat that burdened him like a crown. Few women even for fashion's sake would have worn those weighty parures had they not been jewels (Fig. 7.1). So the jeweller had more freedom than other craftsmen, and he made full use of it. The jewellery of the past is often a fantasy of complexity, and it is bewildering in its variety. This is, of course, why the histories of jewellery that have been compiled are all a little bewildering too. It is difficult to bring order to such chaos.

ANCIENT JEWELLERY

Nomadic man and woman from a very early date almost certainly adorned themselves with stones or seeds threaded on to strings, or attached decorative objects to such clothes as they wore. The earliest systematically manufactured jewellery, however, was produced in those areas where man first settled into communities and grew crops, notably in the Nile valley in Egypt and in Sumeria in the valleys of the Tigris and the Euphrates.

The earliest such jewellery to survive probably dates from about

4000 B.C. and comes from royal tombs in Egypt. It is made of gold set with gem minerals, and among the earliest pieces are some with an obvious mystical significance. It is clear from looking at this jewellery that goldsmiths' workshops existed in ancient Egypt, and that those who worked in them had acquired considerable skills. These early goldsmiths were able to solder, to anneal and to refine gold, and were subsequently to employ the technique of lost-wax casting. The lapidaries of ancient Egypt were also able to polish and shape relatively hard gem material with great precision, no small accomplishment since the only grinding compound available to them was probably silica sand (which the Chinese also used in the early days to fashion nephrite).

It is believed that from its first discovery in Egypt, in the alluvia on the banks of the Nile, gold was considered to symbolise the sun; therefore gold became the prerogative of the kings of Egypt, who were supposed to be descendants of the sun god Ra. Gold was believed to have been used in the first instance to produce symbolic discs, which ensured that the wearer enjoyed the protection of the sun god, and one finds this sun symbol incorporated in many of the talismanic jewels made in Eygpt over a period of some three thousand years. The gems that the Egyptians used (cornelian, lapis-lazuli and turquoise) may also have been thought to have magical properties, though we have no evidence of this. The ancient Egyptians cut these gem materials into variously shaped slabs and set them cloisonné into gold settings to produce a whole range of amulets depicting the whole complex hierarchy of Egyptian deities. The amulets worn by the royal family and their court during their lifetime were buried with them in their tombs. The kings, queens, princes and princesses who wore them were sometimes themselves represented on their jewels in the company of such deities as the Ureas serpent, the dung beetle or scarab, and the falcon god, who they believed protected them from their enemies and the malign fates. A typical example of such a jewel was a pectoral found in the tomb of Tutankhamun (Fig. 7.2). This is in the form of a vulture with outstretched wings, but the head of the bird is replaced by the head of the young king. Also in an early pectoral from the tomb of King Senwasnet III, the king is represented by his name in a cartouche, protected by the vulture goddess Nekhbet above it.

The magical properties of jewellery, and the belief that gold set with gemstones can protect their wearer, have therefore a very long history. The association of jewels with royalty and religion, which is equally deeply rooted in the past, still persists. We still have our royal regalia and our papal rings, 6000 years or more after the priest-kings of Egypt first appeared before their people decked in golden jewels.

Fig. 7.2. Ancient Egyptian pectoral depicting the vulture goddess, her head replaced by a portrait of Tutankhamun; gold, cloisonné set with turquoise, lapis and cornelian (by courtesy of Cairo Museum)

In the early eras of civilisation jewellery became a symbol of privilege throughout the ancient world. This tradition spread from Egypt to Sumeria, to Maecenae and Minoan Crete, to the Persian Empire, to ancient Greece and to Etruscan Italy. In pre-Columbian Mexico and Peru the tradition existed too. The Spanish conquistadors found shiploads of golden treasures in the palaces and temples of the Aztecs and the Incas, and sent them back to their king in Europe.

Aside from the jewellery of ancient Egypt, the early jewellery that has had the greatest influence on the work of subsequent generations of goldsmiths is that of the Etruscans and the Hellenistic Greeks. Both Etruscan and Hellenistic jewels were copied, or used as a basis for their designs, by the Castellani family who had their workshops in Rome in the 1800s, and the influence of the Castellanis, father and sons, is to be seen in much of the jewellery produced in the latter half of the nineteenth century.

The jewellery that the Etruscans produced in Italy between the seventh and first centuries B.C. is characterised by granulated decoration. A great deal of nonsense has been written about the mystery of granular decoration having been discovered by the Etruscans and lost when Etruria was overrun by the Romans. Granular decoration was in fact used by the ancient Egyptians, the Sumerians and the Minoans long before the Etruscans adopted it. The technique presents no great problems to a modern metallurgist. The granules can be readily produced by pouring gold on to powdered charcoal, and the problem of making them adhere to a gold background can be solved in a number of ways. A mixture of copper oxide and fish glue provides a method of sticking the granules in position. Heat is then applied, which drives off the fish glue as a gas and causes the copper to bond the granules to the gold surface by brazing. Another method is to dissolve copper in sulphuric acid and dip the granules in the resulting solution. The acid is driven off by heating, leaving the granules covered with copper. Flux is then applied to the gold background; the little copper-covered golden balls are arranged on it, and heat is again applied (in this case from underneath), producing a neat brazing.

The great achievement of the Etruscans was the fineness of their granular work. They applied as many as a hundred granules to each linear inch of one of their fibulae, the complex safety-pins of the ancient world. But just as we are inclined to underestimate the technical ingenuity of the craftsmen of the past so too we tend to underestimate their patient application.

GREEK FILIGREE

The same metallurgical skill, artistic flair and patience that produced Etruscan jewellery also made it possible for the Hellenistic goldsmiths of the fourth century B.C. to produce those intricate confections of delicate golden wire that we call filigree. They applied filigree to great collars featuring Herculean knots, to penannular bracelets and to ear-rings with terminals in the form of sheep, goats and lions derived from the art of the nomadic peoples living on the northern borders of the Persian Empire.

The Greek goldsmiths, incidentally, obtained more than motifs from Persia. The gold they wrought came from there as well, either as a result of melting down pillaged treasure or from the exploitation of Persian goldmines after Alexander conquered that great empire.

The Alexandrian conquests further provided the Greek goldsmiths with the right intellectual climate in which to work. Many of Alexander's officers married high-ranking Persian women, women of taste and discernment, and brought them back home to Greece. They set the fashions and encouraged the crafts, goldsmithing among them, that flourished in the Hellenistic period.

ROMAN GEMS

The Roman goldsmith never achieved the same dexterity with gold as the Etruscans and the Greeks had done. Rome's contribution to the history of jewellery was the reintroduction of interest in gem-stones. The Romans obtained their gems from every corner of their huge empire, and by trade even from beyond its boundaries. They revived the marriage between gold and gemstones that had charac-terised the jewellery of ancient Egypt. The Romans too were probably the first collectors of gems, many rich Romans assembling consider-able collections of stones either set in rings or kept loose in cabinets.

JEWELS OF THE DARK AGES

Throughout the so-called dark ages, after the Roman Empire was swept away by barbarian invasions, the jeweller's art surprisingly con-tinued to flourish. The jewellers of Europe from 500 B.C. onwards

Fig. 7.3. Shoulder clasps from the Sutton Hoo ship burial, gold set cloisonné with garnets and glass. This type of decoration was widely used in Europe from the fifth century A.D. onwards; these clasps were made in the 7th century A.D. (by courtesy of British Museum)

made jewels for the kings and tribal chiefs, jewels usually set with garnets. In these jewels the stones were polished flat and set cloisonné as the ancient Egyptians had set their stones. The earliest examples of such jewellery to survive come from Romania, the garnets coming probably from those same deposits in Czechoslovakia that are still producing today. The style soon spread throughout Europe and into Scandinavia. The finest surviving examples of this style of jewellery are the pieces from the Viking ship-burial on the banks of the Deben in Suffolk. Those pieces, from what is known as the Sutton Hoo ship-burial, were probably made in Scandinavia in the seventh century A.D. (Fig. 7.3).

While this tradition had been developing on the continent, the Celtic goldsmiths in bronze-age Britain had developed a distinctive goldsmithing culture of their own, producing such technically accomplished pieces as the Ipswich torques and the golden clothing-clasps and golden breastplate that can be seen in the collection of the British Museum.

MEDIEVAL

The jewels of the medieval 'Gothic' period, which were to inspire so many nineteenth century designs, were often functional. The gold-smiths of the period made brooches to hold a cloak at the shoulder, and belt buckles. Most of the brooches were more or less abstract in design, made from gold and roughly cabochoned gems. Some, how-ever, were in the form of miniature pictures in a circular frame, like vignettes created to illustrate some romantic medieval poem. Others were in the form of the heraldic household badges worn by those in the service of the great lords of the period. Some had religious motifs, like the famous Founder's Jewel of about 1400, now at New College, Oxford, which depicts the saints standing in niches under Gothic arches.

Medieval jewellers also made a great many rings, usually set with roughly cabochoned gems, often cruder versions of earlier Roman styles. Some of the shanks of these rings bore inscriptions in black let-ters. Some were made from gold only and carved with motifs familiar to us from Gothic architecture. From this period too came those mar-riage rings carved to depict two clasped hands.

RENAISSANCE PENDANTS

The Renaissance was another age in which the jeweller prospered, and the jewels of this period were again to provide inspiration for many nineteenth century designs. The type of Renaissance jewel that is most typical, and that attracted so much attention from the nineteenth century revivalists, is the pendant. The sixteenth century pendant usually took the form of an allegorical openwork design in gold,

Fig. 7.4. Portrait of Catherine of Aragon painted early in the 16th century shows her wearing typical jewellery of the period (by courtesy of National Portrait Gallery)

set with baroque pearls or other gems and enriched with enamels. The Canning Jewel in the Jewel Room at the Victoria and Albert Museum is a typical and lavish example of the style. It consists of a merman brandishing a scimitar and holding a scrollwork shield. The merman's body consists of a large baroque pearl. His green enamelled tail is set with diamonds and a large cabochon ruby, and more large baroque pearls hang pendant from the piece. Other popular motifs for pendants were lizards, ships, birds, dragons and mermaids. This period also produced elaborate necklaces and collars of gold, pearls and gemstones, and equally elaborate hair ornaments. Indeed contemporary paintings suggest that the pendants were often worn on the side of the head; strings of pearls or chains interspersed with gems attached to the pendants bound up the elaborate coiffures.

The rings of this period were often elaborate too, many continental rings particularly featuring enamel-work. This too was the great age of the signet ring. The Romans probably invented the signet ring, and it has been in use in England since Anglo-Saxon times. Examples earlier than the sixteenth century are rare, but large numbers of beautifully carved heraldic signets were produced in the Renaissance period, to judge from the numbers that have survived.

FLOWERS AND ARABESQUES

The seventeenth century was the age of delicacy, of bows and arabesques and floral themes. People at that time were fascinated by flowers. Many private and public gardens like the Jardin des Plantes in Paris date from this period, and many books were published filled with detailed botanical drawings.

Many pattern-books containing endless designs based on botanical themes were also produced at this time. One sees the influence of this concern with botany on the backs of the pendant miniature-cases that so many of the men and women of fashion of the period wore, containing portraits of their loved ones. These cases were usually decorated with delicate arabesques of flowers and foliage, carried out in champlevé enamels. White enamel was an integral element in most of the designs. One sees the same delicacy of delineation and the same effective use of white enamel in a French necklace from the middle of the century in the Victoria and Albert Museum. This pretty necklace consists of a series of small ribbon bows enamelled white and pastel blue on either side of a large central bow. In the middle of the central bow two flowers, also enamelled in white and blue, are placed, and below it hang a pearl and an irregular pear-shaped amethyst.

INVENTIONS AND INFLUENCES

To understand fully the jewellery of the early eighteenth century one has to try to understand why jewellery is imporant to people who have acquired new wealth and a new social importance. In many periods, and in some countries even as late as the eighteenth century, the wearing of jewellery was restricted to a privileged few. Not only were the few the only people who could afford to pay for the jeweller's skills and the precious materials in which he worked, but also people who were not members of a royal household, or members of a royal court at least, were often specifically forbidden by sumptuary laws from wearing jewellery. So jewellery came to be a symbol of social success, a mark of importance. Jewellery still has this aura about it. It has a significance beyond its intrinsic value. It was something which people who had arrived socially wore as a matter of right, and which people who were just arriving, in a class-conscious society like that of eighteenth century England, naturally wanted to possess.

The early years of the eighteenth century saw the breaking down of the old order in which the landed gentry were the sole privileged class. As the century progressed the circle of the jeweller's customers gradually widened and the jewellery trade grew and prospered as a result of the eager demand from the new merchant middle class. A seventeenth century invention also stimulated the growth of the trade in the eighteenth century. This was the invention, or perhaps more accurately the re-invention, of paste. The ancient Egyptians had made simulants of gemstones in glass, and in 1676 George Ravenscroft discovered that the addition of lead oxide to flint glass made it possible to produce cut stones which were plausible imitations of the real thing. Ravenscroft's discovery proved to be well timed. The late seventeenth and early eighteenth centuries saw, as has been pointed out, the birth of a new middle class, which made its money from trade. Some of the members of this new class could as well afford diamonds, rubies and sapphires as the landed gentry. But there were many whose fortunes were not as large as their pretensions, but who nevertheless wanted to put on a show at Ranelagh Gardens, in the Assembly Rooms at Bath, and at the candlelit evenings in the salons of their friends. Ravenscroft made it possible for them to do this without impoverishing themselves.

The eighteenth century saw a great change of emphasis in jewellery. In the past the mount had been all-important and the stones subsidiary. In the early years of the eighteenth century the stones become all-important, and the older style of mount, often enriched with enamel, gave place to something altogether lighter. It was yet another seventeenth century invention that was responsible for this—the invention of the brilliant-cut. This new cut revealed the full beauty of the diamond by capitalising on its amazing powers

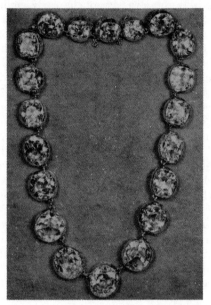

Fig. 7.5. An eighteenth century diamond rivière once belonging to Marie Antoinette

of reflection and refraction (Fig. 7.5). So the diamonds, or paste imitations of diamonds, became the feature of the piece, instead of, as they had been, rather dull highlights in the general design.

THE EIGHTEENTH CENTURY

New styles always owe at least some debt to the past. This was certainly true of the innovations of the eighteenth century, a century which revered the classical past, believing it to be the well-spring of reason and order. The eighteenth century gentleman sought to live his life in classical surroundings. All decoration was drawn from what he believed to be the fount of classical culture, the Renaissance art of Italy, which was a declared re-birth of the cultures of the Roman and Greek civilisations.

This then was the cultural background against which eighteenth century jewellery was produced. A popular piece in the early years of the eighteenth century was the stomacher, a bodice ornament covering most of the front of a dress. Joan Evans illustrates a particularly interesting example in *A History of Jewellery*. This was made about 1710, probably in England, and consists of a bow brooch from which hang three pendants. The bottom pendant is in the form of a cross, a popular motif at this period. The whole piece is set with large pastes, and the light mount is decorated with scrolling acanthus leaves. The design is perfectly symmetrical, and very similar designs are to be found in early eighteenth century plaster work and on the furniture of the period, though the cross motif seems to have been reserved to jewellery. The acanthus which comes from the Corinthian capital was the most popular motif of the first half of the eighteenth century. It adorned everything.

This piece is interesting in a number of ways. It might be thought unusual to find such a lavish and beautifully-made piece set with paste, but the maker of costume jewellery was often, in those days, the same man who made the real jewellery, and he made his imitations to look as nearly as possible like the real thing. Another interesting feature is that though this piece well illustrates the subservience of the mount to the stones, which resulted from the invention of brilliant-cutting, this piece is in fact set with rose-cut pastes. Despite the optical superiority of the brilliant-cut, the pretty rose-cut with its flat base, and pointed crown, cut with triangular facets, remained popular right up to the end of the nineteenth century.

Finally, this piece is interesting because, being set with paste, it has survived to give us a good idea of what the lavish jewellery of the period looked like. Had it been set with diamonds it is highly unlikely that it would have stayed out of the 'melting pot' for two and a half centuries. Someone, sooner or later, would have felt that the diamonds were worthy of a more fashionable setting. Few diamond pieces indeed survived the century in which they were made, and we have for the most part to make our judgements on the jewellery of the past on the basis of the less important pieces set with small coloured stones, and on the basis of imitation jewellery of this kind.

About 1735 the classical baroque symmetry, of which this stomacher is an example, gave place to a new, and asymmetric, fashion from France. The rococo (it derives from the French word for pebble work) fashion pervaded jewellery as it did most other applied arts at this period. Rococo design was much freer than the baroque which it superseded. It derived its imagery direct from nature, not from Renaissance ornament. A typical rococo piece is a riot of imagery, shells and scrolls, flowers and foliage, the whole design often held together by a central cartouche. The fashion was not long-lived in England, and not a great deal of jewellery in this style has survived.

About the middle of the eighteenth century coloured stones, which had been out of fashion for 50 years, became very popular again. The rococo phase, whatever else it had achieved, had freed design from the classical conventions. It had made naturalism acceptable, and in its wake came a period when jewellers sought to reproduce nature in gold and coloured stones. The 1750s and 1760s saw the production of flower brooches, roses with petals of topaz,

Fig. 7.6. Diamond-set feathers made in the second half of the eighteenth century

leaves of emerald and buds set with rubies, many of the stones having foil placed behind them to improve their colour. Another popular subject at this time was the feather (Fig. 7.6). The feather brooches of the eighteenth century, set with small diamonds, are among the most charming pieces of jewellery created between 1700 and 1800.

By this time the making of imitation jewellery was becoming a separate craft, and new materials had been discovered and were being exploited. The most interesting of these was pinchbeck (page 13). This copper–zinc alloy provided a plausible and inexpensive substitute for gold, and it was used until in the nineteenth century rolled-gold and electroplated gold replaced it.

Iron pyrite, inaccurately called marcasite, was first used in the eighteenth century as a diamond simulant, but before long it became accepted as a gemstone in its own right. It was sometimes set in glass plaques, but more usually it was *pavé*-set in silver. Marcasite was simulated, later in the century, by cut-steel. Cut-steel nails were faceted to resemble the rose-cut marcasites, and these nails were then riveted to the mounts. This was an expensive way of doing things, and before long cut-steel jewellery was being die-stamped all of a piece in a press. Matthew Boulton, who founded his famous factory at Soho Hill in Birmingham in 1762, was one of those who made cut-steel buckles to decorate the shoes of the fashionable men and women of the day.

A minor innovation belonging to the middle years of the eighteenth century was a paste imitation of opal. Quite a lot of jewellery was set with it, and although not a very convincing imitation its appearance in obviously genuine period mounts might puzzle anyone who does not know about it.

All the standard forms of jewellery, necklaces, earrings and brooches were worn during the eighteenth century, but this age also saw the production of pieces peculiar to itself. One of the most interesting of these peculiarly eighteenth century pieces was the chatelaine. The chatelaine was originally the lady of the castle who, during the Middle Ages, carried all her keys on a chain suspended from her girdle. Subsequently the chain she wore became known as a chatelaine. During the eighteenth century new uses were found for the chatelaine, and it became so ornate that it ceased to resemble a key chain, and developed into a complicated pendant. The main new use for chatelaines was as watch chains, but they were also used for étui, the decorative sewing cases of the period. The watch, or étui, was suspended from a clip attached to the lower end of the chatelaine, and at the top a hook was soldered on so that the chatelaine could be hung from a girdle; or sometimes a brooch pin was soldered on instead. In addition to the clip to hold the watch or étui, other clips were usually provided so that perhaps a watch key, a seal, or a thimble case, could also be attached.

Because the chatelaine was usually a watch chain, it followed the fashion in watch cases. In the middle years of the century when repoussé-chased cases were in fashion the chatelaine consisted of a series of repoussé-chased plaques, joined by short lengths of chain. Towards the end of the century, when those pretty enamelled watch cases with a circlet of half pearls round the outside were high fashion, the plaques on the chatelaines were enamelled to match the enamel decoration on the watch case. Chatelaines were made in gold and silver and in base metal, usually pinchbeck.

An enormous number of buckles must have been produced between 1700 and 1800. Set with diamonds, with paste, with marcasite or with cut-steel, they were used not only for shoes, but also for belts, and to buckle velvet bracelets and collars.

In the last quarter of the eighteenth century came a great classical revival movement in all the applied arts, sparked off by the discoveries of Herculaneum and Pompeii. One of the results of this movement was a demand for classical cameos, and it was at this period that Josiah Wedgwood began to produce his ceramic cameos at his famous pottery in Staffordshire. They were used for necklaces, bracelets and brooches.

THE NINETEENTH CENTURY

The turn of a century does not always bring with it a radical change of style, and the styles which we associate with the nineteenth century were already emerging in the eighteenth. A reaction against the Age of Reason had begun well before 1800. The romantic revolution and the industrial revolution both had their beginnings in the eighteenth century, and it was these two revolutions, one artistic the other materialistic, that were to affect everything made in the nineteenth century. The industrial revolution was to result in the mass production of cheap wares, jewellery among them, for a new buying public.

A new stratum of society came into existence in the nineteenth century, a stratum below the rich merchant middle class that had grown increasingly powerful during the eighteenth century. From this new class, which the sociologists call the lower middle class, were to spring the *nouveau riche* of Victorian England, while its less successful members were to live comfortable lives in those staid Victorian villas still to be seen on the outskirts of our towns.

This new class, like the merchant middle class before it, was eager to ape its so-called betters. It was to supply this new class with inexpensive copies of the worldly possessions of the rich that men, women and children laboured for long hours in the stygian gloom of the new factories in Birmingham and Sheffield. Cause and effect were interwoven. The industrial revolution created this new society, and the demands of the new society kept the wheels turning and the wealth flowing.

The nineteenth century was proud enough of its material achievements, but the Victorians wanted something else from life beyond success. They wanted to escape sometimes from their own mundane surroundings, so they fostered the romantic revolution, and the romantic revolution brought to those monotonous new streets a breath of distant places and earlier times. The artists and craftsmen presented their customers with a romanticised view of the world.

They did not show the Victorians an India of teeming poverty, but an endless parade of panoplied elephants on which maharajahs swayed in golden howdahs. Medieval England was revealed as a fairy tale time, peopled with courtly knights and gracefully wimpled ladies.

As the century progressed the romantic images became mingled and confused. Minarets grew out of gothic castles which were entered through Byzantine gateways. Sir Matthew Digby Wyatt, writing in 1851, observed that: 'We design and execute in every conceivable style. We are equally at home in the reproduction of Classical and Byzantine . . . Etruscan ware and Majolica; we can execute Chinese or Athenian with the same facility. . . .' Ernle Bradford who quotes this passage from Wyatt in his book *English Victorian Jewellery,* comments: 'It is not that the collector or the student is likely to be deceived into thinking that a piece of Victorian "Gothic" enamelling or a Renaissance pendant is other than nineteenth century in manufacture.' He then goes on to define the tell-tale differences as 'regularity of finish' and 'a certain mechanical coldness'. This is true, but more important these pieces look wrong, as all revivalist art looks wrong.

A man working in a period when a style is alive will have a fundamentally different attitude from that of a craftsman reproducing the superficialities of that style centuries perhaps after it has died. And one can see this difference of approach at a glance, one can perceive the lack of conviction, the lack of understanding in the composition, sometimes even in a single line of chasing. This is not to say that a latterday copy of a past style cannot have a charm of its own, in the way that eighteenth century chinoiseries, which no one would ever imagine were made in China, have their own charm. And, nowadays, we are beginning to discover more and more this charm in nineteenth century art and craftsmanship.

The nineteenth century jeweller did not just raid the lumber rooms of the past, and look to lands afar for inspiration. The romantic revolution was more than anything else a return to nature as the prime source of artistic inspiration. Its exponents conceived of it as a great turning away from the artificialities of the last age. Much of the jewellery of the nineteenth century was taken from nature, but the Victorians had their own way of looking at nature. To the Victorian artist it was no harsh cycle of life and death, but an ever-continuing sunny summer afternoon. So the flower jewellery of the period depicts full-blown symmetrical flowers, stiff and orderly. There is no pretence of reality about these gem-set sprays, even when every detail, every vein and stamen are reproduced.

They were consummate craftsmen these Victorian jewellers

and some of their flower jewellery has never been rivalled for sheer technical virtuosity. And though this jewellery is stiff, there is something endearing about the simple, almost childlike, approach. Simplicity is not a quality which is usually associated with Victorian art, but there is an underlying emotional simplicity about much of their work, and sometimes too they produced designs which had a great simplicity of line (Fig. 7.7). In this connection one

Fig. 7.7. An example of the charming romantic jewellery of the early nineteenth century

thinks of those brooches consisting of a large stone, usually an amethyst, surrounded by a circlet of tiny pearls. Then there were the rivières, those necklaces that consisted of a single row of graduated stones in the most self-effacing of settings.

It is extremely difficult to place the styles of the nineteenth century in any chronological order, or to date a particular piece within 20 years. It is sometimes possible to pinpoint the inception of a new style, but styles tended to linger on, and to be revived from time to time. That curious jewellery made from human hair for instance was first made in the eighteenth century, when it was used as mourning jewellery. This hair jewellery was still being advertised in 1850. Then there was the great classical revival. The discovery of the ruins of great classical cities in Italy had been the inspiration of the Adam style back in the eighteenth century, but it was not until the first decade of the nineteenth century that the clearing of the ash and the basaltic débris from Pompeii was anything like completed, and the ruins became the showplace they have been ever since. So there was a second classical revival at the beginning of the nineteenth century, and a great vogue for classical jewellery. And at no period during the nineteenth century were classical motifs entirely out of fashion.

The classical cameo was the great Victorian standby. The real classical cameos had, of course, been carved from gemstones, usually agates, but the typical Victorian cameo was a shell one. These shell cameos, which were cut from mollusc-shell, were imported in very large numbers from Italy to be set by English jewellers. Some of them were exquisitely carved, the classical figures clothed in flowing drapes were depicted in fine detail. But the majority of shell cameos were of poor quality, mass produced for a mass market.

Another result of the popularity of Pompeii was the Etruscan

Fig. 7.8. Granulated gold ear-rings in the Etruscan style,. made by Carlo Giuliano, one of the followers of the Castellanis (by courtesy of Christies)

style. Gold filigree work and granulation in the Etruscan manner were probably first seen in England in the 1820s. Castellani, the greatest exponent of the style, had set up a workshop in Rome in 1814, and Etruscan work retained its popularity for over half a century. It was still very much in evidence at the Paris Exhibition of 1867. Granulated work, the production of a pattern of minute grains of gold on a gold surface, is a technique which has intrigued goldsmiths down the centuries since the Etruscans perfected it. Castellani and a few of his fellow Italians managed to master the technique, and their work created a considerable stir both in Paris and in London, but the process of making this jewellery was too difficult and too painstaking to be readily copied, and therefore only a limited amount of granulated jewellery was produced in other workshops.

One can date the beginning of yet another nineteenth century fashion from the time when Queen Victoria discovered the Highlands, and began to make her regular pilgrimages to Balmoral. Thousands of mezzotints of Highland cattle and stags at bay were hung in drawing rooms and parlours all over England, and the jewellers began producing the Scottish jewellery that has been popular ever since: the mounted grouse claws and the big silver brooches chased with Celtic motifs and set with a single cairngorm or amethyst. It was this interest in all things Scottish, fostered by Victoria's love of the Highlands, which also focused attention on the pretty freshwater pearls found in the mussels of the Tay and the Spey.

For much of her reign Victoria was a Queen in mourning. In this, too, her subjects followed her example and sombre mourning jewellery became a feature of the Victorian scene after the death of Albert. So great was the demand for the sleek black jet that the deposits around Whitby, which had first been worked in Neolithic times, were virtually exhausted in the second half of the nineteenth century. Albert, incidentally, had created a jewellery fashion, by wearing a heavy gold watch chain, and this heavy linked chain has borne his name ever since.

Perhaps because much of the finest diamond jewellery of the last century has not survived, one possibly gets the false impression from looking at collections of Victorian jewellery that the most magnificent work of the period consisted of suites, or parures as they were called, set with richly-coloured amethysts or glossy garnets. Diamond jewellery there was, and lavish suites set with rubies and emeralds. But just as they were prodigal in their use of styles, so too they used the whole palette of gem materials. Mineral collecting was a popular Victorian hobby, and clearly the jeweller found no resistance to the lesser known gems among his customers. One finds every conceivable type of stone in Victorian jewellery, and now that many stones have become hard to find in nature this jewellery has become a major source of fine examples of such stones as demantoid garnet and peridot.

Certain stones at certain times had a particular vogue. Turquoise was popular during the second half of the century, and was often used as an alternative to pearls for those circlets that framed a large stone, an enamel or a cameo. Coral was very popular in the first half of the century. Coral from the Mediterranean was beautifully carved in the workshops of Naples, and the Neopolitan carvers enjoyed a flourishing export trade with Britain. The big opal finds in Australia in the 1870s provided the Victorian jewellers with beautiful black opals to mount, and the discovery of the great pipes in Africa at the same period created a new interest in diamonds.

The variety of stones used by the Victorian jewellers was rivalled by the variety of cuts produced by the Victorian lapidaries. The diamond saw was a nineteenth century invention, and the whole cutting industry became more mechanised at this time. The lapidaries made full use of their new equipment, producing beautiful variations on the brilliant-cut, like the marquise. They sometimes complicated the brilliant-cut also by multiplying the facets, and the pendeloque, which already had had a vogue in the eighteenth century, now enjoyed a revival. But perhaps the 'cut' which was particularly Victorian was the cabochon. Victorian cabochons range from tiny symmetrical turquoises to huge tear-drop cabochon rubies. Strangely, in the last two decades of the century, when the mathematics of diamond cutting were first beginning to be appreciated (though they were not finally set out until Marcel Tolkowsky published his *Diamond Design* in 1919) there was a great vogue for the old rose-cut.

The settings and the mounts used by the Victorian jewellers were as varied as the stones set in them. Claw, millegrain, thread, pavé and box were all used for nineteenth century jewellery, while every technique was introduced to elaborate the mounts. The jeweller engraved and chased and carved his gold. He used the coloured golds now readily available to him, often as inlays, and in addition to painted enamel work he revived the old enamelling techniques of the Middle Ages: cloisonné, champlevé and encrusted enamelling, and the more sophisticated basse-taille, which was the placing of translucent enamel over a relief design, and plique-à-jour, which consisted in removing the backing from behind the enamel to let the light shine through it as through a stained glass window.

The nineteenth century saw a great increase in the mass production of jewellery. The fly-presses in the Birmingham factories bumped out jewellery components in their thousands. Gold jewellery was stamped out in this way, but mass-production techniques really came into their own in the production of imitation jewellery, in particular rolled-gold jewellery. The end of the century saw the foundation of the great rolled-gold factories of Pforzheim in Germany. Most of these factories began as specialist producers of chain, but soon turned over to manufacturing rolled-gold jewellery that sold throughout the world. The meteoric growth of these factories during the 1880s and 1890s is an indication of the popularity of their products.

A great deal of paste jewellery was made in the nineteenth

century, marcasite also was popular, imitation pearls were made in increasing numbers, mosaics were imported from France and Italy, while the imitation cameos made by Wedgwood, and the glass cameos invented by the Scotsman James Tassie, rivalled the mollusc cameos from Italy. The imitation jewellery of the Victorians differs, however, from much of the costume jewellery of our own day in that it was intended to be a replica of the real thing, a substitute for what was beyond the pocket of the purchaser.

ART NOUVEAU

In the closing years of the nineteenth century another artistic revolution began. It grew out of the enthusiasms and beliefs of the Arts and Crafts Society, whose figurehead was the talented William Morris. Their avowed aim was to reassert the standards of craftsmanship which they felt were being eroded by the growing industrialisation of methods of production. They achieved only a limited success, for in the materialistic society of the late Victorian period their idealism found little response. The only really important effect of the movement was to introduce the *art nouveau* style into this country.

The greatest exponents of *art nouveau* among the European jewellers were Georg Jensen in Copenhagen and Lalique in Paris. *Art nouveau* has been described by Graham Hughes as: 'the most exotic jewellery style ever', and in the hands of an artist of the calibre of Lalique it certainly was. The *art nouveau* movement, like most new art movements, was described by its followers as a return to naturalism. Its motifs, the most common among them being tulips, daffodils, butterflies, wasps, serpents and lizards, were not essentially different from those used by the earlier Victorians, but an *art nouveau* flower is something very different from a flower delineated by a mid-Victorian craftsman. The *art nouveau* flower is not a static idealisation but a lively and sensual creation.

The movement petered out as so many art movements do when its motifs became clichés in the hands of uninspired copyists. Its tulips and daffodils lingered on to decorate dado friezes and twine up and down cast-iron fireplaces. It ended up by being somewhat of a joke, and only in the past few years has the best work of the *art nouveau* jewellers really received its due appreciation as some of the finest jewellery that has ever been produced.

TWENTIETH CENTURY

The Edwardian period saw the production of a profusion of formal jewellery set with magnificent stones, immaculately cut. It was a period of great wealth when entertainment among the rich was still almost as formal as it had been at Louis XIV's Versailles. So great

Fig. 7.9. Typical of jewellery produced between 1900 and 1939; fine coloured stones like the emeralds featured in these pieces are surrounded by equally fine diamonds

necklaces and tiaras of matching brilliant-cut diamonds, emeralds, rubies and sapphires were produced to a standard of workmanship unrivalled before or since. It was at this time that houses such as Cartier, Boucheron and Asprey came into prominence, and when one sees in the salerooms the jewellery made by such famous houses in the first forty years of this century they seem to belong not to the threshold of our own times, but to some long-forgotten age. So much has our conception of jewellery been changed by fashion and economics in the past few decades.

Precious jewellery in the period 1900–1939 was in some ways like the jewellery made in the eighteenth century. All the emphasis was on the stones, and the less setting there was on view the better. This jewellery was geometric in design and beautifully composed, though it lacked any great artistic merit. It is hardly surprising, therefore, that some latter-day designers have described it derisively as 'portable wealth'. The influence of *art nouveau* lingered for a time, and the *art deco* movement resulted in some jewellery in that style being produced, but generally fashions in the fine arts had little effect on jewellery design. Innovations were few, the most important being the clip, followed by the double clip. In the period immediately after World War II this style of jewellery lingered on for a decade, different only in that the later designs tended to be asymmetrical rather than symmetrical.

The more modest jewellery of the period continued to be made to late nineteenth century designs. These lingered on up to the beginning of the 1914–1918 war. Bar brooches, for instances, which were so popular in the 1890s, continued to be made in their thousands. Indeed in the form of riding crops impaling fox masks they were still very much in vogue in the 1930s. Then in the twenties cultured-pearl necklets and ear-rings became jewels for all people and all occasions.

THE DESIGN REVOLUTION

In the 1950s a revolution in jewellery design took place. The existence in Britain of 100 per cent purchase tax inhibited the production of new designs in the old lavish style, but a group of young designers, Andrew Grima prominent among them, conceived jewellery that would appeal on the basis of its artistic content, rather than its intrinsic worth.

This new jewellery was sculptural in concept, and was indeed sometimes described as sculpture in miniature. It certainly owed more to the work of Henry Moore and Reg Butler than to the jewellery traditions of the past. All it really had in common with earlier jewellery was that it was fashioned from gold and gemstones. It was indeed very much *gold* jewellery, such gemstones as were employed being highlights in the design and no more than that. The new designers disliked the sleek shininess of polished gold, and they textured it or finished it so that its surface resembled that of a nugget recovered from alluvia. More and more, too, the new designers turned their backs on faceted stones, and set their pieces with uncut crystals, tourmaline and amethyst crystals, uncut emeralds and dioptase, agates and slices of ruby crystals from Tanzania.

The initial reception of this new jewellery in the trade was luke-

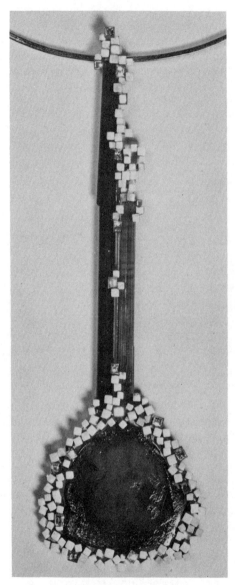

Fig. 7.10. Pendant of watermelon tourmaline slice on sticks of pink and green tourmaline held by bricks of 18-carat gold and square diamonds on a gold necklet; typical of Andrew Grima's designs

warm, and it seemed to appeal only to a limited public. Gradually, however, people began to respond to these new designs, and more and more established manufacturers adopted the texturing and set their pieces with unfaceted minerals. At the same time another form of decoration made its appearance, diamond milling, which broke up the surfaces of the gold into brightly polished facets. Eventually virtually all jewellery offered to the jeweller was either textured or diamond-milled, from watch bracelets to gem rings.

In 1974 a new fashion was born, to cater for a new interest in jewellery among the increasing number of young women who began to buy jewellery for themselves instead of waiting to be given it in the time-honoured way. This new fashion was born in Italy; it was based on chain, which Italian goldsmiths produce in such a variety of patterns. Fancy gold and silver chains were made up into necklets and

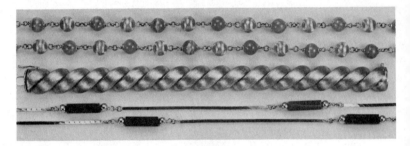

Fig. 7.11. Modern Italian jewellery, showing use of fancy chain and gemstone beads   necklace beads (top) are rhodochrosite; bracelet illustrates texturing of gold

bracelets, interspersed with beads cut from a variety of gem materials—chiefly coral, and agate dyed black to simulate onyx, but also sodalite, lapis, rhodonite, rhodochrosite and jade. These chain necklets often featured pendants carved from the same materials, sometimes framed with small diamonds. Rapidly, as it became clear that this new fashion was enjoying a phenomenal success, a whole range of inexpensive real jewellery featuring these decorative minerals was produced in France, Germany and Britain. The Idar Oberstein cutters were soon hard put to it to cater for the demand for beads and polished pieces of these materials. Even those factories equipped with ultrasonic bead-drilling machines were quoting long deliveries, while the factories making chain were finding similar problems in meeting the unprecedented demand. Throughout the world, it seemed, more and more people were buying jewellery, and the jewellery they wanted was real jewellery of an informal kind that could be worn with anything on any occasion.

CHAPTER 8

The Making of Jewellery

THE MAKING OF JEWELLERY: MAN AND MACHINE

Not so many years ago a great gulf existed between the fine jewellery, made by handcraft methods, and the cheap and usually mundane jewellery made by machine techniques. Today the gulf has narrowed, and for three reasons. The jewellery trade is making more imaginative use of the machine techniques available to it. A shortage of skilled labour has forced the firms in the trade to use machinery to achieve an adequate turnover. The spread of wealth into many more pockets has created an increased demand for a middle-class jewellery. As a result of these three factors well-designed, well-made jewellery is being mass produced today, and more and more manufacturers are exploring every possibility of replacing hand work by machine work (Fig. 8.1). One manufacturer, once well known for his fine hand-made pieces, has carried this so far that he now describes his firm as 'engineers in precious metals'. He is not untypical.

THE DESIGN

Every piece of jewellery made begins as a design. It is no coincidence that most of the great craft workshops of the past were set up and run by designers of more than average ability. Design is after all very important, for if the original conception is poor, all the skills of all the craftsmen in the world could never make a good thing of it. This was a fact often lost sight of in the first half of this century. At that period jewellery making was changing from a craft to a business, run not by a designer–craftsman but by a businessman who probably had never sat at a bench. Sometimes such firms brought in good designs from Paris, but more often than not they employed an underpaid and underprivileged draughtsman to produce an endless succession of variations on time-worn themes. The great revival of public interest in jewellery which has taken place in the last twenty years has been in great measure due to the re-emergence of the designer as a key figure in the industry. There is no doubt that the importation of Italian jewellery into this country, jewellery made in the workshops of designer–craftsmen in

Fig. 8.1. Light engineering techniques are being increasingly applied to the production of jewellery. This picture shows automated link assembly in a German watch bracelet factory

the little town of Valenza on the banks of the Po, was at least partly responsible for this revival of interest. This jewellery was not only made to a price that many people could afford, but it was well designed. It was fresh and it was interesting. The success which this Italian jewellery met with made it possible for a new generation of designer–craftsmen in this country to set up their own workshops with the prospect of selling what they produced. It also emphasised to the established firms here the importance of the designer. Today, more and more of these firms employ their own designers, and give them much more opportunity to impose their ideas on the production.

There are exceptions to any rule, but to be a really successful designer of jewellery one has to be a trained jeweller. Only a man who has worked in precious metals can fully understand their limitations and appreciate their possibilities. And it seems, too, that only a jeweller can have the right feeling about jewellery. Painters and sculptors have designed jewellery in the past, but almost never successfully. Jewellery is not just a work of art, a piece of miniature sculpture—it is a part of dress, a fashion accessory. It is also many other things to many people. It is a symbol of love, a mystic symbol, a symbol of wealth and a symbol of security. All this the jewellery designer has to understand. He has to understand, too, the functional problems: his necklaces must be comfortable to wear; his earrings must not be too heavy; his rings must not ladder stockings; and his brooches must not tear flesh. In addition to all this he must have inspiration. He must be capable of creating something both different and beautiful, and he must develop a personal style. His work must bear the signature of his personality. One should be able to recognise it, as one recognises a piece of Lamerie silver, even before one looks at the hallmark. A good jewellery designer is, in fact, a remarkable man, and at long last he is again being given his due.

Designers work in different ways. Some of them, particularly those who work for houses making pieces set with important stones, make a wax model and stick into it the actual stones that will be used. Some designers make the roughest of sketches and work out the interpretation with the man at the bench. Others get an idea, sketch and sketch away until they are satisfied with the design, and then produce a drawing so detailed that any craftsman who had to make the piece should be able to see at a glance how it should be made. Nearly always, however, there is consultation between designer and craftsman during the making. Any drawing, no matter how detailed, is subject to interpretation, and a craftsman could alter the whole feeling of a piece in the course of making it.

The designer who designs for a mass market needs a different approach from the designer whose work is to create one-off pieces. The one-off piece bears only the cost of the raw materials and the craftsman's time, and it has to find only one customer. The mass-produced piece may well have to bear the cost of £1000 worth of tools, which will use the valuable time of the toolroom for as much as a month. This jewellery must find many, many customers, otherwise the cost of the tools will bear too heavily on the cost of the pieces produced from them.

A failure to produce a suitable design means that the most important department of the factory, the toolroom, has laboured in vain. The designer for the mass market must therefore be a student of public taste. He must be something of a prophet, too. It is not enough to be able to see a trend and follow it. The time lag from the conception of a design to the appearance of the first piece in the firm's sample tray could take as long as 18 months or more. The designer of the mass-produced piece must therefore have the ability to anticipate the taste of tomorrow. But equally he must not leap too far ahead, otherwise the public will not buy and his design will be a commercial failure.

The responsibility for producing a commercially successful design often makes the designer over-cautious. In fact, however, the complex impulses that persuade people to buy jewellery, nowadays, often result in the designer of mass-produced pieces lagging behind public taste, while the adventurous designer of one-off pieces has the opposite problem. Those who can afford to buy important jewellery are usually the older, more conservative people, and the people who are looking for value for money. It is the young who are the makers of manners these days, the leaders of fashion, the eager buyers of the new and the different. The teenagers are not outraged by novelty, and the wife of the up-and-coming and not too wealthy young executive is much more adventurous than were her parents; more concerned with what is effective now than what will be acceptable in ten years' time, less bothered about potential resale value.

The designer, having solved these complex sociological, aesthetic and commercial problems, and having produced his design, leaves the scene except as a consultant. The man at the bench or the production manager of the factory now takes over.

THE MAN AT THE BENCH

The craftsman who is to make the one-off piece, the mounter as he is called, is issued with the necessary raw materials, such as gold sheet, gold wire, gold tube, ready-made pins perhaps, and of course any stones that will eventually be set into the mount.

The raw material may be bought in ready sized form from a bullion dealer, and so may the joints and catches, and even the settings for the stones—all those things known as 'findings'. Some manufacturers, however, alloy their own gold, rolling it out between mirror-polished flatting rolls to make a sheet. They roll out rod between grooved rolls to make wire, and then draw it down to size. Most firms, although they buy in sheet, rod, wire and tube, roll and draw it to the required size and shape. They require such a variety of dimensioned material that it would be neither economic nor feasible to buy material specifically dimensioned for each job undertaken. Rationalisation in the jewellery trade always finds itself at loggerheads with diversification. A craft workshop thinks in terms of producing dozens of a line at the most, and the large mechanised factories, who do go in for longer runs, nevertheless usually have hundreds of patterns in current production. Take for instance a firm producing wedding rings from drawn wire, and consider the many different sections a wedding ring can have, square, rectangular, oval, D-shaped and so on, also the different widths and sizes. So in a wedding ring factory there are grooved rolls, and the walls are hung with draw-plates, with holes of gradually diminishing size, the holes shaped to correspond with the different sectioned wires that the firm uses. The ring maker buys in rod of the different carat qualities and from this he produces the great variety of wire required.

Having been issued with the raw materials the mounter sets about fashioning them. Already, from looking at the design, he has decided how it can best be made up and what materials he will need. The tools which he uses are as old as his craft, the same tools can be seen in drawings and paintings of jewellers' workshops done thousands of years ago. He uses hammers, for these are the basic tool of any smith, whether he works in iron or in gold. He uses drills, and many craftsmen still favour the sensitive bow-drill, invented no one knows how many centuries ago. He uses piercing-saws with slender blades, gravers and files, all tools as old as history. He uses a gas-torch it is true, which is a relatively modern invention, but this is only a different form of fire from that used by the smith through the ages.

The mounter will first perhaps cut out the outline of his piece from sheet gold with a saw (Fig. 8.2). He may well want to dome the sheet. This he does over a metal block, a doming block looking rather like a large dice with hollow depressions of different sizes on the different faces. He takes a punch and a hammer, places the head of the punch on the metal which has been positioned over one of these depressions, and then taps the punch with the hammer. With successive blows he steadily drives down the metal until it follows the shape of the depression. If he wants to dome or depress smaller areas he places the gold sheet on a bed of lead and uses the hammer and punch in the same way. The lead will give under the blows of the hammer, but will still support the gold and prevent distortion.

Very rarely is a piece of jewellery made in one piece. Small pieces will be carved and filled up, and added to the main structure. Wires will be bent and soldered on.

The design may call for part of the gold sheet to be cut away, and this will be done with the piercing-saw. Where stones are to be set, collets will be soldered on, or the sheet will have holes drilled in it to receive the stones.

Every piece made calls for different skills, those that the mounter learned during his five-year apprenticeship and has been improving on every since. But one, which he will have to employ on every piece he makes, is his skill in soldering. The goldsmith's skill with the blow-torch is just as important as his skill with the hammer. At

Fig. 8.2. Making jewellery by hand. The mounter cutting the outline of a brooch with a saw

every bench in the workshop a blow-torch rests on its stand, kept alight always ready for use.

The soldering of jewellery consists of joining two pieces of gold or platinum together by heating a metal of the same quality, but with a lower melting point, and then letting it cool so that it forms a bond (Fig. 8.3). This solder has to be of the same quality as the metal it joins, because with a few exceptions this is called for by the hallmarking laws. The joint is fluxed with borax to make the solder flow; a little piece of solder is placed in position and heated with the torch. The skill is to get the temperature just right, and to use just enough solder to give a neat but strong joint.

When the mounter has finished his work, having decorated perhaps some parts of the piece with texturing or engraving (which is imparted to the surface with strokes of a steel graver), it goes forward to the finishing shop. Here perhaps some parts of the design are given a mirror brightness by pushing them against a rotating steel lap and using finely powdered diamond or carborundum as an abrasive. Then the piece is polished. First it is either roughed against a revolving wire brush, or it is mopped, that is to say it is held against a revolving felt mop, a coarse rouge

Fig. 8.3. Assembling a hand-made bracelet

compound being used as a polishing agent. The polishing is finished against smaller mops revolving on their spindles, and for this process a finer rouge is used. Interior surfaces that are hard to get at are polished by drawing over them a thread loaded with rouge. The pieces are then cleaned in a cleaning bath. An ultrasonic bath is often used these days.

If a particular colour of gold is required, or if as sometimes happens there are slight differences in the shades of the gold wire and the sheet, it is a common practice to hard-gold plate the piece. Platinum and white gold jewellery are nearly always rhodium-plated to improve their colour.

THE SETTER'S SKILL

The mount is now ready to have the stones set. The setter's work looks deceptively simple, as do so many jobs in the hands of a skilled craftsman. When he is seen opening up the claws of a claw setting, which looks like a miniature crown, cutting little seatings inside the claws to hold the girdle of the stone, with a file or a dentist's drill, picking up the stone with his wax-stick, placing it between the claws

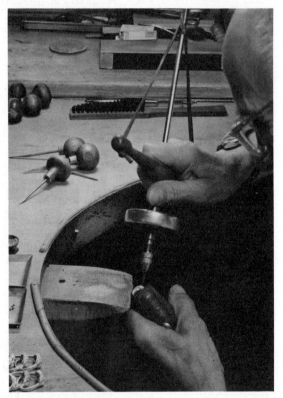

Fig. 8.4(a). Stone setting using an ancient bow-drill to drill a mount to receive the stones

and bending them over to hold it, it all looks very easy (Figs. 8.4(a), (b)). But the stone must be perfectly flat, the claws must be evenly bent, just tight enough to grasp the stone, but not tight enough to damage it. Many stones, though they are hard are also brittle. Emerald particularly could easily be chipped or fractured by a heavy-handed setter, while opal is soft enough to be bruised by the pressure applied by the scorper to the claw.

There are many ways of securing a stone in a metal mount. In the cheapest of imitation jewellery the paste stones are just glued into the holes prepared to receive them. In most of the jewellery sold by the jeweller, however, the stones are set in some form of collet. Most engagement ring stones are set in claw settings. These

Fig. 8.4(b). Stone setting—using a scorper the setter pushes the metal up and over the girdle of the stone

are usually lost-wax cast nowadays. Those required for important pieces, however, are still made in the workshop by bending up a strip of metal so that it forms a section of a cone. This is then pierced with a piercing-saw to create the claws. A little bezel is soldered to the foot of the claws to allow the setting to be firmly soldered on to the shank. To create illusion settings a flat sheet of polished metal with slotted edges is soldered between the claws, and a tiny stone set in a hole in the middle of the plate. This gives the illusion that the stone is bigger than it in fact is. More sophisticated illusion settings nowadays employ a diamond milled plate which has highly reflective facets.

A common variation on the claw setting is peg setting. This as its name implies has little pegs to hold the stone, and it has the advantage of hiding less of the stone than the conventional claw setting.

The girdle of the stone is held by the sides of the claws, instead of the claws being bent over the stone. Pavé setting is used where the designer has ordained that a lot of small stones are to be sprinkled over the surface of the metal. The stones are dropped into holes drilled into the mount, and the setter then raises little grains of metal round the perimeter of each stone to hold it in place.

The rub-over setting is that used for signet ring stones. The stone is dropped into a cup of metal and the rim of the cup is rubbed over it to produce a narrow gold frame round the edge of the stone.

Millegrain setting is achieved by drawing a little serrated hardened steel wheel round the metal close to the stone to produce a little circlet of grains. Thread setting is done in the same way but a plain wheel is used to create a thread of gold to hold the stone. Pearls are usually set by being drilled part way through and then attached to a metal peg with an adhesive.

MECHANICAL METHODS

There are many ways nowadays in which hand work can be replaced by factory processes in order to reduce production costs. Apart from the fact that labour is in short supply, it must be appreciated that labour costs these days range very high in the production bill. Unless a piece contains important stones, the cost of raw materials will represent only a relatively small proportion of the total costs.

STAMPING

Two techniques increasingly used today to economise on labour and labour costs, are stamping and lost-wax casting. Stamping is no new process to the jewellery trade; it has been used for a long time in the production of inexpensive jewellery. In the past, however, jewellery produced by stamping mostly looked a poor machine-made imitation of the real thing. Today, the use of much more intricate tools and more imaginative designing, have led to the production of stamped jewellery hardly distinguishable from the hand-made article. The textured gold watch bracelets made by leading firms illustrate this. Originally, the hand-made appearance achieved by these firms was the result of a lot of hand finishing, but now hand work is being gradually reduced to a minimum by improved tooling. A bracelet can be made from components stamped out in the press and then given a hand-made look by hand texturing. But it has now been proved possible to produce much the same effect entirely from the tools. When the bracelet had been polished it would be extremely difficult, except by an expert, to see that it was not hand made. The major drawback to the machine-made product is that hundreds of identical bracelets will have to be produced to pay for the tools. If production methods are used exclusiveness has to be sacrificed.

DIFFERENT SKILLS

The production of jewellery by mass-production techniques does not take away the skill from jewellery making; it just means that the skill is vested in different hands. It is the toolmaker who is the skilled craftsman in the modern jewellery factory, and the works manager who needs the skill and training to see at a glance how best a piece can be made, how best quality and economy can be reconciled. When the works manager has done this, the die-sinker begins to sink the design in blocks of hardened steel, working to the very fine limits essential for efficient production. He works with a mixture of traditional hand tools and machine tools, files and gravers, modern milling machines and spark erosion machines.

Mass-production techniques are more exacting than are hand methods. A thousandth of an inch or two error here and there are of no great importance in a hand-made piece. The goldsmith can offer up his components and make minor adjustments in a few minutes. In mass production thousandths are important. Production does not end in the press shop. The piece has to be assembled. If this assembly has to be entrusted to highly skilled goldsmiths, and if they have to waste much time in making minor adjustments, then all the economies resulting from stamping out the components will be cancelled out. The assembly of mass-produced components calls for mass-production methods, the employment of semi-skilled labour aided by ingenious jigs, which de-skill and speed up the work. The components from the presses must fit these jigs exactly or they must be scrapped or expensively corrected.

If many jewellery manufacturers have moved out of the world of handicraft into the world of precision engineering, many more firms are making use of an old process, revived a few years ago, which needs less expenditure in capital equipment than a modern press-shop and its attendant tool room. This process, which is also more flexible than stamping, is known as the lost-wax process.

LOST-WAX PROCESS

This process was first used by the ancient Egyptians thousands of years ago. The capital equipment required to carry out this process in a modern workshop is very modest. All that is required is a small vulcanising press, a wax injector, the equipment for preparing and pouring the 'investment', a centrifuge and an oven.

The production cycle begins with the making of a model of the piece to be produced. This model is made in exactly the same way as a one-off piece of jewellery, with the ancient tools and techniques of the goldsmith's craft. The model may cost as much as £100 to make, but this is far less than the cost of a complicated set of dies needed to make the same piece by stamping.

Once made the model is placed in the middle of a small square frame (Fig. 8.5(a)). Rubber is then packed round it, after which the frame is put into a vulcanising press, where the rubber is heated so that it flows round the model and is vulcanised into a solid block. This rubber mould is then sliced in two and the model removed. The two halves of the rubber mould are put together and the channel created to link up the outside of the rubber block with the mould in the middle of it, is placed over the nozzle of a wax injector. The wax injector is a can containing molten wax. By pressing the nozzle at the base of it molten wax can be spurted under pressure into the rubber mould (Fig. 8.5(b)). When the rubber mould is opened again a wax replica of the original model is found inside it. When a number of these wax replicas have been cast, they are mounted on a base to form a 'tree' (Fig. 8.5(c)). This tree is then placed in a metal flask, and an investment, consisting mainly of crystobalite, which is mixed with water to form a white liquid looking rather like and setting like liquid plaster of Paris, is poured into the flask. The wax tree is now totally invested in a solid cylinder (Fig. 8.5(d)).

The next step is to lose the wax, the operation which gives the process its name. This is done by placing the investment in an oven, where the wax becomes liquid again and just pours out of a hole in the base. We now have a hollow plaster mould, and this is mounted on a centrifuge. This consists of a rotary arm mounted in the centre of a metal shield, and rotated by an electric, or a clockwork, motor. On one end of the arm is a small crucible made of refractory material, like that used to make firebricks, that will stand great heat without cracking. The crucible has a hole at its outside end. The investment is fixed behind the crucible so that the hole in the latter corresponds with the pour hole in the investment.

The quantity of gold needed for filling the investment is calculated,

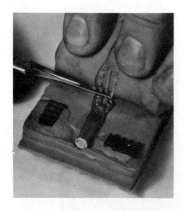

Fig. 8.5(a). Lost-wax casting—making a hollow rubber mould

Fig. 8.5(b). The rubber mould placed over the nozzle of a wax injector to produce a wax replica of the original model

Fig. 8.5(c). Wax replicas built up to form a 'tree' (by courtesy of the Mond Nickel Co. Ltd.)

Fig. 8.5(d). An investment poured round a tree in a metal cylinder. After heating in an oven the wax melts and is 'lost'

Fig. 8.5(e). The cylinder containing the investment is placed in the centrifuge against a crucible into which gold is put, and melted with a blow-torch

placed in the crucible, and melted by playing a blow-torch on to it (Fig. 8.5(e)). When the gold is molten, the centrifuge is rotated and the gold is flung by centrifugal force into the mould.

After cooling, the investment is broken away from the golden tree in its centre, and the final traces of investment are removed with hydrofluoric acid.

The individual gold replicas of the original model are now broken away from the tree and cleaned up. From this one invest-ment alone perhaps twelve perfect copies may result. Sometimes complicated designs have to be soldered up from a number of components made by lost-wax casting, but it is much easier to produce complicated three-dimensional designs in this way than in the press. It is also quite simple to produce ring mounts for gem-set rings, complete with claw settings. A typical firm now makes 90 per cent of its gem rings by this process, and though they are slightly inferior in finish to the firm's hand-made mounts, they cost only a quarter of the price to make. The old techniques of sand casting and casting in cuttlefish still survive in the jewellery trade, but they are not much used nowadays.

It has been implied perhaps that the manufacturing jeweller is faced with a simple choice of methods. He can, perhaps, use hand work, or press-tool, or he can use lost-wax casting. In fact he can, and often does, use all three methods to make one piece of jewellery. It is, for instance, a common practice to use a lost-wax head and solder a drawn wire shank on to it to produce a gem ring. The drawn wire shank has more elasticity than has a cast one, and will better stand up to the stretching entailed in sizing it. If the ring is a fancy one, a stamping could be incorporated in the head. Finally the skill of a traditional craftsman will have to be called upon to set it with a stone or stones.

TEXTURE

Texture has revolutionised jewellery. It is always hard to dif-ferentiate between cause and effect in these matters, but texture is either the result of a revolt against the bright and shiny, or it is the cause of this revolt. In the jewellery trade, texture began on the Continent, or rather it would be true to say that its revival began there. The leading modern designers borrowed texture from the painters and sculptors, for whom it has long been as important as colour and form. After a few years the designers of Swiss watch cases borrowed the idea in their turn from the *avant garde* jewellery designers, and it made its first commercial appearance in this country as a method of watch case decoration. Today, texture is to be found on almost every piece of jewellery coming on to the market. The texture revolution came at a most convenient moment. Mass production was threatening to result in too much monotony — texture made it possible to make one pattern look like a dozen different patterns. It brought variety to the machine age.

Texture can be achieved in many ways. Wrinkled textures can be produced by heating gold up to a critical temperature and just letting the surface of the metal flow, or by letting molten gold fall on to a smooth gold surface and bond itself to it. The textile texture of shantung engraving can be produced by hand or by machine engraving. Bark finish can be hand cut or produced on a diamond milling machine or ground into the gold with dentist's drills.

Texture as has been said can also be applied from the tools in a press, and of course if a hand-made model used for lost-wax casting is hand textured, this texturing will be reproduced on the surface of the jewellery resulting from the process.

The manufacturers of textured articles are inclined to be secretive about methods used to produce their finishes. Most textures can, however, be produced by fitting different tools into a dentist's drill.

Fig. 8.6. Two bracelet watches illustrating various textured finishes on cases and bracelets

Perhaps, anyway, the precise method by which the scores of different finishes seen on modern jewellery are achieved is not important to the man behind the counter for whom this book has been written. If the technical intricacies are not important, however, the effects produced are very important indeed. One of these effects has been to turn what once was rather dull merchandise into something interesting and therefore saleable. Gold watch bracelets were not so long ago a relatively unimportant contributor to retail turnover. Now texture has turned this line into an exciting quick-turnover item (Fig. 8.6).

DIAMOND MILLING

What texture did for the watch bracelet and the cuff-link, diamond milling did for the wedding ring. Diamond milling, as it is used for decoration on jewellery, is an alternative to engine-turning (Figs. 8.7(a) and (b)). A diamond tool is brought to the work, and as a result of the way the milling machine is set up it makes a pattern of sharp bright cuts in the metal. The shape of these cuts depends on the size and shape of the diamond used, the angle at which it is presented to the work and the ratio of the gearing used.

Before diamond milling the ranges of wedding ring manufacturers were very limited, and a retail jeweller might stock as few as half a

Fig. 8.7(a). *Diamond milling—operator setting up the machine into which a diamond tool is fixed.*

Fig. 8.7(b). *Typical examples of diamond milling applied to wedding rings*

dozen patterns. Today, the designs available from the manufacturers are counted in hundreds, and retailers carry much bigger ranges. More recently, textured wedding rings have become popular. Originally the texture was cut into these, but they are now sometimes produced by casting the whole ring from a textured model.

Varying the finish is not the only way in which variety can be given to the ranges of manufacturers using mass-production techniques. By varying the stones in a standard mount, by building up stamped or lost-wax cast components in different ways, a range of jewellery can be achieved from a relatively few standard units.

TRADITIONAL DECORATION

Side by side with the new processes of decoration, traditional methods of decorating jewellery are used. Enamelling of various kinds (see pages 119–120) is still used as a jewellery decoration. Niello wares, imported from the East, are widely sold today. These are produced by cutting a pattern into the metal and filling it with a black niello compound consisting of silver, copper, sulphur and borax. Hand engraving still provides an effective method of decorating jewellery, and inlaying patterns of coloured gold is another popular form. A pattern of tiny pieces of coloured gold is fitted together like the pieces of a jig-saw and soldered on to a gold surface. Then attempts have been made from time to time to revive the ancient art of granular work.

CHAIN

Chain has always been an important component of jewellery. The largest of Pforzheim's jewellery firms all began as chain makers in the nineteenth century, and like most things in the jewellery trade chain can be made by man or machine.

For hand-made chain, wire is bent to form the links, and the chain laboriously built up link by link, each joint being soldered. It takes a chain maker about a day to link 85 gold links by hand to produce about 7 ft of chain. The large links of modern watch bracelets are sometimes made by lost-wax casting and then hand decorated.

By machine some 50 ft of the same chain can be produced in an hour. It is fascinating to watch these chain-making machines working away unattended. The wire is fed to the tools, which bend it to form a link, hold the link in position and form the next one through it. It all happens so quickly that the machine has to be slowed down for the process to be demonstrated, and one can watch a simple trace chain consisting of oval links pouring out of the machine like a string of sausages.

There are many types of chain, too many to do more than mention the most common here. There is for example Milanese, an Italian chain as its name suggests, which consists of interwoven rows of links, like a miniature version of the chain-mail worn by the warriors who fought at the Battle of Hastings.

Brazilian chain is a round chain which consists of a series of linked cups that fit into one another to form a sinuous golden snake. For this reason it is sometimes known as snake chain. Brick bracelets consist of little squares or oblongs of gold cut from seamless tube of square section, which are wired together internally to produce a broad flat chain. There are also many variations on trace, which have different names: belcher has wide links; curb has twisted links; Alma has broad-ribbed links; fetter has long links. There are also a variety of chains consisting of mixed links.

CHAPTER 9

The History of Watches and Clocks

DEVELOPMENTS DOWN THE YEARS

The ancient Egyptians probably made the first time-measuring devices. Observing that the sun, on its journey across the sky from dawn to dusk, threw lengthening and shortening shadows, they built sun clocks. It has been suggested that the famous needles, such as Cleopatra's needle now standing on the Thames embankment, were the gnomons of enormous Egyptian sundials, casting their shadows on huge dials. These first sundials were the forerunners of the more compact sundials (Fig. 9.1) which were still used well into the eighteenth century to check the timekeeping of mechanical clocks.

The Egyptians also devised other ways of measuring the passing of time. Among these were the water clocks, clepsydra as they were called. In their simplest form clepsydra consisted of vessels with holes in their bases and a scale marked on their interior. As water trickled out of the hole, the level in the vessel fell, and by reading off the level against the scale the owner could tell how much time had passed since he filled up his clock. There is an alabaster cast of one of these primitive clepsydra in the British Museum, the original of which is said to date from between 1415 and 1380 B.C. It looks like a giant flower-pot decorated on the outside with hieroglyphs, the ancient Egyptian picture writing.

Later civilisations made much more sophisticated clepsydra. In the last century B.C., in Alexandria, clepsydra were being built with a wheel train, a pointer and a column dial, and highly developed clepsydra must have some claim to be deemed the first mechanical clocks. Most horologists, however, consider the first mechanical timekeepers to have been those clocks, built in the last quarter of the thirteenth century, which were fitted with a mechanical

Fig. 9.1. Copy of tenth century portable sundial
(by courtesy of the Science Museum)

Fig. 9.2. Alarm clock fitted with a verge
escapement. Said to be a fifteenth century
monastic alarm clock

escapement. No one is certain who invented the first real mechanical clock, but he was most likely a monk, for in those days all learning was enclosed within the walls of the monasteries. The first clock might not have been a clock as we know it, with hands and a dial, but probably just a mechanism that rang a bell at the appropriate time to call the inventor's fellow monks to attend matins, vespers and the other canonical hours.

THE MECHANICAL CLOCK

When a little later in history a dial was added to this mechanism, the essential elements of the weight-driven clock, as known today, already existed (Fig. 9.2). All the horological inventions affecting the weight-driven clock, made in all the centuries since, have been only improvements. Fundamentally, the weight-driven clock remains just as it was at the beginning. There was a source of power,

Fig. 9.3. A foliot from the Salisbury Cathedral clock said to have been made in 1386 (by courtesy of the Keystone Press Agency Ltd.)

a rock suspended from a rope coiled round a pulley. There was an escapement, the purpose of which was to check the fall of the rock, to stop all the power from escaping all at once as the rock plummeted to the end of its rope, and to divide the power up into regular impulses. The first type of escapement was known as the 'verge escapement'. It consisted of a crown-shaped wheel, against the teeth of which two flag-shaped plates set at right-angles called pallets, acted. These engaged and released the wheel alternately, so halting and releasing the weight on its downward journey.

The pallets of the verge escapement were attached to an upright rod, on top of which, above the rest of the clock mechanism, was fixed either a metal bar or a wheel. This was called the foliot, and as the pallets of the verge wagged back and forth so did the foliot (Fig. 9.3). The foliot was in fact the equivalent of the modern balance wheel to be found in every watch today. Its back and forth swing, like the back and forth swing of the watch balance, beat out the regular rhythm on which timekeeping depends.

This regular beat was transferred to a set of wheels and toothed pinions, which translated the beat into minutes and drove the single hand of the clock round and round the dial.

The timekeeping of these early clocks was by no means accurate by present-day standards, but seconds and minutes were not important then, and the early clockmakers put no minute marks on their dials, but only calibrated them for hours and quarter hours.

Fig. 9.4. A sixteenth century example of the drum clock with the dial on top and a single hand

This practice continued until the latter half of the seventeenth century, and any clock which stylistically belongs to a period earlier than this but has either a dial calibrated in minutes, or two hands, should be viewed with suspicion.

The clock with the falling weight as a source of power was all very well if one wanted to install it in the turret of a castle, or to mount it permanently on the wall of a great hall or chamber, but it was not easy to move about. Not until the fifteenth century did it become possible to build portable timekeepers, other that is than portable sundials. A new source of power a good deal less cumbersome than the weight and line had to be devised. At some time during the second half of the fifteenth century some unknown man discovered this alternative source of power. He found that if he coiled a ribbon of steel it would naturally seek to unwind itself, and he found that this uncoiling action, which T. P. Camerer Cuss described as 'the pent up power of a ribbon of steel', would provide enough power to drive a clock (Fig. 9.4). Again, of course, it was necessary to have an escapement to prevent the spring from just flying open in a fraction of a second, and at the same time to set the balance beating a steady rhythm.

Many of the early spring-wound clocks were in the shape of drums with the dial on the top, and it was inevitable that sooner or later someone would have the idea of making a little drum clock small enough to wear on the person.

THE FIRST WATCHES

There has been considerable controversy about who can be considered the inventor of the watch. The controversy has never been

Fig. 9.5. Detail from a portrait painted in Germany in 1560, which shows one of the first watches ever made

finally settled but Peter Henlein, a Nuremberg watchmaker, is thought to have a strong claim. He made 'horologia' from 'a trifling amount of iron . . . which both indicate and strike for forty hours . . . even if they are carried on the bosom or in the purse (Fig. 9.5). Henlein's little horologia date from early in the sixteenth century.

Many of the early watches were made in fanciful shapes of musk-balls, shells and skulls. They were very poor timekeepers and were regarded more as toys than as instruments for telling the time. One reason for the great inaccuracy of the early spring-driven timekeepers was that the power output of a fully wound spring was far greater than the power output from one that was almost uncoiled. This variation in power output had a serious effect on the performance of the verge escapement. During the fifteenth century the clockmakers and watchmakers devised two mechanisms designed to overcome this problem of power loss. One of these, a German invention, consisted of a spring acting on a snail-shaped

Fig. 9.6. A watch given by King Charles I to Lord Panmuir

cam. This was called the stackfreed. It has been described by one modern writer as 'a most brutal arrangement', and it was short-lived. The other device, a drawing of which was made by Leonardo da Vinci, was much more satisfactory, and became a standard component of good-quality spring-driven clocks and watches up to the time when the verge escapement was finally dispensed with in the nineteenth century. This power compensation device was called a fusée. It consisted of a grooved cone, which was in effect a stack of graduated pulleys. A gut line, later a fine chain, was used. This was wound on to the barrel containing the coiled spring, the main-spring, that powered the clockwork. The gut line was then attached to the fusée. As the mainspring unwound, the gut passed on to bigger and bigger grooves on the fusée and this provided ever-increasing leverage to compensate for the ever-diminishing power of the spring.

The seventeenth century witnessed a horological revolution (Fig. 9.6). At the beginning of the century the watch was, as mentioned, more of a toy than a timekeeper. A typical watch of the first quarter of the century, the kind being produced by David Ramsey, one of the best watchmakers of the period, was very small, perhaps 2½ in. across. It might have an engraved metal case, or the case might be made of two hollowed-out pieces of rock crystal held in gilt-brass rims. The dial would probably be made of silver and engraved, or it might be decorated with champlevé enamel. On the dial would be a tiny chapter-ring with rather stumpy Roman numerals incised in it. The single hand would be made of steel and would be dart-shaped. The movement would almost

Fig. 9.7. Two clocks illustrating the development of the English brass lantern clock

certainly be fitted with a fusée and chain, and the verge escapement would wag a wheel foliot back and forth.

By the second quarter of the seventeenth century, such makers as Edward East were turning out watches that looked much more like the pocket watches of later periods. These watches were bigger than those made earlier in the century, the flattened spherical cases sometimes decorated with leather and sometimes with biblical or mythological pictures painted in enamel. The movements of these watches, though bigger and more robust than those used by Ramsey for his little watches, were still poor timekeepers.

SEVENTEENTH-CENTURY CLOCKS

During the seventeenth century a clock, probably continental in origin, made its appearance in England. It was called the lantern clock, because it looked like a brass lantern (Fig. 9.7). This clock was produced for over a century, and consisted of a brass box with turned brass pillars at the corners. These pillars terminated in baluster-shaped finials, and ended below the case in little turned feet. Above the brass box, which had hinged sides to give access to the movement,

Fig. 9.8. A pendulum version of the lantern clock made about 1680

were two intersecting arches. Another baluster finial rose from the junction of these arches, and an alarm bell was suspended below it. Above the case, between the arches, were decorative frets. The dial usually overlapped the case, and it tended to get bigger as the century progressed. Also the Roman numerals on the chapter-ring became progressively taller and more graceful. These clocks, which were hung on the wall, were from 6 to 16 in. tall (Fig. 9.8). Their movements, which were controlled by a verge and wheel foliot, were powered by a weight that dangled below the clock on the end of a rope, the other end of the rope being coiled round a spiked wheel in the movement. A second, and smaller weight, powered the alarm mechanism. The alarm setting was in the form of a small calibrated disc in the centre of the dial.

The long-case clock was born in the middle years of the seventeenth century. Already, wooden-cased, wall clocks were being produced, and it was perhaps only to be expected that, sooner or later, someone would feel that a weight-driven clock would look much tidier if the weights were enclosed, and so the clock became a piece of furniture that would stand on the floor. All that was

Fig. 9.9. A long-case clock made by Ahasuerus Fromanteel about 1665

necessary was to add what amounted to a narrow cupboard, fitted with a door to give access to the weights, below the pedimented wooden case of the period. These first long-case clocks were small (about 6 ft high), slender, simple and classically proportioned, and examples by such makers as Ahasuerus Fromanteel and Edward East are very desirable collectors' pieces today (Fig. 9.9).

THE PENDULUM

Though undoubtedly better timekeepers than the watches of the period, these clocks made during the first 60 years of the seventeenth century, the lanterns, the wooden-cased wall-clocks and the long-case clocks, were still far from good timekeepers. Then about 1657 a clock with a new regulator made its appearance in Holland. It was almost certainly the astronomer, Galileo, who invented this new regulator, the now familiar pendulum. It is said that when he was a young man, he was sitting one day in Pisa Cathedral when he noticed that one of the lamps was swinging. He became intrigued and began to measure the time of the swings by comparing them with his pulse beats. He found that whether the swings were long or short, they occupied the same amount of time. The swinging lamp was in fact, he realised, a natural timekeeper, it was as the horologists say 'isochronous'. Galileo eventually made a pendulum, which like the suspended lamp was nothing more or less than a

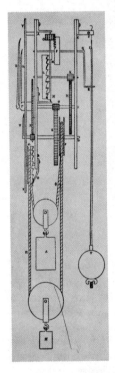

Fig. 9.10. Drawing of the first pendulum clock made in Holland by Samuel Coster to a design by Christiaan Huygens (by courtesy of the Science Museum)

swinging weight. He used his pendulum in connection with his astronomic observations, and had the idea of fitting a pendulum to a clock. Indeed he left a drawing of a pendulum clock, but died before he actually made one. In the end it was the Dutch physicist Christiaan Huygens who became known as the inventor of the pendulum clock, though he was not the actual maker of the clock. It was a fellow Dutchman, Samuel Coster, who made the clock to Huygens' design (Fig. 9.10).

It was soon realised that the pendulum deserved a better escapement than the old verge, the action of which was interfered with by

Fig. 9.11. A Thomas Tompion spring-wound bracket clock movement with fusée

the train. In 1671 William Clement invented a much superior escapement, called the anchor escapement because it looked like the business end of an anchor. This escapement was much less subject to outside influences than the verge, and has been the standard escapement for pendulum clocks ever since. In the next two centuries, between two and three hundred escapements for watches and clocks were invented, some like George Graham's famous deadbeat escapement being successful, but the majority making no lasting contribution to the science of horology and therefore passing into oblivion.

The invention of the pendulum led very quickly to the addition of minute hands to clocks. It then became logical to place five one-minute marks between the hour marks on the chapter-ring, in place of the four quarter marks that had been there for the previous 300 years or more.

The invention of the pendulum and the anchor escapement coincided with the emergence of some of the finest clockmakers who have ever lived. The greatest name among these makers was Thomas Tompion (Fig. 9.11), and his fame was so great, at home and abroad, that some of his Continental competitors paid him the

Fig. 9.12. A Daniel Quare long-case clock of about 1695, illustrating how the long-case developed into a substantial piece of furniture

backhanded compliment of engraving his name on the dials of clocks far inferior to his. It is a tribute to the craftsmanship of this period that so many of the clocks made in the last quarter of the seventeenth century have survived to our own day, and many of them still keep excellent time nearly 300 years after they were made. The two typical clocks of this period were the bracket clock and the long-case. The long-case had grown bigger to accommodate a long swinging pendulum. Its case was enriched with all the fashionable decorative arts of the day (Fig. 9.12). Gilded classical pilasters or twisted columns flanked the dial, beautifully matched walnut

Fig. 9.13(a). A Thomas Tompion bracket clock—typical example of about 1690, with winding squares and cherub spandrels in the dial corners

Fig. 9.13(b). The back of a movement showing the short pendulum used with a verge escapement, and the richly engraved back-plate

veneers, marquetry, or chinoiserie lacquer-work enriched the cases. In the corners of the dials were little applied brass decorative frets called spandrels, often in the form of plump-cheeked cherubs, and the elegant Roman numerals on the applied chapter-rings were cut into the brass and filled with pitch.

The bracket clock, so called because it was designed to stand on a bracket fixed to the wall of a room, was a spring-wound clock with a short bob-pendulum as a regulator. Some of these bracket clocks were made with travelling cases, so that their owners could carry them down to their country estates when the London season came to an end (Figs 9.13(a) and (b)). These were the forerunners of the famous carriage clocks of the nineteenth century.

The cases of the bracket clocks had an elegant simplicity. They were made of ebony or ebonised wood. Above the dial, which was similar to that used on the long cases, was a domed moulding carrying a hinged brass handle. Usually there were a few pierced brass enrichments, but nothing to detract from the classical proportions.

THE BALANCE SPRING

Within a few years of the application of the pendulum to the clock, Huygens also devised a method of rendering the old wheel foliot, the balance wheel as it is known today, isochronous. He attached a coiled spring to this balance wheel, which pulsed like a heart when the balance received its impulse, tightening and then uncoiling again.

That irascible figure of the seventeenth century scientific scene, Dr Robert Hooke, argued and raged by turn. He claimed that he had anticipated Huygens' invention of the balance spring by some years, and the validity of Hooke's claim to this invention is still a matter of controversy, but most of the evidence seems to be in Huygens' favour.

The balance spring did for the watch what the pendulum had done for the clock. It made possible an accuracy undreamed of, and put a minute hand and minute marks on the dial. Soon every man who could afford one was carrying a watch in the pocket of his fashionable embroidered waistcoat.

Because they were the prerogative of the rich, watches were at this period usually heavily ornamented in the style of the period. The repoussé-chasing and the florid piercing, familiar to most of us from Caroline silverware, were applied to the 18 carat gold or silver watch cases. These creations of the goldsmiths' art, carried out in

Fig. 9.14(a). *Eighteenth century pair-case watch by George Graham—showing a richly chased gold case and a similar outer case to protect it*

Fig. 9.14(b). *Decorative outer case which would have a third case, possibly covered with leather or shagreen for further protection*

soft metals, were very liable to sustain damage, and even if they avoided this, the fine detail of the chasing would soon have become blurred from daily wear. So it became customary to provide an outer case for the protection of the ornate inner case (Figs 9.14(a) and (b)). The outer of these so-called pair-cases was more work-manlike than the inner and often it was made of unadorned metal, or sometimes was covered with leather.

TEMPERATURE AND FRICTION

As so often happens in any mechanical science, the solution of one problem tends to draw attention to others. It soon became apparent that though the pendulum and the balance spring brought vast improvements in timekeeping, the full potential of these inventions could not be realised until the errors due to changes of temperature and friction had been greatly reduced. The problem of friction in watch bearings was tackled very early in the eighteenth century. In 1704, a Swiss and two Frenchmen, all living in London, made a joint application for a patent. In this application they stated that as a result of 'great charge and continual labour', they had acquired 'an art of working precious or more common stones . . . so that they may be employed and made use of in clockwork or watchwork . . . not for ornament only, but as an internal or useful part of the engine itself.' These three men, Nicholas Facio, and Peter and Jacob Debaufre, met opposition to their application from the Clockmakers' Company. In fact they shared the fate of so many horological inventors, and became the centre of a long drawn-out controversy, but there now seems little doubt that they were indeed the inventors of watch jewels, which provide hard, and relatively friction-free, cups for the pivot of the balance wheel and the train wheels to run in.

Temperature compensation was not so easily achieved, and it was not until the end of the last century that this bogy was finally laid. The horologists of the eighteenth century did, however, come to terms with the problem. Their work in this field contributed much to the science of navigation, and this in turn laid the foundations of Britain's great programme of imperialist expansion into territories far across the seas.

The main impetus for the eighteenth century experiments in temperature compensation was an Act of Parliament of 1714, an Act which was recommended to the government of the day by, among others, Sir Isaac Newton. The Act aimed to foster the building of a timekeeper that would make it possible for the captains of the ships, upon which Britain depended so much for her wealth and her security, to navigate with much greater accuracy than in the past. A prize of £10,000 was offered for an instrument that would have an error equivalent to not more than one degree of longitude on a voyage to the West Indies. Such a voyage across the Atlantic would of course mean that this timekeeper would be subjected to considerable changes of temperature, and so temperature compensation was one of the first problems that any inventor, who set out to win the prize, would have to tackle.

In 1725 John Harrison, a carpenter's son, devised a pendulum that provided temperature compensation by making use of the fact that brass and steel have different coefficients of expansion. This 'grid-iron pendulum', as it was called, consisted of bars of the two metals lying parallel to one another, five of steel and four of brass, set up in such a way that the expansion of one set of metal bars was offset by the expansion of the other. No matter how hot or how cold it became the pendulum remained the same length. This pendulum was used in high-class long-case clocks and regulators for two centuries, but of course, as Harrison realised, you could not use a pendulum clock on the heaving quarter-deck of a ship. He went on, however, to apply the same bimetallic principle to the balance of a spring-driven chronometer.

Harrison discovered that the balance spring of a watch loses some of its elasticity when heated, and that if the spring is shortened the lost elasticity is restored. So he attached a bimetallic strip to a block holding the curb-pins that determine the effective length of the balance spring. When the temperature rose, the brass on one side of the strip expanded more than the steel on the other side. This caused the strip to bow, draw the curb-pins further along the balance spring, and so shorten the spring. This simple device was fitted to Harrison's famous Number 4 chronometer, which on the voyage of the *Deptford*, from Spithead to Jamaica, in 1761, lost only five seconds.

In 1767, the French watchmaker, Pierre le Roy, achieved compensation, by making a bimetallic balance wheel, the rim of which was cut on opposite sides. Changes of temperature altered the form of the balance wheel, and this compensated for the changes of elasticity of the balance spring. This system was used on good watches until the problem of temperature was solved finally by the Swiss, Dr Charles Edward Guillaume in 1896. He evolved two nickel-steel alloys, one of which he called Invar, short for invariable. As its name suggests it expanded only a negligible amount when heated, and was therefore an ideal metal from which to make balance wheels. Guillaume's other alloy he called Elinvar, which does not lose elasticity to any appreciable extent within the range of temperatures that a watch is likely to encounter. This was just what the manufacturers of balance springs had been looking for.

LEVER ESCAPEMENT

The second half of the eighteenth century saw the invention of a new watch escapement. Of the hundreds invented during the century, the one which Thomas Mudge used for a watch made for King George III to give to Queen Charlotte was by far the most important. About 80 years were to pass before another watch with this lever escapement was made, however. Today, tens of millions of watches are fitted with this escapement every year.

Just what the detached lever escapement achieved was summed up by T. P. Camerer Cuss in his book *The Story of Watches*. 'Every escapement up to 1759', he wrote, 'had been very much under the influence of the watch train . . . Mudge's lever freed, detached, the balance for the greater part of its swing. In fact it is only for a brief moment when it unlocks the train and receives the impulse that the balance has any connection with the rest of the watch.' (See Appendix 3 for a full description of the lever escapement.)

Three other important horological inventions also date from the second half of the eighteenth century: the shock-absorber; keyless work; and the self-winding mechanism. The great Swiss watchmaker Breguet was almost certainly the first to fit a shock-absorber to a watch. It was called the parachute, and worked on the same principle as the modern shock-absorber. The end stones for the balance staff were mounted on springs which gave when the watch received a jolt.

KEYLESS WORK

It was well into the nineteenth century before keyless work became a standard part of every watch, and the owner no longer had to carry on his watch chain a little key that went into a hole in the back of the watch case and fitted over the winding square. The first keyless mechanism was, however, applied as early as 1752 when the French maker, Pierre Caron, made a watch for Madame de Pompadour. He fitted this with a little projecting hook that its owner could draw round the dial with her nail when she wanted to wind it. It was 68 years later before a London watchmaker, Thomas Prest, improved on Caron's idea; in 1820 he took out a patent for the pendant winding system.

SELF-WINDING MECHANISM

In the meantime the eighteenth century horologists had tried to get rid of winding altogether, but it is still not really known who first fitted a self-winding mechanism to a watch. Was it Breguet, a Swiss working in Paris; was it Abraham Louis Perrelet, another Swiss working in Switzerland, or was it a third Swiss, Louis Recordon, who worked in London? All three men made self-winding watches at much the same time, about 1780, and they all worked on much the same principle—the pedometer principle (Fig. 9.15). Like the pedometer, which measures the distance covered by a walker, these watches were fitted with a pivoted weight that swung when the wearer moved. In the self-winding watches this swing of the weight activated a simple train of gear-wheels and pinions that wound the mainspring barrel. This was yet another invention that lay dormant for a long time before its full potentialities were realised.

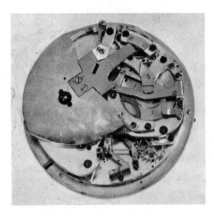

Fig. 9.15. A Breguet self-winding watch (c.1780) with heart-shaped weight

Clocks changed little in their essentials between the early years of the eighteenth century and the middle years of the nineteenth. Their appearance changed, of course, as fashions changed. Round dials replaced square ones in the eighteenth century, and nineteenth century romanticism was reflected in the transformation of the clock case from a sensible wooden box to a confection of marble and brass (Fig. 9.16). In this period, too, many experimental clocks were produced incorporating more or less successful new escapements, none of which, however, enjoyed more than a brief popularity.

In 1840, a Scotsman, Alexander Bain, made an important contribution when he applied electricity to a clock. His patent No. 8783, of October 1840, was not though to be fully exploited until the middle years of the present century, when it was to become increasingly apparent that the days of the spring-wound clock were numbered, and that we were entering the age of electric and electronic timekeeping.

Few horological inventions have not been challenged and, as has been seen, some of them have been acrimoniously disputed. Bain's

Fig. 9.16. A Benjamin Vulliamy clock made at the beginning of the nineteenth century

invention was no exception. Alexander Bain had arrived in London from his native Scotland in 1837 'to seek employment as a journeyman clockmaker'. It was in the same year that Cook and Wheatstone took out their first patent for the electric telegraph, and Wheatstone had certainly, at some stage in his work on the telegraph, considered applying electricity to timekeeping. On August 1st, Sir Charles Wheatstone was introduced to Bain, and on August 18th he bought apparatus for the telegraph from Bain. In November, Wheatstone read a paper to the Royal Society and demonstrated an electric clock. Mutual accusations of stolen ideas followed, but whatever the truth of the controversy there is no doubt that Bain got his patent registered first.

In the first electric clocks, an iron pendulum bob was attracted and repelled by electromagnets, or the pendulum bob was made into a magnet which was attracted and repelled by electrically impulsed coils. In the earliest clocks the electric supply was provided by batteries. Then the mains electrical supply was called into service to power a synchronous electric clock, which, incidentally, the purists say is not a clock at all because it has no escapement.

Fig. 9.17. Drawing of the movement of the John Harwood first self-winding wrist watch

During the period when electric timekeeping was being developed there had been an important breakthrough in mechanical horology. An Englishman, John Harwood, revived the old pedometer system of self-winding, and in 1922 applied it to the wrist watch which had begun to replace the pocket watch in the first decade of this century (Fig. 9.17). Harwood's invention was taken up by a Swiss factory and his watches enjoyed a brief popularity before the firm went bankrupt in the early thirties. The self-winding watch, which is so popular today, is merely an improvement on Harwood's patent.

CHAPTER 10

Mechanical Watches and Clocks Today

THE WATCH

THE SWISS INDUSTRY

Switzerland is still by far the biggest supplier of jewelled-lever watches to the British market. The Swiss industry started in the eighteenth century in the valleys of the Jura. The winters in the Jura are long. The snow often falls in November and may stay as late as the following April. The farmers of the Jura with time on their hands began in those endless winter months to make watches in little workshops, tucked into the low farm buildings which sheltered both their families and their stock.

It was in farm workshops that some of the great watch houses of Switzerland were born. First, the immediate family of the farmer supplied the labour, then cousins and nephews and the sons of neighbours were recruited. In the nineteenth century the more successful of those workshops, which had already gained a more than local fame, became factories, adopting the mass-production techniques which the Americans were teaching the world at that time.

Because in making a watch a very small amount of raw material was turned into a commodity of relatively high value, watchmaking was an industry peculiarly suited to Switzerland, a country with very few natural resources. Soon the Swiss watch industry was making a very important contribution to the national economy. Then came the 1930s, and the blight of world depression infected the industry. Many of the watch houses contributed to their own ruin by embarking in a cut-throat price war, and the whole industry, and the country with it, might have been plunged into bankruptcy, but for the action of a few far-seeing men. They got together and drew up a statute of sound trading, and obtained the blessing of the Swiss Government. An autocratic organisation was set up. The

233

industry was persuaded to agree to sell only at economic prices. The prices of all the components that the involved network of specialist factories sold to the watchmakers—the escapements, the springs, the jewels, the cases and the dials—were negotiated for the year ahead. Prices were related to the cost of manufacturing, and there was no price cutting. The Swiss turned their backs on the destructive anarchy that had brought them to the brink of ruin, and accepted rigid control. Before long the industry was back on its feet again.

In the post-war period one heard this system increasingly criticised in Switzerland. There were rumours of new competitors, and there were those who saw that though a rigid bureaucracy might be advantageous if one had a monopoly of world markets, it would act like a shackle if an industry began to meet serious competition. And serious competition was what Switzerland was soon to face. It was not, however, until 1965 that the pressure of this competition finally persuaded those in power that the industry needed freedom to meet its competitors on level terms. In that year, the old statute ran out. It was not renewed. All the old restrictions were lifted, and once again the Swiss watch manufacturer could make what he chose and sell it at whatever price he wished.

THE RUSSIAN AND JAPANESE INDUSTRIES

The new challenge, which caused the Swiss to accept free enterprise once again, came from two countries—Japan and Russia. There had been a small watch industry in Russia before the war, but when the Russians overran what is now Eastern Germany, they acquired both the machinery and the know-how of some of prewar Germany's most important watch factories. This provided the nucleus of what has become a giant modern industry. From the outset the Russians decided that they would make no pin-pallet watches. Today they are one of the biggest producers of jewelled-lever watches in the world with an annual production of 35 million watches a year (1968). These are produced in five major factories, the biggest of which employs 6000 people. Russia, unlike Switzerland, has no organisation of specialist factories supplying components, but each of these partially automated factories is self-sufficient, making virtually the entire watch under its clustering roofs. And these factories compete with, rather than co-operate with, one another.

The first Russian watches that arrived in this country were sufficiently workmanlike to impress the horological experts, but the finish, at least where it mattered least, was rough, and the styling of cases and dials poor. The finishing of the movements soon improved, and styling more acceptable to our taste soon appeared, though the Russians continued to show no great flair for style. To them the movement was all important, and the old dictum that it is the dial that sells the watch was only gradually brought home to them.

If one of Switzerland's new competitors has lagged behind her in the matter of product styling, this cannot be said of the other. Right from its rebirth after the war, the Japanese watch industry has been almost as fashion conscious as that of Switzerland. They have proved that they can make things as well as, and sometimes even better than, those made in Europe, and their export board set up after the war to improve Japan's image makes sure that her products are up to standard.

The Japanese watch, like the Russian watch, is produced in large self-sufficient manufacturing units, which employ a great deal of mechanisation and automation. And like the Russians they produce no pin-pallets.

Though the rise of the Japanese watch industry has not been as meteoric as that of the Russian—the Japanese had after all a sizeable watch industry before the war—the expansion of this industry has been none the less impressive, and Japan can today claim to have the largest single watch factory in the world, producing fourteen million watches a year (1972).

OTHER PRODUCERS

Both Germany and France have traditional watch industries, the products of which are sold in the British market. The French industry is centred around Besançon, just across the Jura from the centre of the Swiss industry, and the bulk of French production is of jewelled levers. The Germans also produce jewelled levers. Many of their factories, though, have been more or less dependent upon Swiss movements, and in the past at least their main importance has been as an outlet for the vigorous case and bracelet industry of Pforzheim. Since the war, however, the German jewelled-lever watch manufacturers have become increasingly self-sufficient. But it is as a producer of pin-pallets that the German industry has always been better known, and it is still these products, many of them made in the giant clock factories of the Black Forest, that we see most of in this country.

One more watch-producing country should perhaps be mentioned, though few of its products have as yet found their way on to the British market. This is the watch industry of Eastern Germany which seems to be growing rapidly, and the variety of its products suggests that it cannot be dismissed as a future source of supply.

Watches are also produced in Britain by Smiths and by the English subsidiary of an American company, Timex. Timex, who produce inexpensive pin levers, spend far more money on advertising than any other watch brand in the British market, and they sell far more units per year than any other brand—approaching 2 million (1972).

MODERN MANUFACTURING METHODS

The nineteenth century saw the Swiss watch industry change from a cottage industry into a mass-production industry. It was part of the great industrial revolution. The new factories produced watches at a price that many more people could afford to pay, while industrialisation had put money into more pockets and created a new buying public for the watch. But watches continued to be made in much the same way as they always had. People tend to think of the early watchmaker sitting at his bench making his watches by hand, piece by piece, from start to finish. This is, in fact, a romantic conception. In *London Life in the Eighteenth Century*, Dorothy George points out that: 'the making of a watch was chosen as early as 1701 to illustrate the advantages of division of labour'. She goes on to quote Derham who in 1696 referred to 'the invention of cutting engines, fusy engines, etc.' as 'contrivances of this last age'. Writing in 1747, Campbell wrote: 'The springs are made by a tradesman who does nothing else and the chains by another. . . . There are workmen who make nothing else but the caps and studs for watches. . . . After the watchmaker has got home all the parts of which the watch consists he gives the whole to the finisher. . . .' And this, of course, was going on in the Jura as well as in London. So it can be seen that factory production initially meant little more than a gathering together under one roof of a group of specialists. This grouping led to a rationalisation of production, and ultimately to the development of those automatic machines which one sees today churning out pinions, cutting the teeth on batches of wheels and so on, machines that require only to be set up, loaded and checked occasionally (Fig. 10.1).

If component production became gradually more and more mechanised, assembly remained in the hands of the craftsman. If an eighteenth century watchmaker had entered an assembly shop in a Swiss factory twenty years ago, he might have found the clinical atmosphere strangely different from the working conditions that he had known, but he would have found nothing strange about the jobs that the men were doing, or the way in which they were doing them. Assembly had to some extent been broken down so that one man did only a part of a movement, and then passed it on for the next man to make his contribution, but that was really all that had changed.

The eighteenth century watchmaker would, however, find much that was inexplicable to him today if he visited one of the more

Fig. 10.1. The five cutters of an automatic machine cutting the rod to make an arbor

progressive watch factories. Competition has not only led the Swiss industry to getting its freedom once again, but it has also stirred this rather traditional trade into seeking new methods of assembly. A contributory cause of this search has been a growing shortage of skilled labour in the industry. The young people have shown themselves no longer prepared to serve a long apprenticeship to this exacting trade. Nor are they any longer content to live in the little villages of the Jura.

The object of most of the changes which have taken place in the assembly department has been to make it possible to use relatively unskilled labour to put together the components of the watches. This has been done by breaking down the assembly into simple operations that a girl can learn to do in a matter of weeks. And to ensure that the girl does her work as well as the trained watchmakers of the past could have done it, she is provided with ingenious jigs that make it next to impossible for her to do the job badly, also with power tools that call for little manual dexterity in their operation.

Moving belt assembly lines have appeared in some factories while in many others the bicycle-chain units invented by the Lanco

Fig. 10.2. The Lanco assembly system

Company are used. These units have 100 movement holders, and the whole unit is covered with a plastic cover to protect it from dust. The movement holders have toothed wheels below them, and when the operative needs to bring a movement into position in front of her she operates a lever. She then makes her small contribution to the putting together and securing of the parts, pulls the lever again and brings another movement into position in front of her (Fig. 10.2). When she has finished her job on all 100 movements the unit is passed to the next girl who perhaps screws a hundred bridges on to a hundred watches. Then the unit goes to the next girl. There are usually 25 assemblers and inspectors on a chain. The Lanco unit has the advantage over the normal moving belt system because it allows the operative to work at her own speed. A similar unit developed by Ermano can have mechanical equipment attached to it that automates the assembly operations.

Yet another method of using semi-skilled labour in an industry that in the past was the preserve of the highly skilled, is the Walter system devised by the late Professor Walter. He broke down

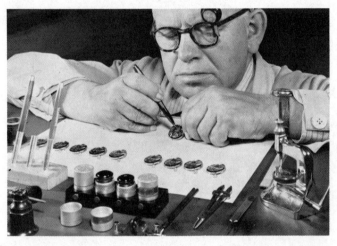

Fig. 10.3. A skilled watchmaker in a modern factory oiling movements and rectifying faults which cannot be dealt with by semi-skilled workers on the line

assembly into operations that took exactly 15 seconds to carry out, and a girl could be trained to do most of these operations in a week.

The watch industry is making increasing use of electronic equipment for timing operations. The electronic watch-timing machine, used both for checking and for preliminary adjustment, saves an enormous amount of time, while electronic equipment for cutting the hairspring means that one semi-skilled girl can today do the work which used to employ six or seven highly-skilled specialists.

The making of the components of a watch has always offered more opportunity for mechanisation than assembly, and it was here that most of the early advances in production techniques were made. Here, too, the past few years have brought even further changes.

Automation has found a foothold in the watch industry. Automatic machines controlled by computers are no longer fed by human beings, but by automatic feeds which are automatically loaded (Fig. 10.4).

The use of automation, and the use of mass-production assembly techniques, mean that factories have to do long runs of one movement. There is no point in setting all this complicated machinery

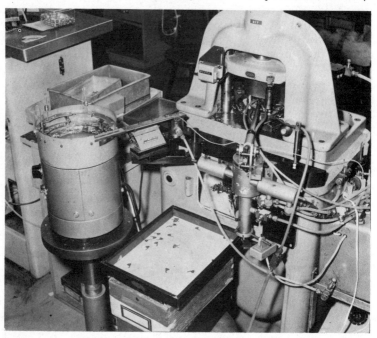

Fig. 10.4. A machine equipped with an automatic feed in the form of a carousel. It will carry out a number of operations on the bridges fed into it and run without attention for many hours

in motion merely to produce a couple of hundred components, or to set up an assembly line for a few dozen watches. Also, movements have to be specially designed if the manufacturer is to exploit fully the possibilities of these new methods. So there is a tendency for factories to concentrate now on fewer calibres.

Many people believed that the application of mass production, once associated only with cheap products, to quality watches was impossible. In theory, the watch produced in a semi-automated factory and assembled by unskilled labour should be better made than that made by the craftsman in the past. The girls become dextrous at their work, and jigs and power tools reduce human error. The recent (1976) recorded high return of watches during the guarantee period suggests, however, that this theory is not always borne out in practice. Then again there were those who deplored any reduction in the number of models produced, feeling that this made for a soulless uniformity. Actually, by using the infinite variety of cases available to them, factories today are producing more models than ever, and if these all contain the same movement there is the consolation that this will mean that in time the repair part situation will become a good deal less chaotic than it is today. There is, too, the not unimportant fact to be borne in mind that had there not been this programme of rationalisation, mechanisation and automation, watches would be a lot more expensive than they are today.

WHAT THE BRAND NAME MEANS

The *Indicateur Suisse*, which is a buyers' guide to the Swiss industry, contains 109 pages in which is listed a staggering total of nearly 8000 brands.

Brand names are put on the dials of watches by three different types of firm. The first type are what the Swiss describe as 'manufacturers'—firms that both make the components of the watch movement, with the exception of a few parts that are bought in, and also assemble the watch. There are only about 25 such firms in Switzerland.

The five Russian factories, the Japanese. factories, and our own British factories also qualify as 'manufacturers'.

The second type of firm is the assembly factory. There are over 700 of these factories in Switzerland alone, scattered all over the Jura, some employing as few as ten people, while others employ hundreds. These assembly factories obtain so-called 'rough' movements from an organisation called Ebauches S.A., which produces between 30 and 40 million movements in any year. These movements made in what are probably the most mechanised factories in the whole watch industry, are known as 'ebauche'. The ebauche consists of the plates, wheels and pinions—in fact, the whole movement except the balance and escapement, which the assembly factory buys from a specialist factory, and the jewels, mainspring and hairspring which are bought from other specialist factories. The assembler also buys cases, hands and dials, which means that he makes nothing, but merely finishes the components, puts them together, regulates the finished movement and puts it in a case.

The quality of the watches depends on the degree of finish imparted by the assembler to the components of the ebauche, and the care taken in assembling and regulating. It depends also on the quality of the components used, for though all the products of Ebauches S.A. are of a high standard, some of their designs are necessarily better than others. More important still is the big difference in quality between different grades of hairspring, jewel, and so on, available to the assembler.

It can be seen that 50 different watches with 50 different brand names on the dial could all be fitted with the same movement made in, say, the A.S. factory of Ebauches S.A. For, with the exception of a few reserve calibres, all the products of Ebauches S.A. are available to anyone wanting to buy them. These watches nevertheless may be as different one from another as chalk from cheese, depending on the standard the assembler sets himself. After all, the difference between one of the top brands selling for £200 or so, and a jewelled-lever selling for £10, is nearly all accounted for by the cost of finishing and regulating.

The third type of firm having a brand name and applying it to the dial of the watches that it sells, consists of the wholesalers and importers. It would not be entirely true to say that these firms neither make nor assemble watches, because quite a number of them case and dial at least a proportion of their range. Some, however, do not even do this.

Often the name on the dial of these watches gives very little clue to the contents. The wholesaler or importer, unless he is tied to a particular manufacturer, tends to shop in the best market, and a brand X watch may have one movement in it this week and a quite different one next week. But in fairness it should be stressed that wholesalers and importers, with rare exceptions, are interested in maintaining the reputation of their brand, and having established it at considerable cost to themselves will not wantonly debase it by associating it with unreliable movements. Also, if watches and service from a supplier are satisfactory, a wholesaler or importer tends to continue with that supplier. Some wholesalers have been dealing with the same supplier over a period of many years. In other words a wholesaler's brand may well be as reliable as any other.

PRICE, QUALITY AND TIMEKEEPING

One of the most difficult problems facing the retailer when selling watches is to justify the considerable variations in price between watches which are very similar in appearance. If a watch has extra features, such as a waterproof case, calendar work, or self-winding work, or if it is fitted with a particularly beautiful dial, or contained in an exceptional case, then it is easy enough to justify its comparatively higher price. Many watches, however, do not have these apparent differences.

The C.F.H. School in Lausanne, set up to improve the standard of watch marketing, is well aware of this problem. Included in the school's syllabus is a series of lectures, with the title 'Defence of Quality', where salesmen who attend the courses are told how the price of an expensive standard watch can be justified. The movement is analysed, component by component. They are told of the different grades of hairspring, for instance, and of jewels. It is explained to them that the more expensive watches are more highly finished, and that finishing costs money. They are told that good watches are adjusted and regulated with greater care and that this work has to be done by skilled and highly paid craftsmen. It is also explained to them that the search for better timekeeping is controlled by the law of diminishing return; that the nearer one gets to perfection the more effort one has to put in to achieve a small improvement.

So far, so good, but the salesman who advances these arguments to a customer is likely to be faced with the logical question: 'How much more accurate is this watch than that which is only two-thirds of the price?' The salesman is now on dangerous ground. Very few firms guarantee the accuracy of their mechanical watches. They may use such advertising slogans as 'Swiss precision', but they seldom back their claim by saying 'we guarantee that this watch will keep time to so many seconds a day or a week or a month'.

It is customary for manufacturers of watches to test their watches before despatching them, and the generally accepted standard for a good watch is that it should not show a gaining rate of more than 15 seconds a day in any one of four positions, dial up, dial down, crown up, crown down. Some of the best factories work to a smaller tolerance than this. For instance, the makers of one famous and exclusive brand regulate their watches so that they have an error of not more than 2 or 3 seconds a day.

The Swiss industry have now set up the Controle Technique Suisse des Montres, which tests the production of the industry and arrives at an index of quality for each firm, based on tests carried out during the year. These tests are not timekeeping tests alone. Such factors as the isochronism of the balance are also checked and affect the index, but obviously timekeeping is an important consideration. Out of 442 firms producing jewelled-lever watches in Switzerland, only nine had an index in 1966 between 1 and 3, but 113 had one between 5·1 and 6 and the index of 350 firms was between 4·1 and 8. Among those 350 firms, there were obviously some producing very popularly priced watches and some producing quite expensive watches. This is a further indication that the relationship between price and performance is a rather tenuous one. Figures submitted by delegates to the International Jewellers' Federation Paris conference in 1976 also tended to suggest that watches in the middle and lower price brackets were more reliable in wear than expensive watches.

Some factories submit a proportion of their production for observatory testing and attach a copy of the observatory certificate showing the performance of each watch to it. They then sell these watches as chronometers. In this case at least there is some guarantee of performance. It must be borne in mind, though, that factory or observatory testing merely means that the watch was performing within certain limits when it left the factory or the observatory. Much may happen to a watch between the time of despatch from the factory to being strapped on to the customer's wrist. It may languish in customs. It may lie in stock on a wholesaler's or a retailer's shelves for months or even years before it is sold. Worst of all it may spend a month or two in the bake-house conditions of the badly ventilated window of a retail jeweller's shop, which could dry up all the oil in the movement in 24 hours. In other words some of that special effort put in by the manufacturer, and some of the advantage gained by the employment of the best components available, upon which the 'Defence of Quality' rests, may be lost in transit.

COMPONENTS OF A MODERN WATCH

Fig. 10.5 shows an exploded diagram of a watch movement with the various components identified, the most important being the escapement. The two parts of the escapement, the wheel and the pallets, act together to control the escape of power from the mainspring (see Appendix 3). Various grades of escapement are available from the specialist factories, but 80 per cent of all jewelled-lever watches manufactured in Switzerland are fitted with a B grade escapement.

THE BALANCE

The balance, the regulator of the watch movement, because its oscillations cause the train to turn at a uniform rate, is also the product of a specialist manufacturer. One company in Switzerland, Fabrique de Balanciers Réunis, make over 50 million balances of various grades a year. There are the Guillaume balances of nickel steel, and brass for chronometers and deck watches. There are the

Glucydur balances of beryllium–bronze alloy, and balances made from nickel silver, often called 'nickel' balances. Most good watches are fitted with Glucydur balances.

One recent improvement has been the surrender of the old balance wheel with its screws for the screwless balance. The screws

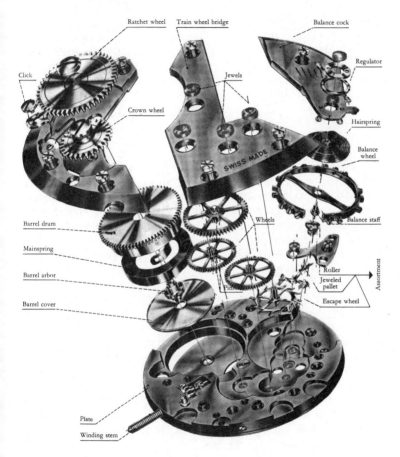

Fig. 10.5. Exploded diagram of an older type of jewelled-lever movement with screwed balance.

on a balance wheel were an archaic survival. The poising of the balance in recent years has been achieved by removing fragments of metal from these screws, not by screwing them in and out, and it is just as easy to remove metal from the rim of a screwless balance as from the screws. Besides this negative reason for giving up the screwed balance, there are positive advantages. The screwless balance is stronger, and less subject to distortion than a balance that has been drilled to take screws; it is also smoother and less air-resistant. In addition it is possible to fit a screwless balance with a bigger diameter, and with the weight further from the centre, in the same space that would have been occupied by a balance with screws round the edge of it.

The balance spring attached to the balance wheel is between three and four times thinner than a human hair, and coils and uncoils over 160 million times a year. These springs are made in various materials, such as phosphor bronze, high conductibility bronze, cupro-beryllium or stainless steel.

JEWELS

The jewels which act as the bearings in which the pinions run, may look simple enough but the making of them again calls for special skills, and the factories supplying them offer a range of 2500 types differing in width and height and so on. There are also considerable variations in the quality of jewels, regarding design, the freedom of the material from imperfections, and the tolerances of dimension. The design of the jewel is most important. It is not only a bearing but an oil reservoir, and some jewels are made, and unfortunately used, which just do not retain oil.

Many members of the public believe that the more jewels fitted the better the watch. This erroneous belief led some firms in the U.S.A. in the 1950s to 'up-jewel' watches by drilling holes in the plates and inserting quite useless jewels. In time, the practice spread to Britain, and 78-jewelled watches were advertised in the national press. A case was brought in a magistrates court in 1962, as a result of which a firm was found guilty of a breach of the Merchandise Marks Act, because many of the jewels had no function. Since this case the practice of up-jewelling seems to have died in this country, but there is still public misconception about what jewels are and what their function is.

Jewels are made of synthetic corundum, the second hardest of all the gem minerals. This takes a very high polish, is resistant to wear and is therefore an excellent bearing material. It is used as a bearing for all the pinions of the train, for the pallets of a jewelled lever and for the impulse pin that impulses the balance wheel. It is also used for certain cap jewels, or endstones, sitting over the bearing jewels, whose function is to take the end thrust of the pivots. They also function as dust caps.

A normal watch is fitted with either 15 or 17 jewels. Automatic watches sometimes are fitted with jewels in the automatic work, and some with as many as 34 jewels are produced, all of which the manufacturer claims to be functional jewels. Some manufacturers also fit jewels to the mainspring barrel, put cap jewels on every pivot jewel and claim that these are functional.

THE FRAMES

The largest components of the watch are the plates, bridges and cocks machined out of brass. These are the frames of the watch. They support the wheels and pinions of the train, the gearing which translates the oscillations of the balance into seconds, minutes and hours. They also house the keyless work. This is another set of gearing, making it possible to wind up the mainspring in its barrel with ease, an operation which would call for considerable force if done directly. Incorporated with the winding mechanism is the set hands mechanism, which allows the hands of the watch to be moved by rotating the winding crown. All that is necessary is to lift the crown, so disengaging the winding mechanism and engaging the set hands mechanism.

THE MAINSPRING

Until recently it was quite usual for manufacturers and distributors to exclude responsibility for broken mainsprings from the terms of their guarantees. This was because no matter how much care was taken in making steel mainsprings, and no matter how rigorously they were tested before being fitted to a watch, they were still liable to break, quite inexplicably, in course of wear. And though the horological research laboratories worked for many years on this problem they never solved it. A few years ago, however, watch manufacturers began to fit cobalt alloy mainsprings, and these so-called 'unbreakable' mainsprings have proved to be almost trouble free. Stainless steel mainsprings are also used nowadays.

TRAIN SPEEDS

A recent development is the watch with a fast train. The application of the 36,000 or 28,000 train to a standard watch is now becoming increasingly common. The normal watch is fitted within 18,000 train, which means that it beats at the rate of 18,000 times an hour, or five times a second. Some makers have been using faster trains, and have claimed improved timekeeping as a result. Stop-watch manufacturers have been using 36,000 trains for many years and have noticed that they had a marked lack of positional error, meaning that there was less than the normal variation in rate no matter in what position the watch was held.

One of the specialist escapement manufacturers supplying Swiss watch manufacturers then developed a 36,000 beat escapement for a normal watch, the balance of which had a very short as well as a very fast swing. This was launched in 1966. Watches fitted with this escapement proved, in practice, to be exceptional timekeepers, and to have a negligible positional error. One of the firms producing these watches issued a guarantee of timekeeping of not more than one minute a month, the same rate guaranteed by the manufacturers of the tuning-fork watch (see page 263).

Some horological experts, however, expressed fears that there might be problems with these watches. They felt that it was one thing to use a fast rate for a stop watch that is run only for a short period, but quite a different matter to use it for a watch which ran continuously. The faster the train, they pointed out, the greater the force required to drive it, and therefore the greater the likelihood of wear.

These watches have not, however, in practice proved so fallible as the sceptics anticipated, perhaps because the dry lubrication used in the escapement successfully coped with the problem of wear. As a result of their proven reliability and their good performance more and more manufacturers have adopted the fast beat.

WATCH SIZES

Watch movement sizes are sometimes expressed in lignes, sometimes in millimetres. A ligne is equivalent to $\frac{1}{11}$ in. or 2·26 mm. The popular $10\frac{1}{2}$ ligne movement is therefore almost an inch in diameter. It is important to appreciate that there is a difference between a round and a shaped movement both of which have the same ligne size. A 5 ligne round movement, which is under half an inch in diameter, is a very small movement made by a limited number of specialist factories, and is an expensive movement to produce. A 5 ligne shaped movement, which is 5 lignes across, but some 8 lignes long, has appreciably bigger plates and all the components are relatively bigger so that it is less exacting and less expensive to produce. Ligne sizes are sometimes written with three dashes after the numeral, for instance 7½‴, and this sign is sometimes confused with the two dashes used to express inches.

JEWELLED LEVER AND PIN-PALLET

More pin-pallets than jewelled levers are still sold in the British market. This is because the pin-pallet is the cheaper of the two to produce, though the modern production methods now employed in the more progressive jewelled-lever producing factories have led to a narrowing of the price gap between the dearer pin-pallets and the cheaper jewelled levers.

The basic difference between the pin-pallet and the jewelled lever is, of course, that the one has steel pins on the arms of the lever which act on the teeth of the escape wheel, whereas the other has synthetic ruby pallets fitted into the lever arms. Synthetic ruby being much harder than steel, the pallets of the jewelled lever are much less likely to become worn, and wear here at the very heart of the movement is likely to have a disastrous effect on timekeeping. This, however, is not the only difference between these two classes of watch. There are good and bad pin-pallets, but the pin-pallet manufacturer is obviously concerned with making to a price, and therefore the standard of his components and of finishing will tend to be lower than those of a jewelled-lever manufacturer. But in justice to the better pin-pallet manufacturers it must be said that a well-made pin-pallet can be a better watch than some of the badly made jewelled levers on the market today. On the other hand the Swiss produce some pin levers that are unworthy of their watch industry.

WATERPROOF, ANTI-MAGNETIC AND SHOCK-RESISTANT

The terms 'waterproof', 'anti-magnetic' and 'shock-resistant' appear on the dial or on the back of many watches. The trouble with these terms is that they are not specific, they are merely relative.

Waterproof

A watch that is marked 'waterproof' may be suitable for wear by a skin-diver deep down below the surface of the sea, or it may be intended only to withstand a brief immersion. There has been an attempt to substitute the term 'water-resistant' for waterproof, but neither the public nor the trade as a whole have proved willing to substitute a meaningless euphemism for a statement of fact.

Watches certificated as waterproofed to withstand pressures of so many atmospheres, or to be waterproof at so many feet, present no great problem to the retail jeweller, but the many watches labelled 'waterproof' without any such guarantee may present difficulties. Customers, if not warned when buying such a watch, may well take the term at its face value and return the watch in disgust when the case leaks or they may sue under the Trade Descriptions Act.

The waterproof problem is further complicated because the waterproof glands which prevent water from seeping down the winding stem tend to wear after a time. Further, when waterproof watches are brought in for repair they are not always adequately tested before they are handed back to the customer. Many retail workshops, in fact, lack the apparatus necessary to carry out such testing.

Many people in the trade are concerned about this uncertainty because it could undermine public confidence in the waterproof watch. The possibility of legal trouble could also discourage jewellers from selling them. This would be a great pity for a waterproof is a very serviceable watch which the retailer should be able to recommend to any customer looking for a watch that will stand up to rough usage, or to a housewife who works in and around water for much of her day. This type of watch is indeed particularly saleable nowadays, for whereas a waterproof was at one time inevitably a bulky watch, this is no longer true. The replacement of the screw-back with a snap-on back, and the introduction of one-piece cases has meant that the modern waterproof can be as slim and as smart as a standard watch.

Anti-magnetic

Magnetic fields used to have disastrous effects on the timekeeping of a watch movement. The hairspring became magnetised, and the coils would stick together. This of course either stopped the watch or seriously affected the timekeeping. This problem has been largely overcome by the use of non-magnetic alloys for the hairspring, and nowadays most watches are marked 'anti-magnetic'. In a British Standard of 1963, tests for anti-magnetic watches were laid down. The watch it was suggested should be submitted 'to a vertical magnetic field of intensity not less than 60 oersteds for a minimum of 5 seconds' in two positions, after having been treated to dispel any residual magnetism.

This degree of resistance to magnetism is perfectly satisfactory for normal use, but the customer who works in high magnetic fields may need a special watch fitted with an inner capsule round the movement to protect it, and such special watches are available.

Shock-resistant

A balance staff which is unprotected is liable to damage if a watch is dropped. For this reason most modern watches are shock-protected. This protection usually consists of a spring device which allows the jewels, in which the balance pivots run, to move and which then returns them to their correct position. Again the British Standards Institution have laid down tests for shock-proofed watches. They say that: 'The daily rate of a watch shall be established, following which the watch shall be subjected to shock forces equivalent to those imposed by a fall (under the weight of its own case and movement and in an unprotected condition) from a height of 3 ft on to a level, solid hardwood floor or base.' The testing of the watch is to be carried out in two positions, and following the test: 'the watch shall not have sustained any internal damage to, nor displacement of, any parts; nor shall the daily rate have changed by more than 45 seconds.'

AUTOMATICS

The early history of the self-winding watch has already been mentioned. In the past 20 years it has ceased to be a mere novelty, and has become a standard, well-tried product, accounting for a very considerable percentage of the output of the watch industry of the world. One of the advantages of the self-winding watch is obvious. More people than one would ever dream forget to wind up their watch, and though the winding up may seem a very small chore, there are doubtless many people who are glad to be relieved of it. Another, and less obvious, advantage is that self-winding watches tend to be more accurate than button-wound ones. It is usually advocated that wearers of button-wound watches should wind them once a day. This brings us back to the problem which faced the first watchmakers, that a fully wound mainspring gives out more power than a mainspring that is wound down. This is not so important in a watch fitted with a lever escapement as it was with the old verge watches, but it does still have an appreciable effect on the performance of the watch. With a self-winding watch worn regularly, the mainspring is kept wound up, so any error due to power output variations is minimised.

Many self-winding watches which appeared in the immediate post-war period were wound by the action of a swinging weight that clunked backwards and forwards between two coiled buffer-springs, but this method of winding was superseded by one where the weight was free to swing through 360 degrees, and which wound the watch whether it was swinging in a clockwise or an anticlockwise direction (Fig. 10.6). Apart from the swinging weight the automatic work, nowadays mostly a self-contained detachable unit, usually

Fig. 10.6. Typical automatic movement incorporating a two-way winding system with the weight swinging through 360 degrees

consists of two reverser wheels and pinions making two-way winding possible, and some type of clutch device which allows the winding mechanism to 'slip' when the mainspring is fully wound.

The jewel bearings in which the pivot of the winding weight ran, gave some trouble in the early days, as they were inclined to crack when the watch was badly jarred. This problem was overcome in a number of ways, including the use of a spring arm for the weight. It was this problem which led one company to fit a tiny ball-bearing to their watches, the steel balls of which are so small they will float on water. This bearing proved highly successful, both in solving the breakage problem and in reducing friction, and a number of other manufacturers have now obtained licences to incorporate this bearing in their movements.

Some ball-races now incorporate synthetic ruby balls instead of steel balls. Many designs of automatic systems have been tried; some have proved successful and have remained in production, others have given trouble and have disappeared. One interesting system, aimed at making the automatic movement really slim, is the mini-rotor. This little rotor, which is only 1 in. in diameter, can be recessed in the movement, and as a result of using a heavy metal and a very ingeniously designed gearing, it provides quite adequate winding to keep the watch going in normal wear and to build up a sufficient reserve.

WATCHES FOR SPECIAL PURPOSES

This is the age of the special watch. Today hundreds of watches are made for timing sports and industrial operations, and it is impossible here even to list them. Most of them belong to one of three main types: the chronographs, the stop watches, or timers as they are usually called nowadays; and the time-elapse watches.

CHRONOGRAPHS

Customers sometimes confuse chronometers, which are very accurate timekeepers, with chronographs, which are watches that both tell the time and can be used for timing. Chronographs differ from stop

Fig. 10.7. Modern chronograph with subsidiary minute and hour dials and a sweep seconds indicator

watches in that the latter is a timer pure and simple, while the chronograph is also a timekeeper. When the user stops the hands on the timing dials he does not stop the watch.

Both wrist and pocket chronographs are made, and they usually have push-pieces on either side of the winding crown to stop, start, and return the timing hands on the subsidiary dials to zero (Fig. 10.7). These operations are performed through a complicated arrangement of cams and levers. The simplest chronographs have only a seconds hand traversing the ordinary dial which is calibrated for fifths of a second. Most, however, have two or three small dials, calibrated for seconds, minutes and hours. Some chronographs have a tacheometric scale which makes it easy to compare distance travelled and speed, and these of course are most useful to rally competitors. Then there are chronographs specially designed for those who do time and motion study and others for those who do chemical analysis and so on. There is, in fact, today, a chronograph made to time almost every human endeavour.

Good chronographs can never be made cheaply. They are made in specialist factories which have a relatively small turnover. The average chronograph contains 360 components as compared with 60–80 in a normal watch, and these components have to be made from very high grade steel of exacting specification, because they have to stand up to surprisingly big forces in relation to their size. Assembly too calls for more than ordinary care. Tolerances are very low, and dust the enemy of any watch movement is deadly in a chronograph mechanism.

TIMERS

The range of timers available today is even more formidable than that of chronographs. There are fifth of a second timers, tenth of a second timers, hundredths of a second timers. There are split second timers with two hands that can time two operations simultaneously, or compare the performance of two athletes, timers for television producers and timers for yachtsmen (Figs. 10.8 and 10.9).

All that a timer consists of is a clockwork mechanism with an escapement and a start, stop, and return to zero mechanism operated either by the winding crown or by push-pieces.

TIME-ELAPSE WATCHES

These watches which look almost as impressive as a chronograph are very popular with young people who never intend to make use of them, but like the timer and the chronograph they are designed as tools (Fig. 10.10). They are normal watches with a movable calibrated bezel round the outside of the dial. Their best-known application is to the diver's watch. A skin-diver wears a tank that supplies him with air for a known period. So he must be aware of how much time has elapsed since he dived. If the tank holds enough air for 20 minutes,

Fig. 10.8. A television timer

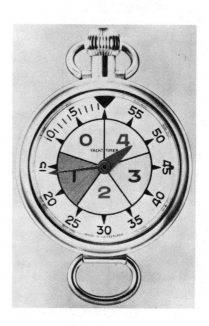

Fig. 10.9. A yachting timer

he sets the indicator mark of the time-elapse dial opposite the time shown on his watch at the time of diving. He can then see at a glance, when submerged, how many minutes of air he has left.

Some of these diver's watches have the time-elapse bezel protected

Fig. 10.10. Waterproof time-elapse watch which is also fitted with a day-of-the-month calendar

under the crystal so that it is less likely to stick due to sea-water corrosion. Some are also fitted with depth gauges.

Another application of the time-elapse watch is for timing the special stages on rallies.

CALENDAR WATCHES

These perhaps hardly rank as special watches, for they are nowadays almost as commonplace as automatics. The simple calendar watch shows the date through a small aperture in the dial, usually either at three o'clock or at six o'clock. The mechanism that makes this possible is fairly simple, consisting of a disc with figures from 1 to 31 inscribed on it, and this disc is geared to the hour wheel so it advances once in every 24 hours (Fig. 10.11). When calendars were first introduced setting them was somewhat laborious. The hands had to be rotated again and again through 24 hours until the right date showed in the aperture. Today, however, many of these watches have more sophisticated systems, and all that needs to be done is to turn the hands back and forth past twelve o'clock. Others are activated by the engaging of a third set of gearing by the winding crown.

Besides these simple calendars some manufacturers produce complicated calendar watches that also show the day of the week, the month, and even the phase of the moon. One or two specialist factories also produce perpetual calendar watches that go on and on, year in and year out, showing the correct date, making allowance

Fig. 10.11. The calendar mechanism added to many modern watches is relatively simple and does not add greatly to the cost

Fig. 10.12. Perpetual calendar watch

for 30-day and 31-day months, and leap years (Fig. 10.12). These marvels of horological engineering are very very costly.

ALARM WATCHES

Many of the watches made in the sixteenth and seventeenth centuries were fitted with alarm work, but the application of an alarm to the wrist watch was not achieved until some 15 or so years ago, when a Swiss company produced an alarm watch which they called the 'Cricket'. In this watch a tiny hammer hit a post attached to the back of the watch, the hammer being operated by a hammer-

Fig. 10.13. Parking timer

release mechanism working from the wheel train. Since then other sounding devices have been used, among them a circular wire gong.

The idea of producing these alarm watches was not so much to wake their owner in the morning as to remind him of appointments. They have, however, a new and more important application since parking meters have spread all over the towns and cities of the world. They serve to remind motorists that their time is up (Fig. 10.13).

THE CLOCK

Many spring-driven, and even a few weight-driven, clocks are still made and sold. One cannot help feeling, however, that these clocks which have remained virtually unchanged for centuries, and have served mankind admirably for those many years, will continue to decline in popularity. Each year that passes the electric clock represents an ever higher percentage of the output of the big clock-making factories here and in other European countries. For some reason people who did not buy electric watches because they were new and unknown and because they needed new batteries every year, are quite happy to buy battery-powered electric clocks, which are just as novel and have the same drawback.

There are various logical reasons for the popularity of the battery electric clock, however, of which one suspects the buying public are only vaguely aware. One is that it is possible to manufacture a battery electric movement with remarkably high timekeeping potentialities at the same cost as a 30-hour spring-driven clock, with a much inferior performance. And with the advent of transistors contact troubles, the main difficulty connected with early battery clocks, have virtually disappeared. Then a problem facing the buyer of a quality spring-driven clock is that the ever-increasing shortage of clock repairers must result in higher costs for servicing. The servicing of mechanical clocks will also inevitably take even longer to carry out.

SPRING-DRIVEN CLOCKS

Spring-wound clocks may well disappear eventually, but they are still with us. Many clock manufacturers indeed offer their models with a choice of two movements—spring-wound or battery electric.

Spring-wound clocks are usually either 30-hour or eight-day, and these categories are roughly equivalent to the pin-lever and jewelled-lever categories in watches. Again, however, as with watches there are great variations of quality in both categories, depending upon the degree of finish and the quality of materials and components used.

Mains electric clocks are still produced but represent an ever-decreasing percentage of total sales.

AUTOMATIC CLOCKS

There have been a number of attempts to remove one of the major disadvantages of the spring-driven clock, that of having to remember to wind it up every day, or every week. One well-known clock harnesses temperature change to this end. This clock has in it a vacuumised capsule, similar to that used in an aneroid barometer, which expands and contracts as the temperature rises and falls, and the expansion and contraction is used to wind the mainspring. A number of clocks fitted with photoelectric cells have appeared on the market and these have electronic circuitry which transforms light energy into electrical energy. The electrical energy is then used to wind the mainspring.

REPLACEMENT NOT REPAIR

The makers of clocks are not unaware of the parlous state of the clock repair trade, and some of them at least consider that factory-reconditioned replacement movements as an alternative to repairing are the inevitable answer to this problem. Indeed, with modern production methods the throw-away movement may even be the answer. It may well prove eventually to be cheaper just to discard the worn or damaged movement and fit a new one, rather than become involved in the handling charges, postage costs, and the cost of individual work to put the movement in working order again. One British firm has produced a movement for a cheap alarm fitted in a plastic container, which has been so designed that the whole movement can be easily removed from the case and a new one fitted in its stead. Many manufacturers of inexpensive mechanical alarms also accept the fact that the repair of movements is no longer economically feasible. It would be cheaper for the owner to buy a new clock.

CLOCK CASES

While discussing the history of clocks, it was pointed out that in the last quarter of the eighteenth century, the making of clock cases fell to the furniture industry, and since then the clock case has tended to be regarded as a piece of furniture, subject to the current fashion of interior decoration. Now that clock movements are very much smaller, the introduction of new materials and some new thinking are slowly changing all this. At least a few of today's designers are beginning to consider the clock as an instrument for telling the time, just as the gramophone is now thought of as an instrument for reproducing music, rather than a piece of furniture (Fig. 10.14). Some of the new clocks look much like the instruments in an aircraft cockpit or on the dashboard of a motor car, and this could well be the beginning of a new and logical trend. The majority of

Fig. 10.14. An example of the designer's growing tendency to treat the clock as an instrument rather than as a piece of furniture.

clock purchases are, however, influenced by women, and women tend to have a more romantic attitude to clocks than men. As a result, clocks such as the reproduction French carriage type tend to be the best sellers in the manufacturers' ranges.

DIALS AND HANDS

In a lecture to an audience of jewellers at a Council of Industrial Design weekend course, Mr Eric Bruton pointed out that an illogical situation has arisen in which we have clocks that would keep time to very close limits, but which are fitted with quite unreadable dials, or with dials where it is difficult to tell the time to the nearest minute. Silvered dials with gilt hands of almost equal length are common, and so are dials without minute marks. There are signs, however, that here again some designers are beginning to treat clock dials as the dials of instruments, and not just as an opportunity for enrichment, for wild flights of the imagination, or for an opportunity to impart a little bit of fashion to an old standby, but again women tend to call the design tune: the traditional dial, like the traditional case, is the most popular with the public.

CHAPTER 11

Electrical and Electronic Watches and Clocks

After four centuries it seems that the mechanical watch is likely to be superseded. Since work on the space programme gave birth to the first electronic watch, the Bulova Accutron, there have been important developments in miniaturised electronic circuitry. The most notable has been the evolution of the electronic chip. These chips look like tiny flakes of metal, but in fact incorporate a complex circuit; they have made possible both the pocket calculator and the solid-state watch.

The other important development has been the miniaturisation of quartz timekeeping technology. In 1880 the brothers Pierre and Jacques Curie discovered the piezo-electric effect in quartz. What this discovery amounted to was that if a quartz crystal is electrically impulsed it will oscillate at a regular rate. In the 1930s quartz clocks based on the Curies' discovery were built by the telecommunications industry, and in 1968 the first quartz wrist watches were shown in prototype form at the Basle Fair. Then in the early 1970s the quartz solid-state watch, i.e. a watch with no moving part whatever, made its appearance. It is these watches, as their price has come down and their reliability has increased, that are taking an increasing share of the world watch market.

THE ELECTRO-MECHANICAL WATCH

The first time that battery power, instead of the power of a coiled spring, was applied to a watch was in 1957, following the invention of electric cells the size of a shirt-button in about 1950. The first electric watch was the result of joint research by the Lip Company in France and Hamilton in the U.S.A. These watches had little commercial success because their timekeeping was not appreciably better than that of a spring-driven watch, the battery had to be changed annually and their reliability was unproven. The first really successful

262

electro-mechanical watch (that is, a watch which though employing an electronic time standard nevertheless contains mechanical parts) came on the market in 1960. This watch, the Accutron, was invented by the Swiss electronics engineer Max Hetzel. He employed as a time standard a tuning fork with a natural frequency of 360 cycles per second, kept vibrating by being impulsed by two coils. The vibrations of the tuning fork were converted into a mechanical drive by means of a small jewel-tipped index spring attached to one of the tines of the fork. This moved an index wheel forward one tooth at each vibration, that is every 1/360th of a second. The index wheel was a marvellous piece of engineering: with its 360 teeth it measured only one tenth of an inch in diameter. The coils used were wound with 30,000 feet of wire one fifth of the thickness of a human hair. The accuracy of the watch was 99·9977 per cent, and for the first time a watch manufacturer was in a position to guarantee the performance of the watches he sold. The watch, however, did suffer from small positional errors, that is to say it performed slightly differently depending on whether it was face up, face down or on its side. Its timekeeping could also be upset by shocks.

When Max Hetzel subsequently joined the Swiss Horological Electronic Centre he worked on the problem of eradicating positional error, using a different form of tuning fork; following an agreement on patent rights between Bulova and Ebauches S.A., the Swiss movement manufacturer, a tuning-fork watch, or 'sonic watch' as it is sometimes called, was produced by the Swiss firm. Bulova, who had the benefit of the Swiss research, subsequently introduced an improved version of the Accutron and later still a woman's version with an appreciably smaller movement.

Max Hetzel next joined Omega, and produced in 1973 an improved sonic watch that was resistant to shocks. A feature of the new watch is what I christened at the time 'Max's magic motor', which is used to translate the oscillation of the tuning fork into mechanical drive to turn the train wheels. It consists of a wheel without pinions, supported by oil in a metal box, the wheel both being impulsed and driving the train by means of an electro-magnetic drive.

The electric watch had also been developed during this period, Ebauches S.A. having produced in considerable quantities an electric watch with a magnetically impulsed balance wheel.

THE QUARTZ WATCH

The first quartz watches, produced almost simultaneously in Switzerland and Japan in 1968, were also electro-mechanical. The Swiss watches when submitted to the Neuchatel Observatory for testing proved to have an average error of only 0·21 seconds per day. The watches employed a bar-shaped quartz with a frequency of 8192 hertz, the frequency being converted by means of a binary circuit to one impulse per second. This impulse was used to drive a stepping motor, which impulsed the train and turned the hands on a normal analogue dial. The quartz, incidentally, was contained in a vacuumised metal box sometimes referred to as an 'oven'.

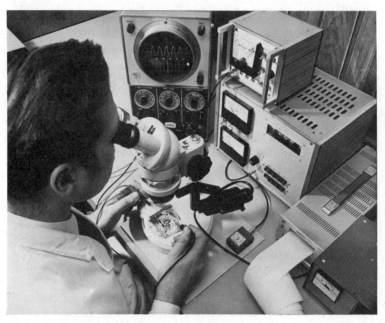

Fig. 11.1. As electronics invades the Swiss watch factories traditional processes are swept aside. The soldering iron becomes the vital tool of the craft and expensive equipment for testing circuits has to be bought. The photograph shows the mounting of a microcircuit in an electronic movement

It has been found in practice that the higher the frequency of the time standard the more accurate a timekeeper is likely to be. Very soon, therefore, the manufacturers of quartz watches introduced quartz crystals with frequencies higher than the original 8192 hertz. Omega in Switzerland and Smiths in Britain have both introduced megahertz quartz watches employing a lozenge-shaped quartz, which besides oscillating at a higher frequency is said to be more resistant to shock because of the method of attaching the terminals. The frequency of the Omega megahertz is 2,359,296 hertz and that of the Smith is 1,548,288 hertz. Most quartz watches, however, employ a quartz of much lower frequency, either 16,384 or 32,768, with the majority of manufacturers tending to favour the higher of the two, claiming that it provides greater accuracy. Many manufacturers of quartz watches claim an error of not more than one minute per year, however, irrespective of the frequency of the quartz they employ.

THE L.E.D. QUARTZ WATCH

In 1972 the next major development in quartz-watch technology took place, with the introduction by Pulsar in the U.S.A. of a solid-state

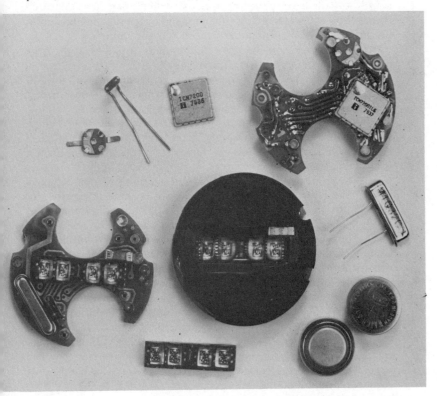

Fig. 11.2. Components of an L.E.D. quartz watch. Centre: assembled module. Below centre: L.E.D. display with epoxy bubbles that protect the diodes and magnify them. Below right: the two batteries that power the movement. Left: the printed circuit, mounted with the display and the quartz in its 'oven'. Above right: the quartz, and the printed circuit mounted with the C/MOS chip. Above centre: the C/MOS chip, and the light-ambient cell that dims or brightens the intensity of the readout to conserve power. Above left: the trimmer for adjusting the module. (By courtesy of Rotary)

quartz watch with a digital readout employing the L.E.D. (light-emitting diode) system, evolved for use in electronic instruments and calculators. These watches, containing printed circuits and chips, produce the time on demand at the press of a button, in the form of an illuminated readout behind a red crystal, and have since become commonplace.

Over a period of two years from 1972, during which a number of large U.S. electronics companies began producing the modules for these watches and a large number of firms became involved in the casing and marketing of them, the L.E.D. watch inevitably suffered some teething troubles. The performance of such watches depends largely on the electronic-chip quality; when they first appeared chip technology was still in its infancy, and out of any batch of chips produced only a small number proved reliable. Supplies of L.E.D. watches proved never to live up to the suppliers' promises, and a large proportion of those that were supplied gave trouble.

Today over 90 per cent of chips produced are said to be up to standard, although still from time to time for inexplicable reasons the producers, as they say, 'lose the recipe'. The design of the whole module has also become more sophisticated, and returns of many L.E.D. watches are now lower, certainly acceptable by watch standards generally. Some bad modules do, however, come on to the market (especially, it seems, from sources in the Far East), and the retailer is well advised to deal with established and reputable companies when buying these watches, especially because it is quite impossible for anyone but an electronics engineer with sophisticated equipment at his disposal to tell good modules from bad ones.

The introduction of the L.E.D. watch has a number of implications for the jeweller. It will essentially tend to reduce his repair business, because these watches will become increasingly reliable and of course do not need oiling and cleaning. Their owners will, however, have to visit their jeweller at least once a year to replace the two cells that power them. This will to some extent offset the loss of traffic through the jeweller's showroom resulting from repair business. In the event of the necessity for after-sales servicing, the jeweller will presumably return the watches to his suppliers so that they can either be trimmed to correct timekeeping errors or completely replaced, which is the only recourse should modules fail.

The price of L.E.D. watches has come tumbling down since their introduction, and this trend is likely to continue. There are only a handful of large electronics companies producing the modules and, as production comes to be counted in millions instead of thousands, inevitably the cost will come down. At the same time, as those who believe that L.E.D.s (or some other type of solid-state watch) will

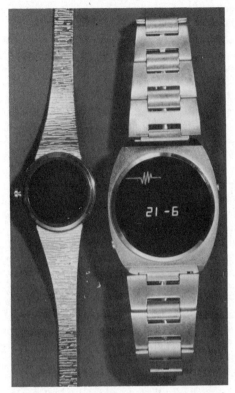

*Fig. 11.3. These two L.E.D. watches, one for men and
one for women, show the L.E.D. display lit up and the
appearance of the watch when the numerals are not illuminated. A button (or buttons) on the right of the dial acti-
vates the readout, a push piece on the left allows the time
and date to be adjusted*

entirely replace the mechanical watch are at pains to point out, the
cost of producing mechanical watches must rise.

The first L.E.D. watches to appear were what are now called two-
function L.E.D.s. They showed only the hours and the minutes. Since
then we have seen the emergence of the multi-function L.E.D. Five-
function watches were produced with a readout for hours and
minutes, a separate seconds countdown and a separate day-of-the-
month and month readout, usually programmed to take account of
months of different lengths. Another added function, the day of the
week, followed, while some manufacturers added an a.m. and p.m.
indicator and called this another function. There is even a multi-function L.E.D. watch and calculator combined on the market. At the

time of writing (1976) a number of alarm prototypes are in existence, as are L.E.D. chronograph prototypes. Also, because with micro-circuits and chips one can do almost anything in the electronics field, the idea of a combined watch and radio transmitter/receiver is being bandied about in the U.S.A., and a prototype wrist-television set is in existence. Some of these multi-function watches have a single but-ton, others two or more buttons to operate the display, and there are obviously arguments for and against the two types. Recently (1975) the British calculator manufacturers Sinclair have produced a low-cost L.E.D. watch with touch panels below the dial instead of buttons, and a number of American companies are experimenting with a time readout that is activated by a flick of the wrist.

One of the snags of the L.E.D. watch, in common with all battery-powered timekeepers, is the need to change batteries, and L.E.D. watches incorporating photo-electric cells (which charge an accumu-lator by converting light energy to electrical energy) are being pro-duced. These watches are, however, even more bulky than the rather portly early L.E.D.s. L.E.D. watches are in fact tending to be both slimmer and smaller, and the battery, small as it is, is all that stands in the way of the production of the wafer-thin or small-diameter L.E.D. The production of women's L.E.D. watches was only achieved at the price of a six-month battery, as against a twelve-month life for a man's watch used in moderation. In practice men who wear L.E.D. watches tend to exhaust their first two batteries within three to six months of purchase, but the second pair usually lasts the full year. Retailers are advised to point out this possibility to their cus-tomers at the time of purchase. Reports from the U.S.A. indicate that improvements in battery design are imminent, however.

THE L.C.D. QUARTZ WATCH

While manufacturers in the U.S.A. have been developing the L.E.D. readout, the Swiss and the Japanese have been working on the liquid-crystal type of display known as L.C.D. This system has the great advantage over L.E.D. that the display of the time is continuous. One does not have to press a button to read the time. The first L.C.D. readouts were not very successful. Not only were they impossible to read in all but ideal conditions of illumination, but they tended to fail entirely after about a year of use, the liquid crystals no longer responding to the electrical impulses that activated them. Brown Boveri, the Swiss firm who did much of the development work in liquid-crystal displays for watches, achieved considerable improvement to readability and greatly increased the life expectancy of their units, and also introduced multi-function units.

The newer L.C.D. displays have larger numerals that appear brighter as a result of the use of a better background tone. Many of the readouts also incorporate date and seconds countdown. The first day dates showed both the time and the date continuously but this was found to be confusing, and the latest versions have continuous

Fig. 11.4. L.C.D. readouts, showing on the right hours and minutes and on the left the time, the day of the week and the date. The basic arrangement of the liquid crystals can be seen in the figure '8'; from this any numeral from 1 to 9 can be produced by electronically impulsing different combinations of crystals

time displays with date and seconds countdown on demand. There is also a day date version in which an indicator below the days of the week is activated as the week progresses. The L.C.D. calendar watches, like the L.E.D.s, are programmed to change automatically at the month's end whether the month contains 31, 30 or 28 days.

There is considerable difference of opinion as to which system, L.C.D. or L.E.D., will ultimately find favour with the public. The production of lower-priced L.E.D. modules in the U.S.A. currently seems to favour the L.E.D., but further improvement of the L.C.D. system and the increasing mass-production of L.C.D. modules could redress the situation in favour of L.C.D.s. There are two other possibilities. The first involves the combination of the two systems, with an L.C.D. continuous time display and additional on-demand L.E.D. functions. (This double system has indeed already been employed by the Swiss chronograph manufacturers Heuer, whose 'Chronosplit' incorporates a tenth-of-a-second split chronograph displayed on light-emitting diodes.) The second, produced by an American firm Suncrux, is an L.C.D. analogue solid-state watch, on the dial of which

Fig. 11.5. L.C.D. and L.E.D. used in conjunction on this complex chronometer from Switzerland: hours and minutes are read out on continuous-display L.C.D., the time to one hundredth of a second is by on-demand L.E.D.

segments of an L.C.D. chapter-ring are activated to indicate the minutes, while an L.C.D. pointer indicates the hours. This dial is not particularly easy to interpret, but it does indicate the possibility of producing a solid-state watch that does not have the drawbacks of the digital display system. Many people find that it is difficult to obtain the information they require from a digital display. The time 10.47, for example, demands the wearer of a digital watch to make a calculation in order to know how long he has before his train or plane departs at 11 o'clock. The wearer of an analogue watch reads this off automatically.

It has often been said that the public are not interested in accuracy of the order that the quartz watch provides, and that to the average member of the public precision to within a few seconds a month is not meaningful. The great advantage of this degree of accuracy is, however, only appreciated by someone who has worn a quartz watch over a period. Quartz accuracy means not only that one can always depend on one's watch always being right, but that one does not have to alter it from one year's end to the next. The owners of quartz watches discover that they have been relieved of another small chore, in the same way that people became accustomed to the boon of not having to wind their self-winding watches. To wind a watch or set it rightly may seem a very small undertaking, but if one has been relieved of the task one never willingly goes back to it again.

ELECTRONIC CLOCKS

The rapid development of the electronic clock in the last twenty years was an indirect outcome of public disenchantment with the synchronous clock, resulting from the unreliability of the mains supply during and immediately after the war. In normal times the synchronous clock is both reliable and accurate, but in that abnormal period it could not be relied upon. So there was a return to the earlier idea of using a battery as a source of power. Battery clocks, in particular battery wall-clocks, soon became very popular, having the advantage over a mains clock of not needing an unsightly lead or a special socket. The early battery clocks had an inherent weakness, however. The make-and-break contact system was liable to failure due to oxidation or dirt. This led designers to explore the possibility of an electronic switching system, and this was achieved by employing a transistor. As a result the electro-mechanical clock came into existence and, unlike the electro-mechanical watch, was commercially an enormous success—so much so that in recent years a number of the major German clock factories in the Black Forest have given up producing mechanical clocks altogether.

Electro-mechanical clocks employed a balance impulsed by electro-magnets, and as time went on plastic wheels and pinions requiring no lubrication tended to replace metal ones. Apart from an annual battery change, therefore, these clocks usually needed no attention for years and were reasonably accurate.

The makers of clocks over the centuries have never ceased to strive for greater accuracy, and today's clockmakers are no exception. There were two ways in which this was most likely to be achieved, by a tuning fork or by a quartz crystal. Though the watchmakers had first opted for the tuning fork, the clockmakers initially ignored this possibility and went straight to quartz. Already in the 1930s quartz clocks had been used in the telecommunications industry; the first of them (following the first application of quartz to a clock by W. A. Morrison, a Canadian working for Bell Laboratories in the U.S.A.) consisted of a series of large cabinets filled with electronic circuits, occupying a sizable room. In the 1960s by using transistors and miniaturised circuits it became possible to produce a domestic quartz clock no

Fig. 11.6. Electronic clock with a digital indication

Fig. 11.7. Inside the case of a British-made mains-powered quartz digital clock. The digital display is provided by valves containing a stack of numbers which light up successively. Shown here are the printed circuit and the push buttons for setting the valves to time. This model shows hours, minutes and second

larger than a small mantel-clock. (Incidentally, the initial research that resulted in the first prototype domestic quartz clocks was carried out in order to produce a quartz ship's chronometer.) The first of the small quartz clocks had an analogue readout, but within a short time a solid-state digital quartz clock was produced, the readout being achieved by means of valves containing a stack of numerals which were lit up as a result of electronic impulses. One Swiss firm, however, produced a clock with an electronic analogue readout employing illuminated bars. In practice the demand for solid-state clocks with digital readouts has been relatively small, and by far the majority of quartz clocks so far produced have been of the electro-mechanical analogue type. If, however, the public becomes more accustomed to

Fig. 11.8. Inexpensive quartz clock movement made in Germany and used by a number of clock manufacturers

digital readouts as a result of the increasing popularity of the digital quartz watch, the quartz digital clock may well be the clock of the future.

The earliest quartz clocks were very expensive, but latterly prices have come down considerably and a number of German firms now produce quartz versions of electro-mechanical movements that add only a few pounds to the price of the clock. In 1974 and 1975 a number of German factories put battery-powered quartz movements into mass production. These, besides being relatively inexpensive, are also very sophisticated. They employ a lenticular crystal with a megahertz frequency, pushing 4, 194, 304 times a second, and a miniature circuit to reduce the frequency, similar to that used in the L.E.D. watch. This circuit impulses a stepping motor driving a plastic train to turn the hands on the dial.

With clocks, as with watches, the problem of producing a solid-state battery movement is to find a readout system that does not drain the battery. The choice lies between L.E.D., which needs to be activated and is therefore not particularly feasible for a clock, and L.C.D., which is still not easily readable in the poor light in which a clock is liable to be placed. It is, however, possible with a clock to use a mains supply and, by providing an emergency accumulator in case of mains failure, to make the clock totally reliable under all normal circumstances.

Fig. 11.9. The majority of quartz clocks being sold in Britain have traditional cases and analogue readout

Meanwhile, however, the Japanese have developed a very successful tuning-fork movement, which has proved both reliable and very accurate; this is being used by a number of British and Continental clock firms.

At the same time as these technical developments have been taking place the nostalgia fashion has resulted in the revival of interest in popular clock styles of the past. The long-case clock and weight-driven wall clocks have been in demand, while metal-cased clocks in the French carriage-clock style or designs based on seventeenth century bracket clocks have been the best sellers in recent years. In fact we have nowadays the anachronistic situation of quartz movements being fitted into carriage-clock cases, because there is little demand for clocks of modern design.

Glossaries

GEMMOLOGY—JEWELLERY—SILVERWARE
—HOROLOGY

*These Glossaries are not intended to be exhaustive
but contain terms which are commonly met in
descriptions of goods*

Gemmology

AMETHYST QUARTZ A massive variety of quartz with amethyst colouring.

AMORPHOUS Unlike a crystal an amorphous material does not have a definite internal structure.

ASTERISM The star-like phenomenon seen in various gems when they are cabochon-cut. Such stones are called star-stones, e.g. star-sapphire, star-ruby, star-rose quartz.

BAGUETTE A simple rectangular cut. Literally translated it means a 'rod'.

BAROQUE PEARL A pearl that is irregularly shaped.

BIREFRINGENCE Another term for double refraction.

BLISTER PEARL A pearly accretion attached to the shell, which is sometimes cut away to produce a half-pearl.

BOULE A mass of synthetic gem material in the form of a carrot, produced by the Verneuil process.

BRILLIANT-CUT The most popular cut for diamonds. A total of 58 facets are cut on the stone including the table and the culet, which last is nowadays optional.

BUTTON PEARLS Round-topped pearls with a flat base.

CABOCHON To polish a stone into the form of a dome. All star stones are 'cut' cabochon.

CAMEO A carved bas-relief. Cameos are carved both on gem materials such as the chalcedonies and on mollusc shells. The latter are properly called 'shell cameos'.

CARAT WEIGHT The standard (metric carat) used for weighing gems. The metric carat equals 200 milligrains (one-fifth of a gram).

CAT'S EYE An optical effect visible in cabochon gemstones: appears like a ray of light crossing the dome of a cabo-chon. The best known cat's eye is the chrysoberyl cat's eye The effect, caused by a series of short tubes or needles, is known as chatoyancy.

CHALCEDONY A micro-crystalline variety of quartz. Agate is chalcedony, where the colour is distributed in bands, and onyx is the straight-banded variety. Most black onyx is stained agate.

CHATOYANCY A band, or streak of light, which moves across the domed surface of a cabochon-cut stone. The phenomenon is known as cat's-eye effect and is due to the reflection of light from cavities or fibres within a stone. Observed in various gem species.

CLARITY The term used to describe the degree of freedom from inclusions of a diamond.

CLEAVAGE Certain gems cleave in definite directions, e.g. diamond has a perfect octahedral cleavage.

CONCHIOLIN Organic material (dark in colour) secreted by molluscs which produce pearls. Known also as conchine.

CRYSTAL A solid having an atomic structure arranged in orderly manner. There are seven crystal systems into which gems are divided.

DISPERSION A term for the 'fire' seen in transparent gems. Due to the ability of faceted gems to separate the colours of the spectrum when light is refracted and reflected within them.

DOUBLE REFRACTION The splitting of a ray of light into two rays, when it enters certain gems belonging to crystal systems other than the cubic. In crystals of the cubic system, and in amorphous substances, light is refracted but continues as a single ray.

DOUBLET A stone composed of two or

277

more pieces of gem material cemented together. Sometimes pigment is included in the cement layer with the object of using inferior material to simulate an expensive stone.

ESSENCE D'ORIENT Name given to a fish-scale preparation used in production of imitation pearls.

FABULITE A common trade name for strontium titanate.

FACET A flat polished area on a cut gemstone, hence a faceted stone.

FEATHER Name given to inclusions in gems (especially sapphires) which are like feathers in appearance. They are layers of crystalline and liquid inclusions.

FIRE-MARKS Hair-like cracks on facets of gems caused by overheating during cutting and polishing.

FOUR C'S An expression evolved to describe the four factors which influence the value of a diamond—colour, clarity, cut and carat weight.

FLUX FUSION A method of producing synthetic emeralds.

FRESHWATER PEARLS Pearls found in mussels in rivers.

GOODS A term commonly used by stone dealers to describe the stones they buy and sell.

GRAIN The pearl grain is one-fourth of a carat.

HARDNESS The usual scale of hardness used in the jewellery trade is the one introduced by the scientist F. Mohs. The scale is:

Diamond	10	Apatite	5
Corundum	9	Fluorspar	4
Topaz	8	Calcite	3
Quartz	7	Gypsum	2
Feldspar	6	Talc	1

The scale is arbitrary and the difference between the hardness of diamond (10) and sapphire (9) is greater than that between that of sapphire and talc (1). There are also intermediary figures, e.g. emerald about $7\frac{1}{2}$, chrysoberyl $8\frac{1}{2}$.

HEAT TREATMENT Many stones have their colour altered by heat treatment. Well-known examples are the production of white zircon, a popular diamond simulant, from brown zircon. Most commercial citrine is heat treated amethyst, and most blue aquamarine is the result of heat treating green aquamarine. Most tanzanites are brown when found; the blue

coloration results from heat treatment.

INCLUSIONS Most gems contain inclusions which may be minerals, liquid or gas-filled libella (bubbles). Diamond often contains inclusions of carbon, garnet, ilmenite and others.

INTAGLIO A seal stone into which a monogram or device has been incised is described as intaglio cut.

LAP A revolving circular disc which can be loaded with abrasive, against which gemstones are held to produce facets. A lapidary is a cutter of coloured stones.

LEVERIDGE GAUGE The most accurate type of gauge for estimating the carat weight of a gemstone by measurement.

LOUPE A small magnifying glass.

LUSTRE This is the surface brilliance of a stone. It depends upon the amount of light reflected from the surface, which is governed by the degree of polish and the hardness. There are various types of lustre, among which are: adamantine, as in diamond; vitreous or glassy, as in ruby and sapphire; resinous, as in amber; waxy, as in turquoise; pearly, as in pearl.

MAKE A term describing the cut of a diamond. A stone will be less valuable if it suffers from faults of make.

MARQUISE Boat shaped. This is a fashionable variation on the brilliant-cut for diamonds.

MATRIX The rock in which a mineral is contained. For instance, ruby is commonly found in a matrix of Zoisite, and the matrix containing the ruby is often slabbed and polished or carved into bowls.

MILÉE Small stones less than $\frac{1}{4}$ carat in weight. A term usually applied to diamonds.

MINERAL An inorganic substance, hence gem minerals as distinguished from organic gems such as pearls and jet.

MIXED-CUT A mixture of brilliant-cut above the girdle and step-cut below the girdle used for coloured stones.

MOTHER-OF-PEARL Material obtained from the inside part of the shell of certain large molluscs.

NACRE Substance consisting mainly of carbonate of lime, which is secreted by certain molluscs. A pearl is composed of nacre.

NATURAL As found in nature. A natural stone rather than a man-made synthetic.

ONYX MARBLE (correctly called MARBLE)

Banded calcite. Not a true onyx, which is a form of crypto-crystalline quartz.

PASTE The glass used for imitation stones.

PAVILION The part of a cut gemstone below the girdle, hence pavilion facets.

PIPE A mass of rock that has solidified in the neck of a volcano, for example the famous diamond pipes of South Africa consisting of 'blue ground'.

PLAY OF COLOUR An effect seen in opal and labradorite, due to interference or scattering of light from thin platelets or spheres near surface of stone.

REFRACTION When a ray of light entering a transparent or translucent stone is bent from its normal path. The refractive index of a stone is a measure of the degree to which light is bent when entering or leaving it. Refraction, and internal reflection, of light in a properly proportioned stone accounts for its 'fire' (see Dispersion).

RHINESTONE A name sometimes given to glass imitations of gems having a slightly iridescent effect.

ROSE-CUT An early cut in which the base of the stone is polished flat and the top has triangular facets cut on it and is pyramidal in profile.

SINE OF AN ANGLE The ratio in a right-angled triangle between the side opposite the angle under consideration and the hypotenuse. Important definition for ascertaining refractive indices of gems.

SOUDÉ STONES French term for soldered. Is usually applied to composite stones (e.g. beryl- or quartz-crown and base with coloured layer between) imitating

emerald. Another version is produced from synthetic white spinel.

SPECIFIC GRAVITY The ratio of the density of a substance to water. The measurement of specific gravity of gemstones is one of the methods used to identify them.

SPECTROGRAPHIC ANALYSIS Analysis of the spectrum produced by a stone in order to identify it.

STAR A rayed effect caused by light reflected from inclusions in a gemstone.

STEP-CUT A cut in which the facets are parallel to the girdle.

STRIAE Another name for growth lines (usually straight) seen in natural gems, and the usually curved growth lines in synthetic gems.

SYNTHETIC A man-made stone. Some synthetics like synthetic corundum closely resemble natural stones in their chemical composition and physical properties. Others, like yttrium aluminate, have no counterpart in nature and should be called simulants.

TABLE The large facet on the top of a stone, parallel with the girdle. Also, the facets cut above the girdle of a stone are described as table facets.

TRANSPARENCY Measure of light penetration in substances. There are transparent stones, semi- or partly transparent, translucent stones through which only some light passes and opaque stones through which no light passes.

WHITE A quite inaccurate adjective used to describe diamonds of high quality, for example 'blue-white'. Such stones are not white but almost colourless, tinted with blue or more often yellow.

Jewellery

AIGRETTE A gem-set head ornament in the form of a plume, worn to one side of the hair.

AJOUR Any setting which enables the pavilion facet of a gem to be seen.

ALBERT A slender chain in precious metal for men's evening wear. Women wore them as guards or muff chains. Named after Prince Consort to Queen Victoria.

ALLOY A metal compound resulting from melting two or more metals together. For example, carat golds are alloys of gold, silver, copper, etc.

ALLUVIAL A metal or gemstone which has been transported from the matrix in which it was formed, usually by water, and is found in an alluvial deposit.

AMULET An ornament worn to protect the wearer from malign influences. The Ancient Egyptians invoked the protection of their gods by depicting them on the jewels they wore.

ARABESQUES Flowing leaf and scroll work, often in low relief.

BANDEAU A narrow head ornament, usually set with gems.

BASSE-TAILLE A form of enamelling in which the surface of metal is recessed to varying depths to receive enamel.

BEADING Round grains or beads formed by a special tool to secure a gem in its setting. Often called millegrain.

BEZEL A thin piece of metal inside the shutting edge of a box. A name given to the surround of metal which secures glass of a clock or watch. The name is also given to the rub-over setting of some rings, and to certain facets in brilliant-cut diamonds.

BOX SETTING A closed form of setting in which a gem is enclosed in a 'box'. The edges of the metal box are pressed on to the girdle of the stone.

BRAZING Another term for hard soldering.

BROACH A tool used for shaping, trimming or enlarging holes.

CAGE-BACK SETTING A gem setting which is cage-like. Often used for cluster rings.

CALIBRE-CUT Stones cut to a special shape to fit a design.

CANNETILLE WORK Gold, sometimes silver, wire-work used for nineteenth century jewellery.

CAMEO A carved gem, or shell, in which the carved design stands out against a darker or lighter background.

CARTOUCHE An ornament in the form of a paper scroll, often used as a surround for a coat of arms.

CHAINS Curb or cable: solid or hollow, circular or oval links slightly twisted. Fetter: long links. Fetter and trace: long links with smaller oval links. Fetter and three: long links separated by three short links. Prince of Wales: U-shaped links soldered in overlapping style. Trace: equal-sized oval links.

CHAMPLEVÉ Recesses gouged out of metal—a ground removed process. The recesses are filled with enamel.

CHANNEL SETTING Metal setting holding stones on two sides only.

CHATELAINE Long chains worn by women for carrying keys, seals, watches, sewing cases and other small objects. A large hook behind the top of the ornament was inserted over the waistband.

CHENIER A name for a joint tube.

CIRE PERDU Lost-wax process of casting.

CLIP A piece of jewellery similar to a brooch, but attached by means of a spring clip instead of with a pin.

CLOISONNÉ Strip is soldered on to metal to create divisions, or cloisons, into which is placed enamel or stones.

COLLET The setting of a stone.

CROWN Upper part of a cut gem.

DAMASCENE An art of decorating a metal by inlaying it usually with a more precious one. Used on sword blades.

DIAMANTÉ An outmoded name for white paste used for imitation jewellery.

DIE The tool used to form a piece of metal in a stamp. Hence die-sinking, meaning to make a die for die-stamping.

DUCTILITY The property of a metal that allows it to be drawn out to form wire.

ELECTRUM A natural alloy of gold and silver. Many ancient wares were made from electrum.

ENGINE-TURNING A machine-engraving process for all-over decoration of a metal surface. Popular forms are 'barley', 'foxhead' and 'straight line'. At some periods it was fashionable to lay translucent enamel over engine-turned surfaces.

ENGRAVING Decorating metal by cutting lines into the surface with a sharp graver.

FILIGREE Ornamentation of fine twisted wire.

FINDINGS Semi-manufactured small parts of jewellery such as settings, catches, galleries, wires, and snaps.

FLANGE A reinforcing rim inside a bezel which acts as a bearing for a gem.

FOIL A thin piece of metallic substance placed at the back of an imitation or natural gem to emphasise its brilliance, or to impart colour to a stone.

GALLERY A decorative border.

GILDING METAL A base metal alloy, mainly of copper (80 to 90 per cent) and zinc (10 to 20 per cent).

GILT The application of a thin layer of gold to a base metal, i.e. mercurial gilding. Nowadays, gilding is invariably carried out in a plating bath.

GIRANDOLE EARRINGS Triple pendant earrings.

GOLD FILLED An American term used to describe rolled-gold.

GOLD PLATING The covering of base metal with a skin of gold. This is done today, electrolytically, in a plating bath.

GRANULATION Individual grains of gold used to decorate jewellery.

GUARD An old name for a long chain.

GUARD RING A ring worn to prevent loss of a more valuable ring.

GYPSY RINGS AND GYPSY SETTING Wide gold ring usually with single diamonds embedded in it. Hence 'gypsy setting'. Effect of being deeply set often increased by an engraved star whose points spread out from the stone.

INTAGLIO Opposite of cameo. A carved design hollowed out of a gem or gem material.

JUMP-RING A wire ring which can be opened to allow another ring to be attached. Commonly used for charms.

LEMEL Sweepings from a jewellery workshop that are melted and re-refined.

LUNATE Crescent-shaped.

MALLEABILITY The physical property of metal that allows it to be stretched by hammering or rolling. Gold is the most malleable of all metals.

MARCASITE A disulphide of iron. Not so common in nature as pyrite, another disulphide of iron which is usually called 'marcasite' in the jewellery trade.

MARQUISE RING Pointed oval shape.

METAL CORE A term formerly used to describe a form of rolled gold. Not acceptable to assay offices.

MILANESE Small links of chain interwoven to form a ribbon effect in the form of a mesh.

MIZPAH RINGS Letters MIZPAH were engraved, or left in relief, on broad gold rings. The word has a biblical reference.

MOUNT The metal part of a piece of jewellery before the stones are set into it. Hence, the mounter is the man who produces the jewellery into which the setter inserts the stones.

NIELLO WORK Incisions cut into metal which are filled with a soft dark-grey compound composed of lead, silver and copper with borax and sulphur. In modern niello the ground surrounding the design is filled in rather than the design itself. In cheaper goods the niello is merely painted on as a background and recesses are not cut into the metal.

PARURE A matching suite of jewellery.

PAVÉ A number of stones set flush with the metal to produce a paved effect.

PENDANT An ornament that hangs from a chain or a pin.

PICKLE SOLUTION Acid diluted with water used for cleaning purposes such as removing coating of oxides formed during annealing.

PINCHBECK An alloy of copper (83 parts) and zinc (17 parts) invented by Christopher Pinchbeck, a London watchmaker (1670–1732). His metal, which was gold coloured, was used for watch cases, jewellery and trinkets.

PIQUÉ D'OR Design formed by driving small gold rods into tortoiseshell or ivory.

PLIQUE À JOUR A rare open form of enamelling. Enamel is laid on a temporary metal ground with colours separated by wires. After heating, the enamel becomes separated from the ground.

REFINING The processes of removing impurities from a precious metal.

RIVIÈRE Gem-set necklaces, with each gem in its own collet graduating in size to a central gem.

ROLLED GOLD Gold is simulated by bonding a block of gold to a thicker block of copper and rolling out the bimetallic block to form sheet from which jewellery and watch cases are made.

SAUTOIR Long ropes of pearls ending with two long tassels of pearls.

SETTER The craftsman who secures stones in a mount.

SHANK The part of a ring that encircles the finger and to which the settings for the stones are attached.

SHOULDER The upper part of a ring shank near the setting which is often decorated.

SLEEPER RING A thin gold ring used to keep open the hole after an ear has been pierced for earrings.

SNAKE CHAIN Often referred to as Brazilian chain. Small metal cups joined to form a flexible chain.

STRASS A name applied to paste or glass imitation stones. Derived from its inventor Josef Strass.

TOUCHSTONE A block of basalt, black quartz or ceramic material. Used for testing metals by the comparison of streaks produced by rubbing the metal on the stone with those produced by needles of known quality.

TRANSLUCENT Passing light imperfectly. For example, translucent enamel.

Silverware

ACANTHUS ORNAMENT A leaf-like decoration derived from classical architecture. Often seen on eighteenth century silver.

ANNEALING Keeping metal in a malleable condition by heating and cooling after work hardening has taken place.

ANTHEMION Ornament introduced by the Adam brothers into England after the discovery of it on the walls of Herculanium. It consists of a stylisation of honeysuckle flowers.

APPLIQUÉ Applied ornament.

BALUSTER From the balusters of a classical balustrade. Used to mean a complex curved form such as is found on the stem of an early eighteenth century candlestick, i.e. baluster candlesticks.

BAROQUE ORNAMENT Ornament inspired by Renaissance architecture. Used on 16th, 18th and 19th century silverwares.

BAYONET JOINT Consists of two projecting lugs fixed to the top half of a cylindrical part, and engaged in two notches in the lower half. Used for casters, cruets, etc.

BEAKERS Normally straight-sided drinking vessels. Some have slightly everted lips.

BLACKJACKS Waxed and blackened leather drinking vessels, somewhat like riding boots, with a silver mounted rim and handle. Mostly date from the seventeenth century. They vary in height from about 7 to 15 in., and hold between a quart and a gallon. Large blackjacks may originally have been used for carrying beer or ale from the cellars.

BLEEDING BOWLS Small shallow silver bowls used by surgeons between about 1670 and 1720. They have bulging sides, a flat everted rim, and a single, pierced, flat handle.

BRITANNIA METAL An alloy used for hollowares consisting of approximately 93 per cent tin, 5 per cent antimony and 2 per cent copper. Wares made of Britannia metal are usually sold with an electroplated deposit of silver on them. Britannia metal is also known in the trade as 'white metal', and sometimes as 'Vickers metal', after James Vickers who is supposed to have first used it to produce tea-pots, spoons, etc., about 1780.

BUFF A cloth or leather mop used for polishing, hence 'to buff' a piece of silverware.

BURNISH To impart a bright finish with a hardened steel tool.

CANDELABRUM A candlestick with two or more branches.

CARTOUCHE An area of plain silver surrounded by ornamental designs to have a coat of arms engraved or chased on it.

CASTER A vessel for holding and scattering pepper, salt, or sugar. The first casters made their appearance after the restoration of Charles II. They consist usually of a body with a separate pierced and domed cover through which the contents can be cast upon food. The method of joining the cover to the body is mostly by means of a bayonet fixture or of a snap-in rim. Screw tops are not common. In the eighteenth century casters were often made in sets of three—two small and one larger. Other types of caster are the spice dredger said, probably erroneously, to have been used in the kitchen. This is fitted with a loop handle on the side, a style still sometimes used for small modern pepper casters. There is also the muffiner, a small caster, often octagonal in form, for spreading cinnamon on hot buttered muffins.

CHASING Decoration applied with a hammer and punch. Repoussé-chased means raised decoration to which the detail has been applied by the chaser. Cast-chasing is a chased up casting.

CHOCOLATE POTS First made after the introduction of drinking chocolate from the West Indies at the end of the seventeenth century. They are rare, and since coffee- and chocolate-pots conformed to much the same shape, distinction between them is often very difficult. Many chocolate-pots were provided with a small additional lid in the cover through which the stirrer (molinet) could be inserted.

COASTER A wine bottle holder. The first coasters date from the late eighteenth century when it was found convenient to place wine bottles in a stand (usually of silver with a wooden base) to protect the table top. The base is usually covered with baize. Pairs were not uncommon, and sometimes two coasters were mounted on a stand on wheels, when they were known as wine wagons or double coasters.

CREAMERS A vessel made to hold cream.

CUT-CARD WORK Form of applied ornamentation consisting of shapes cut from thin sheets of silver and applied to silver articles.

DAMASCENING Method of decoration by inlaying with gold or silver.

DISH RINGS. Usually of Irish make (though the earliest known example was made in England). They served as holders for dishes, and were probably first intended to protect the table from the heat of the dish. Most are spool-shaped with intricately pierced motifs decorating the sides.

EPERGNE A centrepiece for a table. In medieval and Tudor days the importance of a guest accorded him a position above or below the salt which was placed before the host. The use of the great salt died out with dining in the great hall, but the idea of a centrepiece was retained in some households, and towards the end of the eighteenth century the large centrepiece was reintroduced from France. Many of these centrepieces incorporated candelabra and fruit bowls, some even casters and cruet bottles.

FINIAL The ornament topping a piece of silverware. For example, urn finials were placed on the top of Adam silverwares.

FLUTING Vertical channelling used on silverware.

GADROON A lobed border, looking like a series of blobs. Used on silver of the William and Mary period, and at the beginning of the nineteenth century.

HOLLOWARE Dishes, cups, etc., are described as hollowares, spoons and forks as flatwares and knives as cutlery, though this last term is frequently applied also to spoons and forks.

INLAY The cutting away of a metal surface and then infilling usually with a metal or other material of a different colour.

LOVING CUP An urn-shaped cup with two handles.

MAZER A wooden bowl with a silver mount round the rim. Made in the fifteenth or sixteenth century.

MONTEITHS Bowls with a notched rim, which is usually removable. Called, supposedly, after the Scotsman who invented them. The rims were usually elaborately ornamented with scrolls and cherub heads. Made in the late seventeenth and early eighteenth centuries, they were probably used for punch.

OLD SHEFFIELD PLATE Plate made from bi-metallic sheet produced by bonding a block of silver to a block of copper and rolling it down.

PARCEL-GILT An old term meaning 'partly gilt'.

PICKLE SOLUTION Various acids (nitric, hydrochloric, sulphuric) in water, used for removing films of oxide and sulphide from surface of metals.

PIERCING Decoration that is produced by cutting through the metal, originally with a hammer and punch and later with a piercing saw or with press-tools.

PLACE SETTING The cutlery and flatware necessary to set one place at a table. Nowadays, some manufacturers offer their cutlery and flatware boxed as place settings.

PLANISHING Evening out the hammer marks on a hand-raised silver vessel with a planishing hammer.

PLATE A term correctly used to describe silverwares, but 'silver plate' is a term frequently used, incorrectly, to describe silver-plated wares.

PORRINGER Small two-handled bowls introduced about 1650. Some were provided with covers which could be reversed to form a small dish.

QUAICH A shallow bowl with straight handles, of Scottish origin.

REED A pattern often seen on spoons and forks consisting of narrow convex ridges.

REPOUSSÉ WORK Relief decoration hammered up from the back. Detail was added by chasing—hence repoussé-chased.

SCONCE Wall ornament to which candle holders were attached.

SNUFFER Scissor-like implement used for putting out candles.

SPINNING Producing hollowares by forcing metal over a chuck in a lathe.

STANDING SALT A tall salt used as a centrepiece in the sixteenth and seventeenth centuries.

STERLING A silver alloy which is 925/1000 silver.

STIRRUP CUPS These are sometimes still handed to the huntsman while he is on horseback. They have no foot, and are often shaped as a horse's head, fox's head or hound mask.

TAZZA Italian word meaning 'cup'. Often applied incorrectly to flat dishes supported on central stem. The word 'cup' is preferable to tazza.

VINAIGRETTE Small box for containing aromatic vinegar soaked in a sponger.

WAITER A small tray, often footed.

WINE FUNNEL Wine funnels and wine funnel stands were made in silver towards the end of the eighteenth century. The funnel is tapered and bent at the end to direct the stream against the side of the vessel into which the wine was poured, so avoiding undue agitation of the liquid.

Horology

ARBOR An axle in a watch or clock.

AUTOMATIC A self-winding watch.

BALANCE The controller used in watches and clocks. Through the escapement it locks and unlocks the gears to move the hands. The balance is impulsed by the escapement.

BALANCE SPRING The spring which causes the recoil of the balance wheel. Often called the hairspring.

BALANCE STAFF The axle or arbor of a balance.

BANJO CLOCK A clock in the form of a banjo, a style very popular with American makers in the nineteenth century.

BARREL A brass drum holding the mainspring of a watch or a spring-driven clock.

BEAT A normal watch beats 18,000 times an hour, or 5 times a second. The new 36,000 train watches beat 36,000 times an hour.

BEZEL The metal rim holding the crystal of a watch.

BOB The lump of metal on the end of a pendulum.

BRIDGE A metal arch supporting the arbor of a train-wheel or the staff of a balance—hence balance-bridge.

CENTRE-SECONDS A seconds hand attached to the pinion at the centre of the dial of a watch or clock. Sometimes called 'sweep-seconds'.

CHAPTER RING The ring calibrated for hours and minutes which allows the time to be read off.

CHAPTERS The hour marks on a chapter ring.

CHATELAINE An ornamental chain from which a watch was hung. Originally, the chain worn by the chatelaine of a castle from which her keys were suspended.

CHRONOGRAPH A combined timekeeper and timer. The timing mechanism can be stopped and started without interfering with the watch mechanism.

CHRONOMETER A name which horologists would like to reserve for timekeepers fitted with a detent escapement. Nowadays, a name commonly applied to any watch certificated by an observatory or testing bureau.

COCK Like a bridge, but supported only at one end. A balance cock supports the balance staff.

CROWN The serrated button used for winding and setting the hands of a watch.

CRYSTAL Commonly used to describe a plastic watch 'glass'.

CURB PINS Two pins placed on either side of the outer end of a hairspring. They can be moved by moving the index, and in so doing the length of the hairspring is altered and the timekeeping of the watch can be corrected.

EBAUCHE All the parts of a watch movement other than the escapement, balance, jewels and springs. Ebauches S.A. is the giant Swiss company, with many factories, that produces the ebauche for the hundreds of Swiss assembly plants.

ELECTRONIC CLOCK A term loosely used for any clock containing a transistor. A true electronic clock has electronic circuits instead of mechanical gearing. The solid-state clock is a true electronic clock.

END STONE A flat disc of synthetic corundum placed behind a jewelled bearing. Sometimes called a cap jewel, it takes the end thrust of a pivot. The end stones on the balance pivots are spring loaded to provide shock protection.

286

ESCAPE WHEEL The wheel which the pallets of the escapement stop and release.

ESCAPEMENT The mechanism which controls the rate of a watch or clock. In a jewelled-lever watch, the escapement consists of a lever with a square-sectioned synthetic corundum pallet in each arm of the fork, and a wheel with L-shaped teeth on which these pallets act.

FUNCTION A term used to describe the various readouts available on an electronic watch. An hour readout is one function, a minute readout another and so on. A five-function watch might display the hours, minutes, seconds, day of the month and month.

FUSÉE A cone-shaped component with grooves cut in it. A length of gut or chain, attached to the mainspring, is led round the grooves to equalise the power output of the mainspring. Still used for marine chronometers.

GRANDFATHER CLOCK Another name for a long-case clock.

GRANDMOTHER CLOCK A smaller version of the grandfather clock.

HAIRSPRING Another name for the balance spring.

HERTZ A measure of oscillation, i.e. times per second. Quartz crystal oscillations are expressed in hertz. Oscillations of a 'megahertz' quartz crystal are measured in millions of hertz per second.

IMPULSE PIN The ruby pin fixed to the fork of the escapement; it impulses the balance.

INDEX The regulator which moves the curb pins that alter the length of the hairsprings.

ISOCHRONISM Occupying equal time. A pendulum or a balance is described as isochronous if the time of its swing does not vary whatever the arc of the swing.

JEWEL A watch or clock bearing made of a hard gemstone. Nowadays, jewels are made from synthetic corundum. The jewel acts as an oil reservoir and also reduces wear.

JEWELLED LEVER A watch with a jewelled-lever escapement.

KEYLESS MECHANISM The gearing by which a manually wound watch is wound.

L.C.D Liquid-crystal display—a continuous readout system applied to solid-state watches. The liquid crystals arranged as segments of a figure '8' become visible as a result of electronic impulses.

L.E.D. Light-emitting diodes—a method of digital readout. The diodes light up as a result of electronic impulses, displaying numerals composed of dots or lines. Such displays are produced by the wearer of an L.E.D. watch pressing a button, or activating the readout in some other way. This is necessary to conserve the limited battery power.

LIGHT CLOCK A clock fitted with photoelectric cells. The light energy absorbed by these cells is translated into electrical energy and this is used to wind the clock.

LIGNE A measure of the size of a watch movement. It is a measure of diameter, a ligne being the equivalent of just under 2·256 millimetres.

LUG The ears on a watch case which support the lug pins to which the strap is attached.

MAINSPRING The coil spring which provides the power to drive a watch or clock mechanism.

OUT OF BEAT A watch in which the tick is alternately loud and soft because the action is not symmetrical.

PALLET The part of the escapement that detains and releases the escape wheel. In a jewelled-lever movement the pallets are 'jewelled' with synthetic ruby. In a pin-lever the pallets consist of steel pins.

PENDULUM A weight swinging under the influence of gravity.

PERPETUAL CALENDAR A calendar watch or clock which automatically corrects itself for months of different length and for leap years.

PINION An arbor on which teeth have been cut which mesh with the teeth of the wheels of a watch or clock train.

PIN-PALLET A watch escapement having steel pins instead of jewelled pallets attached to the forks. Sometimes called a pin-lever.

PIVOT The end of an arbor or staff. The part which runs in the bearing.

PLATE A brass disc, or plate, with holes in it which forms the frame of a watch or clock.

PLATFORM ESCAPEMENT An escapement mounted on its own platform. Commonly used for small clock movements.

POISE   It is necessary to poise a balance wheel by removing metal from parts of the rim or the screws, so that it will run absolutely flat. An out-of-poise balance results in serious positional errors.

POSITIONAL ERRORS   The time keeping of a watch varies with its being placed with its dial up or its dial down, its winding crown up or its winding crown down. These variations are called positional errors. The main reason for the accurate timekeeping of the 36,000 train is that the faster the beat of a watch the smaller the positional errors.

PUSH PIECE   The push buttons which start, stop and return to zero the timing hands on a chronograph or timer.

RATE   The amount by which a watch or clock loses or gains.

REGULATING   Adjusting a watch or clock to improve its rate.

REPEATER   A clock or watch with a mechanism which could be activated to make the striking mechanism repeat the hour and quarters of its last strike. This device was used when a lamp or candle had to be lit before a clock, or watch, dial could be read at night.

ROSCOPF   The name still used on the Continent for pin-pallet watches. Roscopf made cheap watches in Switzerland in the middle of the nineteenth century.

ROTOR   The eccentric weight in an automatic watch which swings when the wearer moves his arm, and winds the watch through a series of gears. Also part of an electric clock.

SELF-WINDING WATCH   Today, usually called an automatic. A watch with a pivoted weight which swings when the wearer moves, and winds the mainspring through a series of gears.

SET-HANDS   The mechanism which makes it possible to move the hands of the watch without interfering with its movement.

SHOCK ABSORBER   A method of protecting the balance staff from damage by fitting springs behind the end stones to absorb shocks.

SKELETON WATCH OR CLOCK   A watch or clock with pierced plates which allow the action of the movement to be seen.

SOLID STATE   Without moving parts. An L.E.D. watch is an example of a solid-state watch. A quartz watch with hands is not solid-state, because it has a gear train to impulse the hands.

SPLIT SECONDS TIMER   A timer with two seconds hands. One hand can be stopped by pressing a push piece. When the push piece is pressed again this split seconds hand will catch up with the other one. Allows the performance of two athletes to be timed simultaneously.

STOP WATCH   A timer which has no timekeeping mechanism. It is used for sport and industry.

SYNCHRONOUS CLOCK   A clock driven by an A.C. motor synchronised to the mains supply.

TIME-ELAPSE WATCH   A watch with a moveable bezel which allows the wearer to see how much time has elapsed since the watch was set. It is a feature of divers' watches and the watches made specially for rally drivers.

TIMER   A stop watch used for timing sport and industrial operations.

TRAIN   A series of gear wheels and pinions which translate the beat of the escapement into hours, minutes and seconds, and drive the hands.

WATCH TIMER   An electronic instrument for testing the rate of watches.

WHEEL   A gear wheel in the train of a watch or clock.

WINDING BUTTON   The serrated button used for winding and setting the hands of a watch. Often called a crown.

WORLD TIME CLOCK OR WATCH   A watch or clock on which it is possible to read off simultaneously the time in the principal cities of the world.

Appendixes

The Properties of Gemstones and Recommended Trade Names

(by courtesy of the National Association of Goldsmiths)

The nomenclature is not intended to be exhaustive; some of the rarer gemstones and minerals are not tabulated

AMBER—Hardness 3–2½. S.G. 1·04–1·10. R.I. 1·539–1·545

Species	Colour	Recommended trade name
AMBER	All colours	Amber, with or without appropriate colour description

ANDALUSITE—Hardness 7–7½. S.G. 3·1–3·2. R.I. 1·63–1·64

ANDALUSITE	Green, red, brown	Andalusite, with or without appropriate colour description

BERYL—Hardness 7½. S.G. 2·67–2·80. R.I. (Double) 1·57–1·58

EMERALD	Bright green[1]	Emerald
AQUAMARINE	Pale blue, pale greenish-blue	Aquamarine
BERYL	White	White beryl or Goshenite
	Green[2]	Green beryl
	Golden, yellow	Golden or yellow beryl
	Pink	Pink beryl, Morganite

[1] Colour due to chromium.
[2] Colour not due to chromium.

CHRYSOBERYL—Hardness 8½.   S.G. 3·70–3·74.   R.I. (Double) 1·74–1·75

Species	Colour	Recommended trade name
CHRYSOBERYL	Yellow, yellowish-green, yellowish-brown, brown	Chrysoberyl
CHATOYANT CHRYSOBERYL	Translucent yellow to greenish or brownish— showing chatoyancy	Chrysoberyl cat's-eye
ALEXANDRITE	Green to greenish-brown by daylight, red to reddish-brown by artificial (tungsten) light	Alexandrite

CORAL—Hardness 4.   S.G. 2·68

CORAL	Red, pink, white, sometimes black	Coral, with or without appropriate colour description

CORUNDUM—Hardness 9.   S.G. 3·94–4·01.   R.I. (Double) 1·76–1·77

RUBY	Red	Ruby
	Red, with star effect	Star-ruby
SAPPHIRE	Blue	Sapphire
	Blue, grey, etc., with star effect	Star-sapphire
	All colours other than the above	Yellow sapphire, green s., pink s., mauve s., etc.

DIAMOND—Hardness 10.   S.G. 3·52.   R.I. (Single) 2·42

DIAMOND	White, yellowish-white, yellow, brown, green, pink, red, mauve, blue, black	Diamond

EMERALD—See Beryl

FELDSPAR—Hardness 6. S.G. 2·55–2·71. R.I. (Double) 1·52–1·53

Species	Colour	Recommended trade name
ORTHOCLASE	White	Adularia
	Yellow	Orthoclase
MOONSTONE	Whitish with bluish shimmer of light	Moonstone
MICROCLINE, AMAZONITE	Opaque green	Amazonite or Amazon stone
OLIGOCLASE AND ORTHOCLASE *S.G.* 2·66	Whitish-red-brown—flecked with golden particles	Sunstone Aventurine feldspar
LABRADORITE *S.G.* 2·71 *R.I.* 1·55–1·56	Ashen grey with bluish or reddish or yellowish or green gleams	Labradorite

FLUORITE, FLUORSPAR—Hardness 4. S.G. 3·18. R.I. 1·43

FLUORITE, FLUORSPAR	Green, yellow, red, blue, violet, etc.	Fluorspar, Fluorite, with or without appropriate colour description
	Banded blue and other colours	Fluorspar or Blue John

GARNET—Hardness 7½–6½. S.G. 3·3–4·3. R.I. (Single) 1·7–1·9

GARNET	All colours	Garnet
ALMANDINE *Hard.* 7½. *S.G.* 3·8–4·2 *R.I.* 1·76–1·81	Violet-red	Almandine or almandine garnet
PYROPE *Hard.* 7½–7. *S.G.* 3·6–3·8 *R.I.* 1·74–1·76	Red to crimson	Pyrope or pyrope garnet
	Pale violet	Rhodolite or rhodolite garnet
SPESSARTITE *Hard.* 7. *S.G.* 3·9–4·2 *R.I.* 1·80–1·81	Brownish-red, orange-red	Spessartite or spessartite garnet (or spessartine if preferred)

continued

GARNET *continued*

Species	Colour	Recommended trade name
GROSSULARITE *Hard.* 7. *S.G.* 3·5–3·7 *R.I.* 1·74–1·79	Pale green and other colours (translucent) Orange—yellowish-red, Orange—reddish-brown	Grossularite, grossular garnet or massive grossular garnet Hessonite or hessonite garnet
ANDRADITE *Hard.* 7–6½. *S.G.* 3·85 *R.I.* 1·89	Yellow Green, yellowish-green Black	Andradite or andradite garnet Andradite or Demantoid or demantoid garnet Melanite garnet (*R.I.* 1·8–2·0)
UVAROVITE *Hard.* 7. *S.G.* 3·42–3·5 *R.I.* 1·84	Emerald-green	Uvarovite or uvarovite garnet

IOLITE—Hardness 7½–7.   S.G. 2·6.   R.I. (Double) 1·54–1·55

IOLITE CORDIERITE ⎱	Blue and dingy brown	Iolite or Cordierite

JADE (PYROXENE)—Hardness 7–6½.   S.G. 3·2–3·5.   R.I. (Double) 1·66–1·68

JADEITE	Green, whitish with emerald green flecks, mauve, brown, orange, opaque to translucent	Jadeite, or Jade
CHLORO- MELANITE	Dark green or nearly black, with white flecks, opaque to translucent	Chloromelanite, or Jade

JADE (AMPHIBOLE)—Hardness 6½–6.   S.G. 2·9–3·1.   R.I. (Double)
1·61—1·63

NEPHRITE	Green, white, single coloured and flecked, opaque to translucent	Nephrite

LAPIS-LAZULI—Hardness 6–5½.   S.G. 2·45–2·95.   R.I. 1·5

Species	Colour	Recommended trade name
LAPIS-LAZULI	Blue (opaque) often with brassy specks of pyrite; opaque whitish-light blue	Lapis-lazuli

MALACHITE—Hardness 5½.   S.G. 2·3–2·4.   R.I. 1·50

MALACHITE	Green veined, banded	Malachite

MARCASITE—See PYRITE

OPAL—Hardness 6½–5.   S.G. 2·0–2·1.   R.I. (Single) 1·44–1·46

OPAL	Milky with rainbow-like play of colours	Opal or white opal
	The same on dark background	Opal or black opal
	Transparent straw-coloured or colourless, iridescent	Opal or water opal
FIRE OPAL	Fiery red to browny-red	Opal or fire opal
MATRIX OPAL	Flecks of opal in matrix	Opal matrix

PEARL—Hardness 3½.   S.G. 2·71

PEARL	All colours	Pearl, with or without appropriate colour description

PEARL (CONCH)—Hardness 3½.   S.G. 2·84

CONCH PEARL	Pink, white (no pearly lustre)	Conch pearl, with or without appropriate colour description

PERIDOT, OLIVINE—Hardness 7–6½. S.G. 3·3–3·4 R.I. (Double) 1·65–1·69

Species	Colour	Recommended trade name
OLIVINE	Yellowish-green, olive green, brown	Peridot

PYRITE AND MARCASITE—Hardness 6½–6. S.G. 4·9–5·1

PYRITE MARCASITE	Brassy-grey with metallic sheen	Pyrite or Marcasite

QUARTZ—Hardness 7. S.G. 2·65. R.I. (Double) 1·54–1·55

ROCK CRYSTAL	Colourless	Quartz or rock crystal
AMETHYST (natural colour)	Light to dark violet	Amethyst
AMETHYST (heat-treated)	Yellowish, brownish-yellow	Citrine or golden or yellow quartz
	Reddish, reddish-brown, reddish-yellow	Quartz with or without appropriate colour description
	Green	Green quartz
CITRINE	Yellow, brownish-yellow	Citrine or golden or yellow quartz
SMOKY QUARTZ	Smoky or brownish-yellow to black—when brownish-yellow to brown or smoky brown	Smoky quartz
		Cairngorm, or brown quartz
ROSE-QUARTZ	Milky rose-pink	Rose-quartz

QUARTZ (with inclusions)

PRASE	Leek-green	Prase
CHATOYANT QUARTZ	Whitish-grey, greyish-green, greenish-yellow, blue, with shimmering streaks of light	Quartz cat's-eye
CROCIDOLITE (pseudo-morph)	Yellowish-brown, brownish-golden yellow with shimmering streaks of light	Tiger's-eye

continued

QUARTZ *continued*

Species	Colour	Recommended trade name
CROCIDOLITE (pseudomorph)	Like tiger's-eye but greyish-blue	Falcon's-eye
AVENTURINE QUARTZ	Yellowish-browny-red, yellow, brown, red, or green, with small flakes of mica	Aventurine quartz

QUARTZ (Cryptocrystalline) CHALCEDONY GROUP

Species	Colour	Recommended trade name
CHALCEDONY (translucent)	Grey to bluish	Chalcedony
CHRYSOPRASE	Apple-green and light green	Chrysoprase
CORNELIAN	Red in various shades	Cornelian
HELIOTROPE	Dark green with red spots	Bloodstone Heliotrope
JASPER	Whitish, yellow, red, green, brown, etc.	Jasper
PLASMA	Leek-green	Plasma
AGATE *Hard.* 7. *S.G.* 2·59–2·67 *R.I.* 1·53–1·54	Banded in various colours, white, yellow, grey, red, brown, blue, black, etc.	Agate, onyx, sardonyx, etc., as appropriate
	Milky with green or rust-coloured moss-like inclusions	Moss-agate

RUBY AND SAPPHIRE—See CORUNDUM

SERPENTINE—Hardness 2½–5. S.G. 2·5–2·7. R.I. 1·57

Species	Colour	Recommended trade name
SERPENTINE	Translucent green	Bowenite
	Emerald-green with black spots	Williamsite
	Green, grey-green, whitish- and reddish-brown rock	Serpentine

SPHENE—Hardness 5–5½.   S.G. 3·45–3·56.   R.I. 1·9–2·05

Species	Colour	Recommended trade name
SPHENE	Yellow, green, brown and grey	Sphene, with or without appropriate colour description

SPINEL—Hardness 8.   S.G. 3·58–3·65.   R.I. (Single) 1·72

SPINEL	All colours	Spinel; or red s., pink s., orange s., etc., respectively

SPODUMENE—Hardness 7–6½.   S.G. 3·18.   R.I. (Double) 1·65–1·68

SPODUMENE	Yellowish-green, brownish-green, pale yellow	Spodumene
HIDDENITE	Bright green[1]	Hiddenite
KUNZITE	Rose-pink, lilac, violet	Kunzite

[1] Colour due to chromium.

TOURMALINE—Hardness 7½–7.   S.G. 3·0–3·20.   R.I. (Double) 1·62–1·64

TOURMALINE	All colours	Tourmaline; or red t., green t., parti-coloured t., etc., respectively

TOPAZ—Hardness 8.   S.G. 3·50–3·56.   R.I. (Double) 1·61–1·63

TOPAZ	All colours	Topaz; or white t., pink t., blue t., etc., respectively

TURQUOISE—Hardness 6–5.   S.G. 2·6–2·9.   R.I. (Double) 1·60–1·65

TURQUOISE	Sky blue, blue, bluish-green, greenish	Turquoise
TURQUOISE MATRIX	Flecks of turquoise in matrix	Turquoise matrix

ZIRCON—Hardness 7½. S.G. 3·95–4·70. R.I. (Double) 1·79–1·99

Species	Colour	Recommended trade name
ZIRCON	All colours	Zircon; or blue z., red z., etc., respectively

ZOISITE—Hardness 6. S.G. 3·35–3·38. R.I. 1·703–1·696

Species	Colour	Recommended trade name
ZOISITE	Crystals usually brown but changed to blue by heat treatment. Also found in massive green form	Zoisite

Exemptions from Hallmarking

This appendix lists the articles exempted from compulsory hallmarking under Part II of Schedule I of the Hallmarking Act 1973, as amended by the Hallmarking (Small Silver Articles) (Exemption) Order 1975, and the Hallmarking (Exempted Articles) (Amendment) Order 1975.

EXEMPTED ARTICLES

1. An article which is intended for despatch to a destination outside the United Kingdom.
2. An article which is outside the United Kingdom, or which is in course of consignment from outside the United Kingdom to an assay office in the United Kingdom.
3. Any coin which is, or was formerly at any time, current coin of the United Kingdom or any other territory.
4. Any article which has been used, or is intended to be used, for medical, dental, veterinary, scientific or industrial purposes.
5. Any battered article fit only to be remanufactured.
6. Any article of gold or silver thread.
7. Any raw material (including any bar, plate, sheet, foil, rod, wire, strip or tube) or bullion.
8. Any manufactured article which is not substantially complete, and which is intended for further manufacture.
9. Any article which is wholly or mainly of platinum, and which was manufactured before 1st January 1975.

ARTICLES EXEMPT IF OF MINIMUM FINENESS

10. Any article which
    (a) is wholly or mainly of gold or of silver or of gold and silver

assaying in all its gold parts not less than 375 parts per thousand and in all its silver parts not less than 800 parts per thousand; and

(*b*) was manufactured before the year 1900 and has not since the beginning of the year 1900 been the subject of any alteration which would be an improper alteration if the article had previously borne approved hallmarks.

11. Any musical instrument, where the description is applied to the mouthpiece, and the mouthpiece is of minimum fineness.

12. Any article containing only one precious metal, being a metal of minimum fineness and of a weight less than that specified in the following table:

Gold	1 gram
Silver	7·78 grams
Platinum	0·5 gram

13. Any article which is wholly of one or more precious metals of minimum fineness and which is so small or thin that it cannot be hallmarked.

14. Any article which is of minimum fineness and which is imported temporarily (whether as a trade sample, or as intended for exhibition or otherwise) and for the time being remains under the control of the Commissioners of Customs and Excise.

14A. Any article, any precious metal in which is of minimum fineness, and which either

(*a*) contains gold and platinum but not silver, and the weight of the gold parts of which exceeds 50 per cent of the total weight of the precious metals in the article, that total weight being less than 1 gram; or

(*b*) contains silver and either gold or platinum or both gold and platinum, and the weight of the silver parts of which exceeds 50 per cent of the total weight of the precious metals in the article, that total weight being less than 7·78 grams.

14B. Where an article described in paragraph 12 or paragraph 14A above contains materials other than precious metals the article shall not be taken as falling within that paragraph unless it complies with Part III of Schedule 2 to this Act.

EXISTING EXEMPTIONS

15. The following articles of gold, if manufactured before 1 January 1975, and (except in the case of articles mentioned in sub-paragraph (d) below) of minimum fineness:

   (*a*) rings, except wedding rings, pencil cases, lockets, watch chains and thimbles,

   (*b*) articles consisting entirely of filigree work,

   (*c*) articles so heavily engraved or set with stones that it is impossible to mark them without damage,

   (*d*) jewellers works, that is the actual setting only in which stones or other jewels are set, and jointed sleeper earrings.

16. Subject to the exceptions below, the following articles of silver, if manufactured before 1 January 1975, and (except in the case of articles mentioned in paragraph (e) below) of minimum fineness ·

   (*a*) lockets, watch chains and stamped medals,

   (*b*) mounts the weight of which is less than 15·55 grams,

   (*c*) articles consisting entirely of filigree work,

   (*d*) silver articles the weight of which is less than 7·78 grams,

   (*e*) jewellers works, that is the actual setting only in which stones or other jewels are set.

17. Articles of gold or silver manufactured before 1 January 1975, other than articles mentioned in paragraphs 15 or 16 above, and being of such descriptions as, under any enactment in force immediately before the passing of this Act, to be specifically exempt from hallmarking.

NOTE

'Minimum fineness' means for gold the standard of 375 parts per thousand, for silver the standard of 925 parts per thousand and for platinum the standard of 950 parts per thousand.

The Lever Escapement

(Text and illustrations by courtesy of the British Horological Institute)

THE PARTS (Fig. A.1)

The lever escapement consists of the following parts:
Escape wheel, usually with 15 teeth.
Pallet assembly. Pallet staff 9; lever 7, with notch and horns 12; pallet stones—entrance 10, exit 8. The pallet stones or jewels are generally of synthetic sapphire or ruby. They are assembled firmly in the slots of the pallet frame and are generally secured by shellac to make adjustment easy. The lever terminates in a notch, flanked by two horns, forming part of the safety action (see Fig. A.1).
Banking pins 6, which limit the movement of the lever.
Balance assembly. Balance spring 2; large or impulse roller 4; small or safety roller 5; impulse pin 14. The large roller carries the impulse pin, or ruby pin as it is sometimes called, which operates on the notch of the lever and unlocks the escapement, and also receives impulse.

The small roller with the guard pin or dart forms the main part of the safety action to prevent overbanking. A crescent-shaped piece, known as the passing hollow, is cut out of its circumference.

ACTION OF THE ESCAPEMENT (Fig. A.2)

The balance rotates in the direction of the arrow. The locking corner of tooth B of the escape wheel rests against the locking face of the entrance pallet. The impulse pin is clear of the lever notch, the lever resting against the left-hand banking pin. The angle at which the pallet stone is set in relation to the locking face of the wheel tooth is such as to draw the stone into the wheel and hold it there, so that a knock will not cause the lever to move; thus the guard pin is free of the roller.

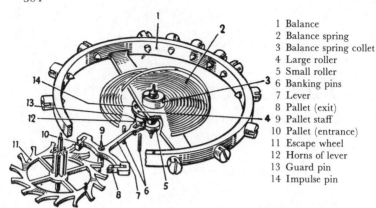

1 Balance
2 Balance spring
3 Balance spring collet
4 Large roller
5 Small roller
6 Banking pins
7 Lever
8 Pallet (exit)
9 Pallet staff
10 Pallet (entrance)
11 Escape wheel
12 Horns of lever
13 Guard pin
14 Impulse pin

Fig. A.1. Parts of lever escapement. This is a straight-line arrangement. The escape wheel has club teeth

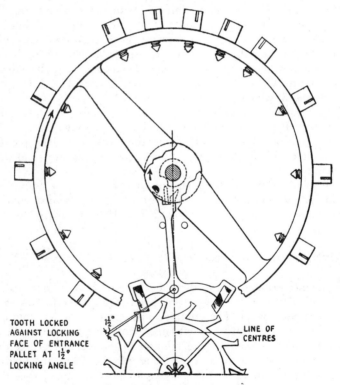

TOOTH LOCKED
AGAINST LOCKING
FACE OF ENTRANCE
PALLET AT 1½°
LOCKING ANGLE

1½°

B

LINE OF
CENTRES

Fig. A.2. The escapement when locked

Unlocking (Fig. A.3). The balance, having completed its swing to the left, is brought to a stop before it starts turning in the opposite direction as a result of the action of the balance spring. The impulse pin enters the notch of the lever and strikes against its right inside face. The pallets are thus caused to turn on the pallet staff and the

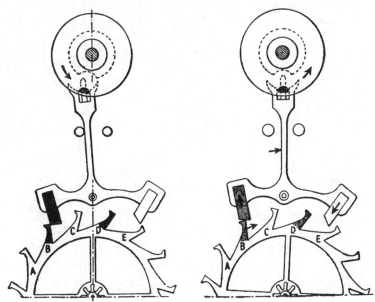

Fig. A.3. *Unlocking commences*   Fig. A.4. *Impulse—first phase*

entrance pallet stone is withdrawn from the shaded tooth B. The instant the locking corner of the entrance pallet stone reaches the locking corner of the tooth, unlocking is complete and the wheel starts to turn.

Impulse (Fig. A.4)—first phase. The impulse is in two phases. As the entrance pallet stone continues to move away from the shaded tooth B, and the lever is forced over the right by the action of the impulse pin in the lever notch, the locking corner or toe of tooth B forces its way along the impulse plane of the stone, thereby pushing the stone out of the way. This action causes the left-hand inner face of the lever notch to press on the impulse pin, and gives impulse to the balance. In unlocking, the impulse pin moves the lever and withdraws the pallet stone from the wheel tooth; in the impulse stage this is reversed and the impulse pin is assisted on its way by the lever notch.

Impulse (Fig. A.5)—second phase. When the locking corner of the shaded tooth B reaches the discharge corner of the stone, the impulse plane of the tooth takes over and continues the impulse by pressing upon the discharge corner of the pallet stone, causing the pallets to continue turning still further. The instant the discharge corner of the tooth reaches the discharge corner of the stone

Fig. A.5. Impulse—second phase   *Fig. A.6. Locking at drop*

impulse is complete, and the useful work of this particular 'escape' is finished.

Locking (Fig. A.6). The escape wheel now moves freely until the shaded tooth D drops on the exit pallet stone. The impulse pin leaves the lever notch. The lever is close to the right-hand banking pin, but not yet quite in contact with it. The balance continues to rotate in the direction of the arrow. This is the supplementary arc. At the same time that the entrance pallet was progressively moved clear of tooth B during unlocking and impulse, the exit pallet was similarly moved into position to intercept and lock tooth D. Drop brings the locking corner of tooth D on to the locking surface of the exit pallet stone and locking at drop takes place. This does not complete the locking action, because the stone has still to be drawn further into the escape wheel, and the lever brought firmly against the banking pin.

Run to the banking (Fig. A.7). Immediately locking at drop has taken place, the run to the banking starts. This movement is caused by the draw action due to the angle at which the pallet stone is set in relation to the locking face of the wheel tooth. It continues until the lever is held against the banking pin and it permits the wheel to turn slightly further after locking at drop. It also ensures that the

Fig. A.7. Run to the banking

guard pin will be held clear of the circumference of the safety roller. Locking at drop, plus run to the banking, give the total lock.

Draw provides safety against random operation of the safety action should the watch receive a knock. If the watch should receive such a severe jar as to cause the lever to be moved away from the banking pin, the guard pin or dart makes contact with the safety roller and this prevents the escapement from being unlocked until the guard pin can enter the passing hollow. This can only happen when the impulse pin is about to enter the lever notch to unlock the escapement at the correct instant. The horns of the notch take over the safety action during the short time when the guard pin is entering the passing hollow and until the impulse pin is safely in the notch.

When the balance makes its next return swing the same action takes place in the opposite direction. Tooth D is unlocked and gives impulse to the exit pallet stone. Tooth A is then locked on the entrance pallet stone—and so the action is repeated.

The balance is absolutely free or detached throughout its swing, except for the comparatively short time the impulse pin is actually in the lever notch, while unlocking and impulse are taking place. The free part of the swing is called the free, or supplementary, arc.

Touchstone Testing in the Workshop

The most effective way of testing metals in the retail jeweller's workshop is to use the touchstone. This has served the jeweller well for many centuries, and allows him not only to identify one metal from another, but with practice will enable him to determine the carat quality of unhallmarked gold.

The touchstone is a slab of basaltic rock, which is harder than most metals, and fine-textured. Good touchstones are extremely difficult to find these days and the jeweller may have to make do with a 'stone' made of ceramic material.

Besides a touchstone the jeweller will require a set of touch-needles of known carat quality. He will also need nitric acid and hydrochloric acid. For the preliminary tests a dilute nitric acid is used, consisting of one part of distilled water and one of concentrated acid. Nitric acid has no effect on gold, but it attacks the base metals, copper and silver, with which it is usually alloyed. The principle of the touchstone test is to make a streak with the metal to be tested and drip a few drops of the acid on it and study the reaction. To ascertain the carat quality of the gold the reaction of the test streak is studied with a streak made with a touchneedle of known carat quality.

To ensure that the sample is not rolled gold or gold plated a scratch should be made in an inconspicuous place with a small file. This will remove the outer layer of gold. The initial test is made by placing a drop of the nitric acid on the streak. If the streak is yellow, the indications are:

(a) Streak dissolved indicates a copper alloy, for example the base metal beneath the gold layer of rolled gold or gold plate.
(b) Streak darkened indicates 9 carat gold.
(c) Streak unchanged indicates 14 carat gold, or a higher carat.

If the streak is white, the indications are:

(*a*) Streak dissolved indicates either a silver, nickel or tin alloy.

(*b*) Streak darkened indicates a 9 carat white gold.

(*c*) Streak unchanged indicates a higher than 9 carat white gold, a platinum or palladium jewellery alloy, a stainless steel, an aluminium alloy or a lead alloy.

The final test is made by adding a drop of hydrochloric acid to the drop previously placed on the streak. The indications are now:

(*a*) A white precipitate in the liquid indicates a silver alloy.

(*b*) A darkened streak, which dissolves, indicates a 9 carat gold.

(*c*) A white streak, unchanged after the initial test, but which becomes coated with a white film, indicates a lead alloy.

(*d*) A white streak unchanged after the initial test, but which dissolves on the addition of hydrochloric acid, indicates an aluminium alloy.

(*e*) A streak unchanged after the first test, but which is very slowly dissolved on the addition of hydrochloric acid, indicates either a higher gold than 9 carat, a palladium jewellery alloy of 950 fineness, or a stainless steel.

(*f*) A streak which is unchanged on the addition of hydrochloric acid to the first drop indicates a platinum jewellery alloy of 950 fineness.

To complete the simple touchstone test, for discrimination among the white alloys, a slip of white blotting-paper is used to absorb the liquid from the touchstone. A faint brown stain indicates a palladium–white gold. A brown stain indicates a palladium jewellery alloy. A faint yellow-green stain indicates a nickel–white gold or stainless steel, where white streaks were not dissolved during the initial test with nitric acid. (See indications white (*c*), and final (*e*).) To distinguish between nickel–white gold and stainless steel the touchstone is cleaned and dried, a new streak is made, the touchstone is warmed, and one drop of hydrochloric acid is added. By this treatment stainless steel is dissolved, but nickel–white gold is not.

An effective confirmatory test for white alloys may be made in the following manner: a streak is made on the touchstone, a little finely-powdered potassium iodate (less than one-tenth of a grain) is sprinkled on the streak, and one or two drops of concentrated hydrochloric acid are added. After one or two minutes the touchstone is washed under a very gentle stream of water and the streak is observed. A 950 fine platinum jewellery alloy streak remains unchanged, a 950 fine palladium jewellery alloy streak shows a red colour, nickel–white gold or stainless steel is dissolved and a palladium–white gold gives a paler colour than a palladium jewellery alloy.

The simple touchstone test does not give any reliable indication of the fineness of a silver alloy; to ascertain this an additional test is necessary, using a solution prepared by dissolving 30 grains of silver nitrate in one fluid ounce of distilled water and adding a drop of concentrated nitric acid. A drop of the solution is placed on a fresh streak. If the streak is unchanged, the indication is sterling silver (925 fineness), or Britannia silver (958·4 fineness). A brown stain on the streak indicates a fineness below 900, and the depth of the colour intensifies as the proportion of base metal increases until, with a white base metal, a black stain is obtained.

A simple distinction between sterling or Britannia silver and nickel silver (nickel–copper–zinc alloy) can be made with a solution of one part by weight of chromic acid, six parts by weight of concentrated nitric acid, and two parts by weight of water. When a drop of this solution is applied to the streak, a red coloration indicates silver, whereas a green coloration indicates nickel silver.

If it is necessary to ascertain the fineness of a yellow gold alloy, a series of test acids is required:

For gold alloys below 9 carat—One fl. oz of distilled water is mixed with 1 fl. oz of concentrated nitric acid, a few drops at a time.

For gold alloys from 9 to 14 carat—One fl. oz of No. 1 acid (above) is mixed with 3 drops of a saturated solution of common salt in distilled water.

For gold alloys from 14 to 18 carat—One fl. oz of distilled water is mixed with 2 fl. oz of concentrated nitric acid and 10 drops of a saturated solution of common salt in distilled water.

For gold alloys above 18 carat—One fl. oz of No. 3 acid (above) is mixed with 1 grain of potassium iodide.

In addition, a set of test needles of alloys of known carats is necessary so that comparison streaks can be made near to the streak of the alloy under examination. Thus, the reaction of the alloy under test to the appropriate acid can be closely compared with the reaction of a known alloy.

Experience and good judgement are required for reliable evaluation of gold alloys.

An indication of the fineness of a platinum alloy may be obtained by using a test acid made up of 1 fl. oz of concentrated hydrochloric acid, one-third fl. oz concentrated nitric acid, one-sixth fl. oz distilled water, and one-third oz of ammonium chloride crystals. This test acid must be allowed to stand until it has a yellow colour; it is then ready for use. The streak of a platinum alloy, of fineness below 950, is attacked in proportion to the relative amount of base metal present in the alloy.

The indications of the touchstone tests may be found to depend somewhat on the conditions of test, e.g., on the type of touchstone used, the temperature of the reagents, and the experience of the operator. Reliability in the identification of alloys may be ensured if a series of touchneedles of the standard alloys is available, so that comparison tests may be made.

If a touchstone is not available, spot tests may be made by the application of the reagents to a small area which had been filed at an inconspicuous place on the article. Owing to the somewhat limited area available, in comparison with a touchstone test, it may be advantageous to watch the course of the spot test through a magnifying glass, and finally to note the extent to which the metal has been stained or etched by the reagents.

All the chemicals used in the touchstone tests are poisonous, and the acids are highly corrosive to the skin and clothing. Inhalation of acid fumes must be avoided.

Recently, testing sets that eliminate the need to use a touchstone and needles have become available; gradually, because they are more convenient and easier to use, they are tending to replace the touch-stone.

Some Useful Tables

Weights for Precious Stones and Pearls

The metric carat of 200 milligrams is the unit used for precious stones other than pearls, which are generally reckoned by grains which are quarter-carats (i.e. 50 milligrams).

4 grains = 1 metric carat
1 metric carat = 200 milligrams
5 metric carats = 1 gram

A useful comparison is:
141¾ metric carats = 1 oz. avoir.

Troy Weight for Precious Metals

The ounce (oz.) is the unit of weight for precious metals and all fractions of an ounce are expressed in decimals.

The gram has been suggested as the unit of weight for gold and silver when metrication generally is used in the U.K.

Troy, Avoirdupois and Grams

	Troy grain	Troy dwt.	Troy ounce	Avoir. ounce	Avoir. pound	Grams	Kilo-grams
1 troy grain	1	0·04167	0·00208	0·00229	0·00014	0·0648	0·00006
1 troy dwt.	24	1	0·05	0·05486	0·00343	1·55518	0·00156
1 troy ounce	480	20	1	1·09714	0·06857	31·1035	0·03110
1 avoir. ounce	437·5	18·22917	0·91145	1	0·06250	28·34954	0·02835
1 avoir. pound	7,000	291·66666	14·58333	16	1	453·59264	0·45359
1 gram	15·43235	0·64301	0·03215	0·03527	0·00220	1	0·001
1 kilogram	15,432·349	643·0145	32·15073	35·27394	2·20462	1,000	1

313

Some British Coins as Weights

Gold coins	Standard weight (grains)	Remedy (grains)
Sovereign—£1	123·27447	0·20
Half-sovereign—10s.	61·63723	0·15
Silver (up to 1946)		
Crown—5s.	436·36363	2·000
Half-crown—2s. 6d.	218·18181	1·216
Florin—2s.	174·54545	0·997
Shilling—1s.	87·27272	0·578
Sixpence—6d.	43·63636	0·346
Threepence—3d.	21·81818	0·212

Oz. Troy and Grams Equivalents

Oz. troy	Grams	Grams	Oz. troy
1	31·104	1	0·0321
2	62·207	2	0·0643
3	93·310	3	0·0964
4	124·414	4	0·1286
5	155·517	5	0·1607
6	186·621	6	0·1929
7	217·724	7	0·2250
8	248·828	8	0·2572
9	279·931	9	0·2893

Melting Points of Metals

Metal	°C	°F
Osmium	2700	4892
Iridium	2454	4449·2
Ruthenium	2450	4442
Rhodium	1955	3551
Chromium	1830	3326
Platinum	1773	3223·4
Palladium	1555	2831
Copper	1083	1981·4
Gold (fine)	1063	1945·4
22 ct. yellow	1003	1837·4
18 ct. yellow	905	1661
14 ct. yellow	838	1540·4
9 ct. yellow	830	1526
Silver (fine)	961	1761·8
Silver (sterling)	893	1639·4
Brass	940	1724
Aluminium	660	1220
Zinc	419	786·2
Tin	232	449·6

Specific Gravity

Specific gravity is the ratio of the weight of a metal (or other body) to the weight of an equal volume of water at a standard temperature and pressure, the weight of water being taken as 1.

Osmium	22·5
Iridium	22·41
Platinum	21·4
Gold (fine)	19·36
22 ct. yellow	17·7
18 ct. yellow	15·58
14 ct. yellow	13·4
9 ct. yellow	11·3
Rhodium	12·44
Ruthenium	12·2
Palladium	12·00
Silver (fine)	10·53
Sterling	10·40
Copper	8·94
Brass	8·5
Tin	7·3
Chromium	7·14
Zinc	7·14
Aluminium	2·70

Index